PERSPECTIVES ON CAPITALISM

PERSPECTIVES ON CAPITALISM

Marx, Keynes, Schumpeter and Weber

Edited by
KRISHNA BHARADWAJ
SUDIPTA KAVIRAJ

SAGE Publications
New Delhi/Newbury Park/London

Copyright © *Indian Council of Social Science Research, New Delhi, 1989*

All rights reserved. No part of this book may be reproduced or utilised in any form or by any means, electronic or mechanical, including photocopying, recording or by any information storage or retrieval system, without permission in writing from the publisher.

First published in 1989 by

Sage Publications India Pvt Ltd
M-32 Greater Kailash Market I
New Delhi 110 048

Sage Publications Inc
2111 West Hillcrest Drive
Newbury Park, California 91320

Sage Publications Ltd
28 Banner Street
London EC1Y 8QE

Published by Tejeshwar Singh for Sage Publications India Pvt Ltd, phototypeset by Aurelec Data Processing Systems and printed at Chaman Offset Printers.

Library of Congress Cataloging-in-Publication Data

Perspectives on capitalism: Marx, Keynes, Schumpeter, and Weber / edited by Krishna Bharadwaj, Sudipta Kaviraj.
    p. cm.
    1. Capitalism—Congresses. I. Bharadwaj, Krishna. II. Kaviraj, Sudipta.
HB501.P413 330.12'2—dc20   1989   89-35237

ISBN 0-8039-9619-5 (US-hbk)   81-7036-161-3 (India-hbk)
        0-8039-9620-9 (US-pbk)   81-7036-162-1 (India-pbk)

Contents

Foreword   7
    by Sukhamoy Chakravarty

Introduction   9
1. Keynes as a Theorist of Capitalism   20
   Sukhamoy Chakravarty

2. The Analytical Framework of Keynes   38
   Mihir Rakshit

3. The Resurgence of Political Economy   55
   Krishna Bharadwaj

4. Joseph Alois Schumpeter: A Centennial Appraisal   87
   P R Brahmananda

5. Schumpeter: The Inconsistencies of a Prescient Ideologue   118
   Amiya Kumar Bagchi

6. On Political Explanation in Marxism   132
   Sudipta Kaviraj

7. Politics: The Dialectics of Science and Revolution in Karl Marx   175
   Randhir Singh

8. Weber, Gramsci and Capitalism   185
   Asok Sen

9. Relevance of Max Weber for the Understanding of Indian Reality   211
   Yogendra Singh

10. State Power and Capitalist Democracy   231
    Ralph Miliband

11. The State and Development of Capitalism: The Third World Perspective   247
    Rehman Sobhan

Notes on Contributors 259

List of Seminar Participants 262

Index 266

Foreword

In the history of social thought, the year 1883 was doubtless an exceptional one. The same year saw the death of Karl Marx as well as the birth of John Maynard Keynes and Joseph Alois Schumpeter. During the year 1983, seminars were organised all over the world to celebrate the 'triple centenary'. In planning a national seminar to mark this occasion, the Indian Council of Social Science Research deviated from similar seminars held elsewhere by including Max Weber, even though he was not connected with the other three in a ceremonial way. What influenced the planners of this seminar in this decision was to get an additional perspective on 'Capitalism' which has shaped contemporary sensibility greatly, besides having numerous points of contact and divergences with the view points of the other three.

These four social theorists have 'classical' attributes in the sense Alfred Marshall, a great economist himself, once defined the term. I here quote the following paragraph from Marshall which deserves to be very much better noted than it is. Marshall wrote,

> I do not myself hold a classical author to be one who more than others had said things which are true, as they stand. I do not feel bound to agree with him on many points, even on any point. But he is not for me classical unless either by the form or the matter of his words or deeds he has stated or indicated *architectonic* (emphasis added) ideas in thought or sentiment which are in some degree his own and which, once created, can never die but are existing yeast ceaselessly working in the Cosmos.[1]

Any social theorist, who has even a minimal familiarity with the writings of his authors would recognise the presence of 'architectonic ideas' in the writings of these authors. Who, indeed, can deny that Marx with his concept of 'Homo Faber', Keynes with his profound analysis of 'uncertainty' in the shaping of economic institutions, Schumpeter with his ideas on 'novelty' and Weber

[1] Alfred Marshall's letter to James Bonar, in A.C. Pigou, ed., *Memorials of Alfred Marshall*, London, 1925, p. 374.

with his ideas of 'rationalisation' have profoundly influenced our understanding of 'Capitalism' as a mode of social and economic organisation, even when we may have many points of disagreement with anyone or with all of them?

Furthermore, while all these authors were born in a Western milieu, and, tongue in cheek, Marx may be described as an eminent Victorian, Keynes and Schumpeter as cultural Edwardians, and Weber, a German nationalist, their influence is very marked in the thinking of all non-Western theorists who are trying to understand their contemporary historical situation, even though they may have plenty of scope to innovate. It is precisely because of this living influence that the ICSSR could collect a number of scholars belonging to different disciplines to examine in depth the thoughts of these authors and assess their contemporary relevance. Thanks are due to the commendable work done by the editors of this volume, Professors K. Bharadwaj and S. Kaviraj, through whose efforts we are now in a position to present a selection of the papers presented at the seminar for a wider public.

I may put on record here the great interest taken by the then Chairman of ICSSR, Mr. G. Parthasarathy and the then Member-Secretary, Dr. D.D. Narula in making the seminar possible. I must also thank Dr. Iqbal Narain, Member-Secretary, ICSSR, and Dr. T.K. Majumdar, Executive Director, ICSSR for the work they have put in to render the publication possible. Finally, I dare express the hope that Indian social theorists will find the book of some interest, no matter where their major doctrinal affiliations lie.

March 1989   SUKHAMOY CHAKRAVARTY

Introduction

For social sciences, 1983 was a remarkable year of commemorations: the death centennial of Karl Marx and the birth centennials of Keynes and Schumpeter coincided that year. Although they differed widely in their ideological vision and theoretical perceptions, these towering figures in social science shared a major concern in their intellectual pursuits. They were intensely and passionately engaged in the task of unravelling the structure and mode of the functioning of capitalism, and in exploring the key elements that shaped the dynamics of the capitalist societies. Their intellectual range was vast: not only did they seek to comprehend the logic behind the economic system of capitalism, but also its history and possible future. The Indian Council of Social Science Research held a conference commemorating the three centennials. The subject of capitalism that it undertook to reflect upon, was sought to be given a fuller treatment by the inclusion of Weber and Gramsci in some of the papers presented at the Conference.

In planning the Conference, the Organising Committee felt that the themes taken up should bring out the richness of the theoretical ideas of these Masters, not so much to advance exegetical/polemical scholarly debates on abstruse questions, but to focus upon the influence that their ideas—as living thoughts—have come to bear upon our contemporary perceptions and analyses of social realities. The purpose included, in particular, bringing out the relevance of their theoretical ideas and structures to the understanding of the processes of capitalist accumulation in the developed and developing countries of today. In persuance of this objective, two kinds of papers were sought from the participating scholars. One set, mainly dealing with the methodological and analytical issues, and the second, concerned with the analysis of the experience of India's development, in the application of theoretical tools and methodologies forged and advanced by these thinkers.

The papers presented in this volume are drawn from the first theoretical set. Dealing with such profound and prolific writers and system-builders like *Marx, Keynes and Schumpeter*, and on the wider-ranging theme of the structure and dynamics of capitalism, it is but natural that discussion in any one paper would not be strictly confined within disciplinary boundaries. On the other hand, discussions by specialists on particular themes were also called for, since distinctive elements in their theories have been developed with differing range, depth and intensity in different social sciences. Hence, we find in the papers presented here, specialised, discipline-oriented focus on the aspects of the theory chosen by the authors. These papers, also, have not been organised to concentrate on pre-selected problems, common to the three theorists. A comparative analysis of the differences and similarities in their perspectives and approaches inevitably informed most of the papers in their different thematic contexts. The papers, thus, represent the authors' reflections on problems and aspects of the theories of their choice, the commonality being the broad theme of capitalism. Consequently, while the volume perhaps lacks a concentrated focus on selected themes, it makes up for it, we hope, by offering a glimpse into the social theory enterprise among scholars in India.

At the centre of the concerns of Marx, Keynes and Schumpeter, was the analysis of the economic structure of capitalist economies and their fluctuations-ridden growth process. The papers by Sukhamoy Chakravarty, Mihir Rakshit, Krishna Bharadwaj, P.R. Brahmananda and Amiya Bagchi address themselves mainly to their economic-theoretic contributions, although, by the very nature of the wide compass of their work, the 'economies' part can be hardly viewed in pristine isolation. The authors do refer to these wider considerations in their papers. Particularly in the case of Marx, Weber and Gramsci—who integrated their analysis of the state with that of the society—we have papers by Sudipta Kaviraj, Randhir Singh, Asok Sen, Yogendra Singh, Ralph Miliband and Rehman Sobhan, that explore, in greater depth, the political and sociological dimensions of their thought.

The opening paper by Sukhamoy Chakravarty focuses on Keynes as a theorist of capitalism. The author provides an insightful perspective, placing Keynes' contribution in the light of his relation with prominent predecessors—Marshall and Marx—and with his contemporaries, Schumpeter and Kalecki. Highlighting Keynes' distinctiveness of analysis in identifying the instability of capitalism as mooted in the twin phenomenon of 'money' and 'uncertainty', Chakravarty sees Keynes' analytical breakthrough in challenging the then dominant sanguine view of the capitalist economy as a self-regulating, market-governed mechanism. Chakravarty brings out, at the same time, the Marshallian elements which continued to influence Keynes' view of prices and his acceptance of their efficient resource-allocative role. It was the continuance of these Marshallian (marginalist) strands that paved the way for the neo-classical synthesis which followed soon after the publication of the *General Theory*. (A similar view is expressed in the papers by Rakshit and Bharadwaj.) Chakravarty also draws certain striking similarities, as well as differences, of capitalist investment in shaping the process of accumulation and its volatile character. For Keynes, unlike Marx, however, the crisis of capitalism was manageable through a proper devising of the monetary and fiscal policies. Chakravarty concludes that while Keynes' analysis of long-run dynamics of capitalism was in some ways, much less satisfactory than that of Marx, or Schumpeter, he successfully forged a set of tools to advance coherent thinking on the macro-analysis of capitalist economies.

Mihir Rakshit's essay elaborates the analytical framework of Keynes, bringing out the positive contributions that Keynes made, through his *Treatise* as well as the *General Theory*—the dominant message of both the works being the primacy of investment, rather than of saving, as sources of economic growth and fluctuations. Rakshit outlines the differences in the approach and methodology of the two works; the former uses the disequilibrium dynamics, emphasising the different speeds at which price-and-quantity adjustments take place, while the *General Theory* employs essentially the short-run equilibrium methodology. In the *Treatise*, he discusses many interesting questions of dynamics, which anticipate in a more primitive form, the discussions in macro-economics of today. The two works led, however, to major differences in their conclusions: The *General Theory* established that the under-employment equilibrium is the rule rather than the exception in capitalist economies while the *Treatise*, taking the full employment equilibrium as a point of reference for its disequilibrium analysis, presumed the long-run tendency to full employment. The rudimentary dynamics and sequential analysis of the *Treatise* did indicate that unregulated capitalist societies could not but be plagued by problems of inflation and unemployment. While many of Keynes' specific analytical results might have been challenged and his 'fiscalism' as an effective policy brought to question in contemporary capitalist reality, Rakshit suggests that one area of Keynesian economics that has proved more enduring is his demonstration of the fallacy of composition; namely, that individual experiences cannot be simply aggregated into collective experiences so that macro-economics is ridden with isolation paradoxes. Such situations are increasingly encountered in the economies of the world today, which warrant collective action.

Krishna Bharadwaj discusses the recent revival of classical and Marxian political economy wherein the theoretical approach is attempted to be reconstructed and posed as an alternative to the mainstream neo-classical theory. The paper argues that the surplus-based approach of Marx has possibilities of fruitful adaptations and extensions in terms of a logically coherent theory of distribution and accumulation, as also of handling more meaningfully changing historical conditions within which development takes place. The paper holds that a consistent explanation of distribution is central to a logically coherent analysis of accumulation, and a weakness of Keynes' critique is seen to lie in the marginalist vestiges that remained in his treatment of capital and of distribution. This weakness was to lead to the 'counter-revolution' in the form of the 'neo-classical synthesis'. The paper also includes a comparative study of Schumpeter and Marx on the question of technical change. Both writers acknowledged the prominent role of technological change in capitalist dynamics, but they employed radically different frameworks and theories of value and distribution, with consequent differences in analytical perceptions and conclusions. The paper concludes expressing a view that the more 'open' structure of political economy, particularly as comprehensively extended in Marx, allows for the possibility of integrating historical changes with logical abstraction, and leads to a richer and more meaningful analysis of output, employment and technical change.

P.R. Brahmananda's appraisal of Schumpeter follows next. The author pays a warm and fulsome tribute to Schumpeter's originality of contributions—in his view, not adequately acknowledged—in developing concepts like the circular flow, in the conceptualisation of innovation and the theory of development based thereupon, in bringing out the role of credit and forced savings in stimulating development, and in the explanation of business cycles as formed of different periodic cycles (particularly, the Kondratieff long-wave).

Brahmananda draws comparisons—parallels and contrariness—between Schumpeter and Keynes, as also Marx. He suggests that the Schumpeterian analysis has a long-ranging relevance and creative role in the theory of development, and regards the Schumpeterian system as having triumphed over Marx, and certainly over Keynes. He views the modern emphasis on technological dynamism, and on mass consumption per capita, as a criterion for evaluating the worthwhileness of development as Schumpeterian legacy. Viewing the Indian development experience, Brahmananda maintains that while certain elements of the innovational process might be active, the Indian experience, so far, cannot be brought under the rubric of the Schumpeterian development theory.

Amiya Kumar Bagchi's assessment of Schumpeter is markedly in contrast with Professor Brahmananda's. He considers Schumpeter as the 'most self-aware' and 'successfully self-concealing' theorist, much of whose 'analytical work and even a considerable part of his work in the history of economic thought can be seen simply as a reaction to what he took to be the current fashion.' Bagchi illustrates his standpoint by discussing how Schumpeter, especially in his early phase, borrowed some powerful concepts from the classical writers, particularly from Marx, and attempted to assimilate these within his Austrian/Walrasian theoretical framework, and within the philosophical approach of methodological individualism. These were: concepts such as 'circular flow'; the significance of the entrepreneurial function in shaping the dynamics of capitalism, the disequilibrium induced by innovations generating super-profits; and the rise of monopoly and its effects on the investment behaviour of capitalists. Bagchi considers that the Schumpeterian contribution, particularly to the understanding of monopoly capitalism, arose only after the 1920s, and that Schumpeter could explain the rise of monopoly for reasons apart from those traditionally discussed, namely, economies of scale and finance, by adding to the list the transaction-costs and risk-bearing aspects of monopoly. Schumpeter's discussion of the process of creative destruction, and of the monopolistic practices, and his attempt to relate market structures and innovations, did advance the understanding of monopoly capitalism in interesting and novel ways. Bagchi argues that these essentially dynamic and systemic forces were attempted to be analysed by Schumpeter in a Walrasian theoretical mould, and within the approach of methodological individualism. This, in his view, led to a number of inconsistencies in his understanding, interpretation and analysis of the real phenomena of capitalist dynamics—the phenomena, Schumpeter could be credited with, for insistently highlighting.

Although initial developments in Marxist theory occurred in the field of economics, there has been, of late, much discussion about the possibilities of a Marxist political theory. Two, somewhat different strategies, have been tried out by scholars who have considered what a Marxist theory of politics would look like; both these approaches are represented in the present volume. Sudipta Kaviraj's paper tries out a line of argument which implies that, though Marx's observations on politics were highly suggestive, they need to be structured into a formal theory before their applications can be properly controlled, and there are some logical problems which have to be carefully attended to in any construction of this kind. He proposes a distinction between empty and determinate ideas, which are bound to exist in any theory of such large, explanatory ambitions. He suggests, further, that we look upon the concept of 'relative autonomy' of the political as an empty concept which does not offer us a substantive doctrine, but makes a logical gesture that a theory is required at this place. The related concept of 'determination', Kaviraj suggests, is a negative concept which does not yield an outcome, but something like an alphabet, out of which an outcome would have to be constructed. The last section of the paper tries to deal with problems of methodological individualism by making a distinction between explicit and abstract structures, and combining an empirical primacy of explicit structures with an explanatory primacy of the more abstract ones

While Kaviraj's paper emphasises the underdetermined spaces in Marx's political theory, and suggests that some of the logical implications of these are still to be clearly brought out, Randhir Singh's contribution emphasises what is available in the classical Marxist tradition. Marxism is seen as an inheritor of the philosophical arguments in the German tradition which emphasise the methodological principle of the totality. Concentration on the phrase 'relative autonomy of politics' may, in Singh's view, lead to serious empiricist and liberal reformist errors in Marxist thinking on political questions. He prefers using the idea of the relative autonomy of the state, indicating the possible autonomy that the political formation of the state might enjoy in a particular historical conjuncture, particularly one in which no basic class is in a position to exercise hegemony over others. But it is never autonomous from the socio-economic structure of a society of unequal classes.

Randhir Singh's paper also points emphatically to the specific way in which the cognitive and practical interests of Marx's theory are jointed together. Forms of Marxist discourse which tend to give excessive importance to its 'scientific' aspect, often lead to a practical emasculation of the revolutionary perspective. Marxist theory seeks to have cognitive grasp over historical processes, not for scientific analysis alone, but to see the shapes of liberating political action that are possible. It also sees such liberating praxis as being able to constitute and modify historical processes. While human subjects act within the relative constraints of historical structures, their political actions are not calculable with the precision common to natural science; and the historical tendencies that Marxist theory outlines, are only 'real possibilities and strong probabilities'. The work of Marxist theory should be evaluated, Randhir Singh argues, not in terms of their academic, scholastic sophistication, but according to the extent to which such work is able to damage the structure of power and inequality in class societies.

Though not directly on Marx's contribution to political theory, Asok Sen's paper connects these general questions on politics and the State to a set of related issues which dominated theorists of a generation after Marx. By bringing together the concerns of two such different thinkers on the destiny of capitalist society as Max Weber and Antonio Gramsci, Sen is able to reveal some interesting comparative structures in Marxist and Weberian social thought. Taking Gramsci together with Weber is particularly apt, because Weber's critical remarks about the relative neglect of ideological structures in Marxist theory, is answered (though not in direct polemics) by Gramsci's highly original reflections on the processes of the formation of ideology, and the fundamental relations of sustenance and reinforcing between structures of thought and modes of production. Weber and Gramsci could, thus, be seen as sharing a common question which they answer in different ways.

It is rather common in Marxist discussion to focus on the central methodological differences between the two authors and show their divergent assessments of the destiny of capitalism in history by emphasising Weber's earlier work with their more optimistic vision of rationalisation. Sen's paper does an analytical operation on the two theories, which chooses to go in the opposite direction. His discussion draws upon the wealth of recent research on Weber's thought which has shown the complexity of his intellectual evaluation and made us more sensitive to its internal lines of rupture. In the later years, Weber is shown moving away considerably from his earlier optimistic assessments of a capitalistic civilisation governed and structured by rationalistic principles. Although he continues with his belief that capitalist development means increasing rationalisation of society, it is evaluated quite differently, with increasing scepticism about its rationalistic claims, and deeper anxiety about its results in human freedom.

Using the vital conceptual couples in Marx's theory—of productive forces/relations, base superstructure and civil society/state in an innovative way, Gramsci formulates a new answer to the problem of capitalist impasse in European history. Sen argues forcefully that the reason why Weber remained imprisoned in a pessimism of the intellect, and Gramsci found a new optimism of the will, is because Weber did not accept, or consider, a political solution to the capitalist predicament.

The influence of Max Weber on academic sociology in India contains a paradox. Weber offered large sociological explanations, not only of the capitalist social forms of the modern type, but also of major forms of Indian religious consciousness. Although Indian sociologists, trying to analyse processes of modernisation in today's India, have often turned to Weber for theoretical implements, there is no comparable interest in his suggested explanatory scheme about traditional society.

Yogendra Singh's paper on the relevance of Max Weber for the understanding of Indian reality offers an explanation of this paradox. Part of the reason lies, according to him, in the difficulties of Weber translation. Singh attends to the revived debate on Weber's writings on India, arising out of Detlef Kantowsky's claim that much of the criticism Weber attracted from Indian scholars was for no fault of his. His translators put his admittedly difficult text through an infelicitous translation, which, sometimes, in the light of the predominant functionalist influences in American sociology, took it through a subtle but significant methodological mistranslation, taking Weber's primarily interpretative philosophical presuppositions through a distorting functionalist and positivist reading.

Singh has also documented the recent shift in the general understanding of Weber's theory of history; from the earlier view that it advanced an aggressive theory of national superiority of capitalism, his theories are now seen as increasingly sceptical about rationality claims. As a corollary, modern scholars sharply contest the idea that Weber's theory provided a hierarchical placing of cultures; on the contrary, it is seen as advancing a strong theory of cultural relativism, which denies any linear structure to history. There is no one paradigm in Weber's sociology, Singh claims; rather, a number of paradigms contest for dominance. Two specific difficulties are discussed in some detail. First, Weber's larger historical curiosity was about the significance of capitalist forms in Europe, and studies of Indian society were secondary, complementary analyses. Second, on a strong interpretative theory of society, for an outsider, grasping the internal significance of social concepts is, admittedly, difficult. However, Yogendra Singh maintains, in conclusion, that the problem of Weber's relevance to India could be divided into substantive and methodological questions. While there could be serious problems about Weber's substantive formulations about Hindu and Buddhist religious communities, his project of an interpretative yet causal understanding of social processes in history would be of enduring relevance to Indian sociology.

The last two papers in this volume, by Ralph Miliband and Rehman Sobhan, fall into a category of their own. They do not address the questions of exegesis or extension of the theories under consideration; they provide largely theoretical general frameworks for the workings of the State. This is the reason for their inclusion in this volume. The two papers are complementary in several ways. Both use a primarily Marxist frame for analysing the modern State in advanced and underdeveloped capitalism. Both papers argue that in order to understand the modern State, reductive economistic explanations are inadequate, and consequently, both make theoretical presentations of what they consider to be the preferred form of the concept of the autonomy of the State.

Ralph Miliband extends his earlier statements on the capitalist State considerably by claiming that in societies of advanced capitalism, the State enjoys, what he calls provocatively, an absolute autonomy in decision-making. The paper argues that the generally accepted idea that the State tries to guarantee the conditions of existence of the social form of capitalism as a whole, and not reflect passively the political choices of a narrow class, is quite correct. However, within its rather wide terms, there is need for a greater and more sensitive registration in Marxist literature of the real margin of choice that the wielders of decision-making powers within the State create possibilities in which the State could go against the express interests and intention of a dominant class.

Conventional Marxist analyses of the capitalist State took as paradigmatic the relation existing between the State and the capitalist class in the 19th century, and exaggerated their structural differentiation and conflict in concrete decision-making processes. But developments in both the structure of the capitalist economy and its class formation, and of the political regimes and the State, ensures a different kind of congruent relationship. It is false, Miliband argues, to image this relation in the old form. The capitalist State, particularly its decision-making strata, enjoy a great degree of real choice in policy-making, and when it acts in ways congruent with interests of the capitalist class, it is not because it is driven to do so, but it wants to do so. The task of the State is seen increasingly as defence of a given social order, and not of the interests of the capitalist class. And the formulation of what are the interests of defence of the social order is left to be defined primarily by the State. Finally, Miliband extends this thesis to argue that this theory could be turned round to claim that given its great power and autonomy, a radical government, if it comes to power in these states, could use these considerable powers to carry through radical policies.

Rehman Sobhan's paper is complementary to Miliband's in the sense that it sees the Third World states as posing a common theoretical problem for Marxist theory, and seeks to offer an outline of a general theory. The major argument in Sobhan's paper is that in a significant way, one of the primary strategic relations in state explanation in capitalism has to be inverted in the case of Third World societies. In advanced capitalism, the State acts out, in the interests of, and through pressures from, a highly articulated and self-conscious capitalist class. In Third World societies, economic development prior to independence from colonial rule, does not produce a bourgeois class with clear structural boundaries, internal cohesion and self-consciousness. The relation between the capitalist class and the State is both chronologically and analytically reversed. It is the State which works—using its policies after independence—to produce, bring into existence a real capitalist class. The paradox of Third World social structuration, therefore, is that within them, a capitalist society is sought to be created in the absence of a pre-existing bourgeoisie by the State, following some general policy and institutional models. It is the military and bureaucratic groups within these states which act as a proxy for the absent, or really nascent capitalist class. The question of the autonomy of the state in the conventional form is really redundant in this historical context; it should be formulated as a question of the autonomy of the weak capitalist class from state support.

As mentioned earlier, the papers included in this volume form only a part of those presented at the conference. Another major set of papers, which do not appear here, were primarily concerned with applications to problems of development. Besides, there were written comments on all papers presented at the conference, which, for lack of space, we have not been able to include in this volume. The conference generated stimulating discussion in all its sessions, and some of the critical suggestions made in the debates have been incorporated by the authors in the reworked versions of their papers.

We would like to thank those who were associated with the conference at various stages of its planning and execution. Thanks are due, particularly, to G. Parthasarathy, former Chairman of the ICSSR, D.D. Narula, its former Member-Secretary, Sukhamoy Chakravarty, K.N. Raj, P.C. Joshi, Yogendra Singh and Randhir Singh, who were members of the organising committee. An ICSSR group, consisting of T.K. Majumdar, S.C. Srivastava, Partha Ghosh, K.K. Siddh and N.K. Talwar, handled the considerable work of actually organising and arranging such a large seminar, Dr. T.K. Majumdar has looked after the conference proceedings from the ICSSR side. Finally, we would like to thank Yashwant Singh, particularly, for helping in the organisation of the seminar, and typing the final manuscript through its various stages.

1

Keynes as a Theorist of Capitalism

SUKHAMOY CHAKRAVARTY

I

For the sake of convenience of presentation, the central propositions of this paper can be listed as follows. First, *General Theory*[1] is the single most important contribution that Keynes made to our understanding of the capitalist economic system. Second, Keynes' understanding of what constitutes the 'economic method' was very much more Marshallian than Walrasian. As such, the search for a Walrasian micro-foundation for Keynes' economics is largely misplaced. Third, Keynes tried to understand the logic of functioning of a *specific* system of economic organisation which is best described as 'liberal capitalism'. His understanding of capitalism as a socio-economic formation was distinctly his own, even though it has some overlaps with the understanding displayed in the works of Marx and Schumpeter. Fourth, on the technical plane, while Keynes' major contribution was the theory of 'effective demand', he established this proposition via a different route from the one followed by his contemporary M. Kalecki, who can be said to have arrived independently at a theory of 'demand for output' as a whole. In contrast with Kalecki's, Keynes' analysis was derived from his understanding of what constitutes a 'monetary economy' as distinguished from 'a real exchange economy'. Kalecki,[2] it may be recalled, had derived considerable inspiration in his early macro-economic work from Rosa Luxemburg, who had grappled with the implications of Marx's schemes of expanded reproduction

---

[1] J.M. Keynes, *The General Theory of Employment, Interest and Money*, London, 1949.

[2] See the English translation of M. Kelecki's early Polish essays, *Studies in the Theory of Business Cycles*, Oxford, 1966. (English translation of the essays originally written in Polish during 1933–39.) See also his *Essays in the Theory of Economic Fluctuasions*, London, 1939.

very early in the century when few had noticed their significance for understanding the logic of the functioning of capitalism. Fifth, the specific policy prescriptions made by Keynes in the 1930s to move out of the 'Great Depression' do not exhaust Keynes' insights. While some of his prescriptions are clearly dated, his basic insights remain vital in more ways than one even today. Sixth, the identification of Keynes' economics as the economics of a mature capitalist economy is somewhat one-sided in its emphasis. Finally, Keynes' work belongs to a philosophical tradition which begins with Hume and has very little points of overlap with the Hegelian tradition which influenced Marx rather deeply, at a crucial formative stage in his intellectual development.

II

The first proposition could have been treated as requiring no explicit articulation but for the fact that as late as June 1983, it was announced by no less than M. Friedman[3] that Keynes' most important work was *A Tract on Monetary Reform*.[4] However, this position can barely be seriously maintained as that book contained hardly any conceptual innovation, even though it had some brilliant observations to make on inflation as a tax, a point of major practical importance. The *Treatise on Money*[5] is undoubtedly more important because of Keynes' treatment of the international monetary system and for including the basic clue to the Kaldorian theory of distribution to which some post-Keynesians attach a lot of importance. On the whole, however, it can be seriously maintained that a large part of the *Treatise* was more concerned with the problem of price instability in a Wicksellian tradition, and did little to illuminate the problem of fluctuations in the aggregate level of output and employment.[6] Whatever may be one's judgement

[3] See M. Friedman in his Keynes Centennial contribution to *The Economist*. 'The Keynes Centenary', *The Economist*, London, 4 June 1983, pp. 35–37. Other articles in this series were by F.A. Hayek (11 June 1983, pp. 45–48); Sir John Hicks (18 June 1983, pp. 21–24); and Paul Samuelson (25 June 1983, pp. 21–25).

[4] J.M. Keynes, 'A Tract on Monetary Reform' (1923), in Donard Moggridge, ed., *The Collected Writings of John Maynard Keynes*, Vol. IV, London, 1971.

[5] J.M. Keynes, 'A Treatise on Money' (1930), in Donard Moggridge, ed., *The Collected Writings of John Maynard Keynes*, Vol. VI (Two Volumes), London, 1971.

[6] The parable of the 'banana grower' in the *Treatise* gives some hint as to possible output adjustment but it is only a bare hint.

about the basic validity of Keynes' system, it has to be admitted that it is as a founder of modern macro-economics that Keynes' claim to ultimate fame rests. The rudiments of the theory of output as a whole were reflected in Keynes' popular writings prior to the *General Theory*. But it is possible to maintain that the main clue to the theory of effective demand was provided by Kahn's theory of the multiplier which influenced Keynes' tract *The Means to Prosperity*.[7] Keynes' ideas on the theory of output as a whole in its formative stage were further strengthened by the access that Sraffa provided him to the Ricardo-Malthus correspondence on the 'glut controversy'. Keynes found in Malthus a kindred soul, in the 'great Cambridge tradition', as he put it in his allocutionary address in 1935. This was done at a time when Malthus had been disregarded as a general economic theorist for nearly one hundred years, a period dominated by what Keynes described as the 'Ricardian orthodoxy'.[8]

III

It is necessary to say a few words about Keynes and his intellectual affiliation to Marshall. That Marshall was a great intellectual influence in the early stage of Keynes' transformation into an economist is well known. One can see the Marshallian influence on the *Tract*. At the time of writing the *Treatise*, Keynes was moving away from Marshall to Wicksell. When it came to writing *General Theory*, Keynes chose to concentrate his attacks on Pigou, Marshall's chosen successor. The crux of this attack lay in the recognition that capitalism had no such self-regulating properties as Pigou and the 'classics' had claimed. In view of this fundamental point of difference, the 'raison d'etre' of *General Theory* itself, it may be odd to say that Keynes never broke with the Marshallian tradition. The fact remains, however, that in several ways, Keynes remained a Marshallian economist. First, Keynes remained a price

---

[7] J.M. Keynes, 'The Means to Prosperity' (1933), in *The Collected Writings of John Maynard Keynes*, Vol. IX, *Essays in Persuasion*, London, 1972, pp. 335–66.

[8] See J.M. Keynes' allocutionary address on Malthus, 'The Centenary Allocution' (1933), in Donard Moggridge, ed., *The Collected Writings of John Maynard Keynes*, Vol. X, *Essays in Biography*, London, 1972, pp. 104–08. This essay is different from his equally important but much longer essay on Malthus, 'Thomas Robert Malthus', also in the above volume, pp. 71–103.

theoretic Marshallian till the very end. His main analytical preoccupation was to extend Marshall's partial equilibrium theory to the theory of output as a whole. His definition of the short period was also entirely Marshallian. Second, quite unlike Harrod and Kalecki, Keynes refused to draw upon the contemporaneous developments in the theory of imperfect competition, even when it would have made his analysis more realistic in some respects. As a matter of fact, in a reply to Bertil Ohlin he explicitly disclaimed any relationship between his work and that of Mrs. Robinson, whose book he had earlier reviewed for publication.[9]

Third, Keynes never subscribed to the Robbins-Knight definition of economics as a science which was an adaptation from the Austrian conception of economics. Fourth, while Keynes professed a lack of interest in the 'long run' in contrast with Marshall, he did not altogether avoid discussing it. On these occasions he permitted himself 'prounciamentos' which were rather Marshallian in nature as in his vision of transformed capitalism when capital had ceased to be scarce.

These basic similarities with Marshall must be clearly borne in mind before one can hope to understand the very distinctive and, in some respects, very radical changes in perspectives that Keynes brought about.

IV

This brings me to a discussion of what Keynes had to say regarding the functioning of capitalism as a mode of economic organisation, which was in several major respects inconsistent with Marshall's understanding. This is also crucial in as much as he fashioned major aspects of his conceptual apparatus with a view to analysing the inner logic of a system with which he was basically in sympathy but which he felt possessed some major flaws. As Keynes saw it, capitalism was basically a *money using* economy. He felt that to understand capitalism, one has to develop a monetary theory of production. This is first clearly indicated in a little known paper of his which came out in a 'Festschrift' in honour of Arthur Spiethoff. The volume came out in 1932 and it clearly shows Keynes' mind at

---

[9] See J.M. Keynes, in D.E. Moggridge, ed., *The Collected Writings of John Maynard Keynes*, Vol. XIV, p. 190.

work while he was moving away from the *Treatise* to the *General Theory*.[10]

What are the predominant characteristics of an essentially monetary economy? In answering this question, Keynes at one stage even made use of Marx's distinction between two circuits of capital. In a unique complimentary reference to Marx, so uncharacteristic of him, he drew attention to Marx's two circuits of capital 'C-M-C' and 'M-C-M', and found the essence of the monetary economy to reside in the latter.[11] While he dissociated himself from the use made by Marx of the latter schema in analysing the self-valorisation process of capital, he was of the opinion that in a monetary theory, money was not a veil but an essential instrument for bringing about necessary intermediations between the present and the future. Capitalism does not remain capitalism if the forward looking aspect of production is ignored along with the concomitant aspect of uncertainty.

The central theme of uncertainty as the principal premise of his theory of effective demand is lost sight of in the mathematical formulations of the Keynesian system given by Lange, Meade, Hicks and others. But Keynes had drawn attention to this aspect of his work in his letter to Hicks, although in a muted manner.[12] But the point is made with such forcefulness in his 1937 article on *General Theory*, which came out in *QJE* in response especially to the criticism made by J. Viner, that one is left wondering how the IS-LM model, elegant as it is, could receive a canonical status as one of the clearest expositions of Keynes' system.

In dealing with uncertainty, Keynes drew on his early work on 'probability' theory, which, I believe, deserves much greater attention from economists than it has received so far, with the exception of Shackle. This is because Keynes' approach to the central question of 'probability' differed substantially from the use made of almost all contemporaneous work done on the subject. While

---

[10] See J.M. Keynes, 'Monetary Theory of Production' (1933), in *The Collected Writings of John Maynard Keynes*, Vol. XIII, *The General Theory and After*, Part I, 'Preparation', London, 1973, pp. 408–11.

[11] This material has recently come to light and is included in J.M. Keynes, *Collected Writings*, Vol. XXIX.

[12] The entire Keynes-Hicks correspondence deserves to be carefully examined. See, 'Keynes-Hicks Correspondence', in *The Collected Writings of John Maynard Keynes*, Vol. XIV, *The General Theory and After*, Part II, 'Defence and Development', London, 1973, pp. 79–84.

Ramsey, for whom Keynes had great respect, criticised Keynes' approach, it is not clear that Keynes accepted this criticism.

We know from the more recent work of Arrow that there exist some systems of postulates defining risks and attitudes to risk following from the Ramsey-de Finetti approach, in the light of which we can deduce the theorem that the market can do an optimal job of risk-sharing. This is not possible with the approach taken by Keynes in his important work *A Treatise on Probability*.[13] For, as Keynes argued there, probability calculus represented a calculus of 'partial belief', which does not, in general, lend itself to a numerical representation. The significance of Keynes' views on this question has also recently been stressed by John Hicks in his methodological tract *Causality in Economics*, a book which is important for understanding Keynes' theory of liquidity. It is not clear, however, whether John R. Hicks would have agreed with Sir John Hicks on this point.[14]

The twin phenomena of money and uncertainty explain, in Keynes' opinion, the structural basis of instability which characterises capitalism. The clue here lies in the volatile nature of inducement to invest along with the high elasticity of demand for hoards at a low enough rate of interest. These factors can also explain how real capital formation can be retarded for significant stretches of time. Further, unlike what Hansen asserted and what Keynes also suggested once or twice, they can also apply to a semi-industrialised economy such as that of India.

Keynes' observations on this set of questions have been developed very recently by Minsky for developed capitalist economies and I believe that they provide a better clue to his mature position than text book theories have generally admitted.[15] Several of us have tried to indicate their relevance to developing countries in contrast with what was asserted, with some justification, by theorists such as V.K.R.V. Rao and A.K. Dasgupta.[16]

---

[13] J.M. Keynes, 'A Treatise on Probability' (1921), in *The Collected Writings of John Maynard Keynes*, Vol. VIII, London, 1973.

[14] See John R. Hicks, *Causality in Economics*, Oxford, 1979, pp. 103–22.

[15] See Hyman P. Minsky, *John Maynard Keynes*, London, 1975 and 1976. See also his subsequent publications on the same theme in collected form, *Stabilizing an Unstable Economy*, Yale, 1986.

[16] See Sukhamoy Chakravarty, 'Keynes, "Classics" and the Developing Economies', in P.C. Joshi and C.H. Hanumantha Rao, eds., *Reflections on Economic*

This, along with the theory of multiplier, would seem to me to constitute the essence of the Keynesian Revolution.

Attempts have been made to describe Keynes' economics as a theory of 'fixed price equilibria'.[17] These efforts seem to imply that the most distinctive feature of Keynes' economics was the assumption that money wages are rigid. Sometimes it is held that Keynes did not introduce any theoretical innovations.[18]

All that he achieved was to introduce a realistic dimension to neoclassical economics, by bringing into sharp focus the fact that wage bargains are made in money and that measured in terms of money, they are largely rigid.

I think that this position is not entirely correct. There is little doubt that the fact that wage bargains are made in terms of money is central to Keynes' argument. But the issue of rigidity of wages is not so clear. There is no doubt that for certain purposes, Keynes did assume money wages to be rigid. This simplifies some part of his exposition by providing a convenient unit for measurement of output. The use of a wage unit was a fruitful idea of Keynes. Measured in terms of wage units, the consumption function can be shown to possess a higher degree of stability as Alvin Hansen showed years ago. But it is not true to say that Keynes relied on money wage rigidity to prove his central proposition that the capitalist system could not be regarded as self-adjusting. In one of the most important chapters in *General Theory*, Chapter 19, Keynes deals with the question of what would happen if money wages were assumed to be flexible. In relation to flexible wage policy, he wrote,

> The chief result of this policy would be to cause a great unstability of prices, so violent perhaps as to make business calculations futile in an economic society functioning after the manner of

---

Development and Social Change, Essays in Honour of Prof. V.K.R.V. Rao, New Delhi, pp. 75–89; and M. Rakshit, *The Labour Surplus Economy*, New Delhi, 1982. A.K. Dasgupta wrote 'Marx and Keynes', in V.B. Singh, ed., *Essays in Honour of Dr. P. Mukherjee*, New Delhi, 1965. Dasgupta's second piece is closer to the position I have taken in the above publication.

[17] In this category E. Malinvaud's work is the most important contribution from a macro-economic viewpoint, although he was preceded by J.P. Benassy. See Edmond Malinvaud, *The Theory of Involuntary Unemployment*, Oxford, 1977.

[18] See P.A. Samuelson, 'John Maynard Keynes', *Econometrica*, 1946, reprinted in Joseph E. Stiglitz, ed., *Collected Scientific Papers of Paul Samuelson*, Vol. II, Cambridge, Mass., 1966.

that in which we live. To suppose that a flexible wage policy is a right and proper adjunct of a system which on the whole is one of laissez-faire, is the opposite of the truth (p. 269).

Keynes came to this conclusion after careful consideration of the transmission channels through which a fall in money wages will affect the level of unemployment. He could find no solid reason to believe that such flexibility will necessarily correct lapses from full employment as it would merely amount to monetary management by the 'trade unions', as he himself put it, in contrast with monetary management by the banking system. While he did not think that the former was a practical possibility in a laissez-faire capitalism, he was willing to entertain the hypothesis for the sake of argument. His conclusion was that the systemic failure to reach full employment was due to deeper structural reasons than mere rigidity in the level of money wages. This is not to suggest that he did not attach any importance to the phenomenon of rigid prices in advanced capitalism. But his main attack on orthodox theory which comes out in his detailed criticism of Pigou is that it had illegitimately transferred to the properties of the system as a whole what could be true for a single firm or at most, to producers of a single homogeneous product. Thus, Keynes felt that *microeconomics* of the orthodox school did not have *macro support*. All evidence according to him pointed to the contrary.

Second, when he looked at the institutional features of the capitalist economy, what struck him most was that investment decisions were taken largely by an independent group of people in comparison with those who did most of the savings. Conventional Marshallian theory postulated an equilibrating mechanism through the rate of interest. Keynes struck a serious blow at the orthodox theory of interest based on productivity and thrift. While it is doubtful whether his effort in this respect was fully successful, he did point out that the equilibrating mechanism in a monetary economy was typically likely to operate through variations in income. Thus, Keynes succeeded in abolishing the supremacy of Say's law, but it has to be admitted that his analytical treatment of capital theoretic issues left a lot to be cleared up. Even such an ardent Keynesian as Roy Harrod[19] believed that Keynes required

---

[19] See R.F. Harrod, 'Review of G.L.S. Shackle's "The Years of High Theory"', *Economic Journal*, Vol. 78, September 1968.

something called the 'neutral' rate of interest,[20] which is consistent with equality between what should be called ex-ante saving and investment at full employment in order to protect himself against the charge that Hicks had brought against the Keynesian theory of interest as an entirely monetary phenomenon.[21]

It is clear that many who call themselves Keynesians today would agree with Harrod, especially those who believe in the 'grand neoclassical synthesis'. The 'locus classicus' for them is of course Hicks' famous article in the *Econometrica*[22] which portrays simultaneous determination of the interest rate and the level of income, given the investment demand function, the consumption function, the liquidity preference schedule and the nominal quantity of money.

The IS-LM presentation of Keynes' thought was undoubtedly an elegant device and lent itself to comparative static exercises. While Joan Robinson and some others regarded this construct as an instance of 'bastard Keynesianism', it is perhaps more accurate to say that it reflects a basic lack of clarity in *General Theory* as to how much of classical orthodoxy he was willing to shed.

He criticised Hicks for not emphasising expectations sufficiently but otherwise he had nothing to say by way of criticism.[23] He never doubted the inverse monotonic relationship between the level of investment and the rate of interest although he was doubtful of its elasticity. Keynes never gave a cogent analysis of the downward slope of the investment demand schedule.

Keynes' reviewers in the 1930s, with the exception of Kalecki, never saw any great difficulty in accepting the investment function. For them, it was a time-honoured notion. It was left to Abba Lerner to attempt a clarification of the postulated relationship.[24] Lerner's derivation proceeds in two steps. First, a downward sloping relationship is postulated between desired capital stock and the rate of interest, based on considerations relating to diminishing returns to capital. Second, it brings in imperfect substitutability of

[20] For an explication of the role of 'neutral rate of interest', see J.M. Keynes, *The General Theory, op. cit.* (note 1), p. 243.
[21] See John R. Hicks, *Value and Capital*, London, 1939.
[22] See John R. Hicks, 'Keynes and the Classics', *Econometrica*, 1937.
[23] See the Keynes-Hicks Correspondence, *op. cit.* (note 12), pp. 79–83.
[24] See A.P. Lerner, *The Economics of Control: Principles of Welfare Economics*, New York, 1947, Chapter 25, and many subsequent publications.

resources needed for producing capital goods and consumer goods, giving rise to upward rising supply price for capital goods. Whatever may be the merits of Lerner's construction, it shows clearly the influence of neoclassical capital theory on a major Keynesian theorist who probably gave the question more thought than any other known to me.

It would appear to me quite fair to state that Keynes himself was partly a neoclassical economist in his treatment of capital theoretic issues and also in his treatment of the demand side of the labour market. While he was willing to reexamine the latter question in his reply to Dunlop and Tarshis,[25] he never had any occasion to reexamine the somewhat obscure treatment of capital theoretic issues contained in Chapters 16 and 17 of *General Theory*.

His statement and belief that the best way of getting rid of the unacceptable features of capitalism was to allow for some more time a steady accumulation of capital so that 'scarcity price' which capital owners enjoyed could be brought to zero (or near zero), reflects the influence of the Ramsey model of growth whose descriptive significance for understanding the capitalist system is non-Keynesian and, some would hold, even anti-Keynesian in character.[26]

Joan Robinson became acutely aware of this inconsistency in Keynes quite early and felt the real need to extend Keynes' analysis to the Marshallian long period. Kalecki, as already alluded to, never accepted it, and in a review of *General Theory*, pointed out the unsatisfactory nature of Keynes' treatment. He used two devices to get around the problem of indeterminacy of the investment function. One is to treat expectation as a sort of average of past experiences. The other is to bring in the principle of increasing risk.

Furthermore, he also brought into the forefront the lag between investment decision and investment completion, thereby making it possible to lay down the basis of an endogenous theory of fluctuations. However, it is not clear that he succeeded in what he had set out to do, namely, a theory of cyclical growth in a growing capitalist economy. His treatment of innovation as a semi-exogenous

---

[25] See J.M. Keynes' reply to Dunlop and Tarshis in *Economic Journal*, 1939, reprinted in *The Collected Writings of John Maynard Keynes*, Vol. VII, London.

[26] See J.M. Keynes, *The General Theory, op. cit.* (note 1), Chapter 16.

element is very important and links up with the work of Marx and Schumpeter to which I now turn.[27]

V

Similarities between some aspects of Marx's thought and that of Keynes were noted very early. While Keynes himself made no distinction between Marx and Silvio Gesell,[28] and in fact showed some preference for the latter, in the atmosphere of the 1930s it was not difficult to avoid comparison with Marx. Probably the most perceptive comparison among the early attempts was the one carried out by Fan Hung in an article where the author acknowledged his indebtedness to M. Dobb and M. Kalecki.[29] Fan Hung emphasised the special relevance of Marx's theories of expanded reproduction as well as his analysis of the functioning of money capital to derive several major propositions of Keynes' theory. He also asserted, contrary to the view expressed at that time by Joan Robinson, that Marx did not accept Say's 'law of the Market', which Marx at one stage described as merely 'childish babble'.

Subsequently, Joan Robinson carried out a critical examination of Marx's economics with considerable discernment and a great deal of sympathy.[30]

Robinson's work, according to her own testimony, was liked by Keynes. However, Keynes had no occasion to comment any further on Marx. There is some evidence that compared with the views expressed in the 1930s, particularly in his article for the *Yale Review*,[31] and also in various writings for *New Statesman*, Keynes had turned somewhat conservative, as is partly evident in his

[27] See M. Kalecki, *Theory of Economic Dynamics* (Revised Edition), New York, 1966; 'Observations on the Theory of Growth', *Economic Journal*, Vol. 72, 1962; 'Trends and Business Cycles', *Economic Journal*, Vol. 78, 1968.

[28] D. Dillard carried out a detailed analysis of the interrelationships between the ideas of Keynes, Proudhon and Gesell. A summary is given in his book, *The Economics of John Maynard Keynes*, London, 1950.

[29] See F. Hung, 'Keynes and Marx on the Theory of Capital Accumulation, Money and Interest', *Review of Economic Studies*, October, 1939, reprinted in D. Horowitz, ed., *Marx and Modern Economics*, London, 1968.

[30] See J. Robinson, *An Essay on Marxian Economics*, London, 1942.

[31] See J.M. Keynes, 'National self-sufficiency', *The New Statesman and Nation*, 8 and 15 July, 1933. (Also in *Yale Review* for Summer, 1933.) Reprinted in *The Collected Writings of John Maynard Keynes*, Vol. XXI, *Activities, 1931–39: World Crises and Policies in Britain and America*, London, 1982, pp. 233–46.

posthumous article called 'U.S. Balance of Payments', published in 1946. The important thing is, however, not what Keynes himself thought of Marx but whether the internal logic of Keynes' analysis was congruent with Marx's.

I believe that here we come across striking similarities as well as major dissimilarities. As early as 1919, Keynes wrote about the 19th century capitalists, 'like bees they saved and accumulated, not less to the advantage of the whole community because they themselves held no other ends in prospect.'[32] This is strikingly similar to Marx's analysis of the role of capitalists as bearers of the accumulation process. However, for Keynes, the system worked on the basis of a 'double deception' as he called it, whereas for Marx, the clue lay in the understanding of the process by which labour can be obtained out of labour power. Keynes thought the Ricardian basis of Marxism particularly objectionable and his follower Joan Robinson also did not find any particular use for the labour theory of value, except as a metaphysical proposition, even though she quite clearly saw that what Marx was getting at was a theory of exploitation, and not a theory of relative prices.[33]

This is not the place to go into a detailed exegesis of the labour theory of value, which has numerous facets. Suffice it only to observe that a theory of exploitation is basic to Marx's system, not merely as an ethical concept, but as an analytical device with a considerable cutting edge. Marx's specific analysis was confined to a relatively earlier stage of capitalism, whereas what most modern Marxists are trying to do is to find a suitable extension to advanced capitalism, while some 'analytical Marxists' are trying to extend it to 'socialism'.[34]

Keynes did not accept any theory of exploitation of labour by capital. What he saw instead was the transformation of bourgeois virtue of thrift into a vice in the changed circumstances of mature

---

[32] See J.M. Keynes, 'Economic Consequences of the Peace' (1919), in *The Collected Writings of John Maynard Keynes*, Vol. II, London, 1971.

[33] It is interesting to note that while Keynes was willing to accept that '*Labour* in the literal sense has been the prime factor of production' (italics in the original), he would surely have sided with Marshall rather than Marx in his value theory. See 'The Dilemma of Modern Socialism', *The Political Quarterly*, April-June 1932, reprinted in *The Collected Writings of John Maynard Keynes*, Vol. XXI, *Activities, 1931–1939*, London, 1982, pp. 33–48. The above sentence appears on p. 38.

[34] On 'analytical Marxism' see J.A. Roemer's numerous contributions, especially, *A General Theory of Exploitation and Class*, Harvard, 1982.

capitalism. He was deeply critical of the hold of Benthamism on contemporary society, even when it had outgrown such a need. Incidentally, Keynes thought Marxism was also a variant of utilitarianism.[35]

Hence, for Keynes, the crisis of capitalism was manageable by a proper management of the interest rate and if need be, by a comprehensive socialisation of investment. He wanted to fight the dark forces of time and uncertainty which, as he said, renders 'foul into fair, and fair into foul'.

For Keynes, the essential point was not to abolish capitalism as such but to bring about a euthanasia of the rentier. He also wanted to determine afresh the agenda of the state, an expression he borrowed from Bentham in his influential essay on 'The End of Laissez-Faire'.[36]

Keynes has been criticised by many Marxists, notably Paul Sweezy for his ahistorical approach. There is doubtless a considerable element of truth in this description. Keynes' treatment of mercantilism is a typical example of his treatment of history when it came to long range theorising but it should be remembered that Keynes showed a very deep appreciation of the financial mutations that capitalism in his days had undergone compared with the Victorian days which Marshall had analysed, especially in the latter's important evidence before various Royal Commissions.

I have already mentioned that the sources of Keynes' thought lie deep in the Cambridge tradition that he had inherited from Henry Sidgwick and others who had a reformist cast of mind. The contrast with Joseph Schumpeter who grew up during the same period in Franz Joseph's Vienna is quite striking. Schumpeter had to reckon with a different philosophical trend, namely, Austro-Marxism, a term first used by an American Marxist, Louis Boudin. Schumpeter accepted quite a few of the basic propositions of Austro-Marxism. For the sake of those who are sceptical, let me quote at some length, from one of Schumpeter's last works which was written to celebrate the centenary of the *Communist*

---

[35] See J.M. Keynes, 'Two Memoirs', reprinted in *The Collected Writings of John Maynard Keynes*, Vol. X, *Essays in Biography*, London, 1972.

[36] See J.M. Keynes, 'The End of Laissez-Faire' (1926), in *The Collected Writings of John Maynard Keynes*, Vol. IX, *Essays in Persuasion*, London, 1972, pp. 272–94.

Manifesto.[37] Schumpeter wrote apropos the economic interpretation of history,

> It must not be forgotten that Marx (deeply rooted as he was in eighteenth century ideas and in the German philosophy that continued eighteenth century traditions), had an enemy to fight and an obstacle to overcome that barred the way toward an acceptable theory of history—the doctrine of the 'general progress of the human mind' that made a purely intellectual process the causally important independent variable in social history, the doctrine that prospered so well from Condorcet to Comte and J.S. Mill. If the economic interpretation had done nothing else except to beat back this kind of thing by compensatory overemphasis of 'objective' economic conditions, it would, because of this merit alone, have to stand high in the history of economic as well as of general sociology.

Schumpeter went on further to praise Marx's doctrine that it is man's being that determines his consciousness and not his consciousness that determines his being as a vast and important step away from uncritical individualism.

It is very doubtful if Keynes would have agreed with Schumpeter's assessment of Marx's thought and the critical appreciation of the long-run historical dynamics that Marx initiated and Schumpeter followed, albeit with many significant differences.

For Keynes, the 'Great Depression' represented a frightful intellectual muddle. He wanted to remould the thinking of his contemporary economists to demonstrate that one could solve the major economic problems of the day provided one could jettison certain pre-existing modes of thinking. It is in the power of ideas that he believed and it is ideas which he wanted to transform.

In this assessment of the power of ideas, Keynes was both right and wrong. Right, because there was an urgent need to get away from an economic theory which rested on the fundamental premise that the economic system was a self-adjusting one. Wrong, because he under-estimated the exemplicity of the power of the vested interests, and the internal logic of the functioning of capitalism as a *mode of production*.

[37] See J.A. Schumpeter, 'The Communist Manifesto in Sociology and Economics', *Journal of Political Economy*, June 1949, pp. 199–212.

Kalecki in a series of articles which he wrote in mid-1940s saw the situation more clearly. In this he was aided by his initial schooling in Rosa Luxemburg's writings. He saw that continuous full employment may not be compatible with the maintenance of the capitalist system as a profit-motivated system. For nearly twenty-five years, it looked as if Kalecki's forebodings were misconceived or at best exaggerated. It was thought that Keynes had shown us the way to a brave new world where cycles were a thing of the past and continued accumulation could bring us into the neighbourhood of the Elysium. Experience from the late 1960s onwards has shown much of this to be untenable. It is to the contemporary situation that we turn now.

VI

What does the contemporary scene connote in terms of the relevance of Keynes' analysis of the 'macro' functioning of a capitalist economy? I should be inclined to answer that there has been little evidence to suggest that the capitalist economic system is a self-regulating one. This, after all, was Keynes' central message. More concretely, Keynes' treatment of time, uncertainty and factors influencing the inducement to invest, their dependence on the state of long-term expectation are all strongly underlined by what we have witnessed in the world as a whole during the last ten years in particular. The major change is the emergence of stagflation. Can Keynes' economics cope with the problem posed by stagflation?

I doubt whether it can, so long as we stick to the competitive paradigm which Keynes used. Keynes may have had some justification for ignoring imperfect competition, partly for meeting the orthodox theory on its own ground and partly from his conviction that allocative inefficiency of capitalism was not its most pronounced flaw. I, however, believe that it is difficult to support the second half of Keynes' reasoning. Increase in market power exercised by large corporations or organised social groups is a factor that cannot be ignored in today's context. If anything, they loom large on the economic scene, and contribute vastly to wage-price stickiness.

Asymmetric price responses of producers in the face of changing demand brings in an additional source of complication into the macro-management of the economy which the original Keynesian system did not envisage. Kalecki, who had allowed for imperfect competition in his analysis from the beginning was prescient enough to make a distinction between 'flex price' and 'fix price' markets. Manufactured commodities according to him belong to 'fix price' categories whereas markets for primary products belong to the 'flex price' group. Kaldor has recently used this distinction to explain inflation and recession in the world economy. Galbraith has used this distinction in regard to his recent analysis of the American economy. While I do not agree with those who maintain that Keynes' theory lacked solid micro-foundation, it is certainly true that a revised micro basis which takes into account the slowness of information diffusion process as well as possession of market power by various agents is essential for comprehending as well as managing the problem of stagflation. This obviously means that Keynesian policies must go beyond mere 'fiscalism'. The moot question is whether the state under capitalism is capable of carrying out comprehensive modes of planning.

Here one has to recognise that, Keynes' treatment of the State is quite unsatisfactory. In his 'The end of laissez-faire', already referred to, he merely redefined the agenda of the State and did not subject the liberal theory of the democratic State to any very close scrutiny. Schumpeter took a rather hard-headed view of the democratic State which some have found cynical. I believe that a concept of legitimation is central to the functioning of a democratic State and Schumpeter may not have sufficiently emphasised this element. However, the essence of the problem of stagflation lies in the fact that what is considered to be one legitimate function of the State, i.e., to preserve the value of the monetary standard, is found to conflict with what Keynes had made into an essential function of the State, namely, ensuring full employment. Hence arises a deep source of cleavage, which Keynes did not envisage.

Efforts have been made by many contemporary economists, especially monetarists, to give up the legitimacy of the concept of full employment with the help of a concept of 'natural rate of unemployment'. This concept has been criticised on conceptual grounds by such moderate economists as F. Modigliani and James Tobin, by no means orthodox Keynesians. Because of such opposition, these efforts have not succeeded in converting the entire profession, especially in the U.S. Hence, Keynes remains a factor to reckon with and one still thinks of a role for employment policy.

However, ideology apart, there is one additional point which requires explicit mention. Throughout his writings, Keynes had very little to say about technical progress. He assumed an important role for enterprise but took something like a 'production function' for granted. While in a purely short period context, this may not have been altogether unjustified, even though Schumpeter found it highly questionable in a 'long-period' context, Schumpeterian objections have greater validity.[38] But in his long-term projections, this feature was bound to lead him astray, as one of the historically specific features of the capitalist system has been its ability to 'revolutionise' its mode of production from time to time as both Marx and Schumpeter in their different ways put it. Marx went to the extent of deducing a law of population specific to capitalism on the basis of induced technical progress whereas Schumpeter described a stationary capitalism as a contradiction in terms.

The experience of post-World War II bears out amply the importance of technical innovations as a factor in sustaining high levels of demand and fuller utilisation of labour, aided presumably by the general acceptance of a moderately Keynesian milieu. With the fading of the Keynesian milieu, some orthodox economists hope that the revival of a climate conducive to long-run investment, especially stemming from revolution in information technology, will make it possible for the system to regain its past dynamism. In my opinion, it is still too early to form any firm conclusion on such a complex subject. My general conclusion is sceptical, not merely because a high rate of growth of output does not necessarily mean a high rate of growth of employment, but because we have also been witnessing a resurgence of the power of 'finance capital', which may not be a merely transitory factor alone. Furthermore, much on the employment side will depend on the conditions of wage bargaining or, as Marx would have put it, on the forms that class struggle assumes. Here too, it is too early to assess the trend of the 1980s.

While Keynes' analysis of long-run dynamism of capitalism is admittedly unsatisfactory, I believe that Keynes performed a great service to economic theory by placing it within the context of history, not merely as a descriptive device but more profoundly,

---

[38] See J.A. Schumpeter, 'Review of Keynes' General Theory', *Journal of the American Statistical Association*, December 1930, pp. 791–95.

by forging a handy set of tools for coherent thinking about problems of the capitalist economy as a whole and by showing how economic action arises in the context of an irrevocable past and an uncertain future.

2

The Analytical Framework of Keynes

MIHIR RAKSHIT

> The object of our analysis is not to provide a machine, or method of blind manipulation, which will furnish an infallible answer, but to provide ourselves with an organised and orderly method of thinking our particular problems; and, after we have reached a provisional conclusion by isolating the complicating factors one by one, we then have to go back on ourselves and allow, as well as we can, for the probable interactions of the factors amongst themselves.[1]

The tale of the sweeping success of Keynesian economics, followed by its rapid decline and fall, has all the ingredients of a classical tragedy. The high points of this story are clearly marked and worth recapitulating. To all important economic problems faced by Western nations since the Treaty of Versailles (1919), Keynes responded brilliantly, seeking to make sense of the contemporary events in order to prescribe suitable policies. The consummation of this process of search for relevant theory and policy was seen to be attained in the *General Theory*, where Keynes broke away from the neo-classical system and put forward an alternative paradigm regarding the macro behaviour of capitalist economies. The majority of the economists were soon converted to his doctrine, and by the end of the Second World War economic policies in almost all capitalist countries came to be based firmly on Keynesian principles. With the success of these policies in maintaining full employment with a fairly high rate of economic growth for more than two decades, Keynes was regarded as the saviour of capitalism, and economists as a group had never had it so good in terms of prestige, power and all the earthly things the 'rational man' strives for.

---

[1] J.M. Keynes, A General Theory of Employment, *Interest and Money*, London, 1936, p. 297.

Failure of Keynesian Economics

Such a happy state of affairs was, alas, too good to last, and by the 1960s Keynesian tools appeared to have completely lost their cutting edge. Since the retreat of Keynesianism over the last two decades is mainly due to the failure of its policy package, we may as well take a quick inventory of its principal contents. The major malady of capitalist economies—business cycles with varying degrees of employment and of capacity utilisation—is attributed by Keynes to the deficiency and excess of effective demand. The government is urged to fight unemployment and inflation through counter-cyclical measures, injecting purchasing power in the economy in times of unemployment, and cutting down expenditure through taxes or other means when the economy is beset with inflation. With the passage of time this simple remedy has been found ineffective because of two related developments. First, the goal of attaining internal with external equilibrium has proved elusive to most countries under both fixed and relatively flexible exchange rate systems. The emergence of such a problem was, indeed, anticipated by the early Keynesians, but they could not suggest any practicable solution to it. Again, rising prices are found to go merrily along with large scale, even growing unemployment—a phenomenon the simple Keynesian theory cannot easily account for. Under these conditions, Keynesian policies turned out to be of little help to capitalist economies in their attempt to solve the problems of unemployment, inflation and balance of payments.

The stage was thus set for the ascendancy of the monetarists under the inspiring leadership of Professor Friedman, whose views, like those of Keynes, are both persuasive and capable of being projected in terms of a few simple propositions intelligible to the lay public and politicians—qualities which, as the history of economic analysis suggests, are essential for the success of any theory. According to Friedman, not only are capitalist economies inherently stable, but Keynes-type anti-cyclical policies, especially monetary policies, also raise rather than reduce the amplitude of fluctuations in the levels of prices and income. Hence, governments are advised to follow a policy of only ensuring a steady growth in money supply in order to maintain price stability, rather than of overall demand management.

The impressive gains in favour of monetarism over the last two decades have not, however, made Keynes irrelevant, either in terms of the search for an appropriate analytical framework for capitalist societies, or in respect of the central economic problems they are confronted with. For one thing, monetarists incorporate in their theories quite a few Keynesian building blocks and draw conclusions which Keynes himself noted in passing way back in 1930[2], but choose to play them down as of minor significance[3]. Again, monetarism seems to have thrived more on the failure of the traditional Keynesian policies than on its positive merits or inherent strength. Stagflation and inflationary depression are as much a puzzle to the monetarist as they are to an orthodox Keynesian. Finally, even the most ardent followers of the Chicago school are unlikely to derive much comfort from the record of Friedmanite policies followed in Great Britain, USA or Chile. Nor is it easy (with any normal definition of 'long run' and 'full employment') to explain, *a la* Friedman[4] or Lucas,[5] the post-Second World War experience of prolonged boom followed by severe and near chronic unemployment in a number of capitalist countries. Thus, the central theme of Keynesian economics, namely, the failure of the market mechanism to ensure full and optimal utilisation of resources, remains as important now as it was in Keynes' days. This, to be sure, does not make the Keynesian theory necessarily relevant. But an appraisal of the ephemeral and enduring features of Keynes' analytical framework may suggest fruitful ways of approaching emergent problems that continue to baffle the present generation of economists.

Keynes' Method: Nature of Adjustment and Equilibrium

The Core of the Keynesian System

In our search for the basic contributions of Keynes we focus on those elements of his work which form an inter-connected schema,

---

[2] J.M. Keynes, *A Treatise on Money*, Vols. I and II, London, 1930.

[3] We propose to return to this theme at a later stage of our enquiry.

[4] M. Friedman, *The Optimum Quantity of Money*, Chicago, 1969; M. Friedman, 'A Theoretical Framework for Monetary Analysis', *Journal of Political Economy*, Vol. 78, 1970.

[5] R.E. Lucas, *Studies in Business Cycle Theory*, Amsterdam, 1982.

or a model, however incomplete. Such an approach forces us to identify the *Treatise* along with the *General Theory* as forming the core of the Keynesian analytical framework. Let us remember that in both his major works, Keynes is concerned with problems of unemployment and trade cycles in mature capitalist economies. In analysing the nature of these problems, the two books, especially the earlier one, bring to the fore the importance of identifying the rapidity of adjustments in prices and quantities in different markets—a point examined at length by Leinjonhufvud[6]. In this respect there is a remarkable degree of similarity in the two Keynesian models. First, money wages in both are taken to be sticky, and the short-run behaviour of the economy is worked out on the basis of historically given levels of wages. Second, contrary to the contentions of Leinjonhufvud, Friedman[7] and Malinvaud[8], Keynes assumes commodity prices to be perfectly flexible[9]. In fact, the *Treatise* employs the Marshallian method where prices are always market clearing at any given level of production, and the difference between the demand price and the supply price initiates a process of adjustment in output and employment.

A related, though curious, feature of the Keynesian treatment of investment in the *Treatise* as well as in the *General Theory* is that, the value of industrial equities is taken as a proxy for prices of capital goods—a procedure that induces Keynes to regard their price level as adjusting instantaneously to market forces[10]. Following Marshall, it is then assumed that the actual price of capital goods equals their demand price, which, in its turn, 'depends on the rate of interest at which the prospective income from them is capitalised'.[11] Since investment is small in relation to the stock of capital in developed economies, the prospective yield is not regarded as sensitive to the current rate of capital accumulation. In both

---

[6] A. Leijonhufvud, *On Keynesian Economics and the Economics of Keynes*, London, 1968.

[7] M. Friedman, 'A Theoretical Framework for Monetary Analysis', *op. cit.*

[8] E. Malinvaud, *Theory of Unemployment Reconsidered*, Oxford, 1977.

[9] In a footnote, Malinvaud observes, however, the price-marginal cost equality condition in Chapter 21 of the *General Theory*.

[10] This was perhaps natural for an economist having an intimate knowledge of the share market. However, few economists will now subscribe to the Keynesian notion, since prices of most investment goods are sticky, even though prices are perfectly flexible.

[11] J.M. Keynes, *Treatise, op. cit.*, Vol. I, p. 154.

these respects the *General Theory* approach closely follows the *Treatise* and emphasises the volatile nature of investment and its crucial role in the generation of trade cycles.

The propensity to invest along with the consumption function lies at the heart of the Keynesian mechanism of the formation of effective demand in the *General Theory*. In the *Treatise*, Keynes does not put forth explicitly an aggregate consumption function, but all its ingredients are to be found in his discussion of the adjustment process where expenditure on consumption goods is related to earnings of workers and capitalists. Keynes also recognises the possibility of a change in the rate of interest affecting saving, but does not consider this effect quantitatively significant.[12]

Again, as Hicks[13] has already noted, the operation of the saving-investment mechanism—in fact, the theory of effective demand itself—comes into its own only when people regard money as a substitute for bonds or other types of assets. One of the important innovations of the *Treatise*, an innovation that is carried over to the *General Theory*, is the formulation of the liquidity preference function. This enables Keynes to forge a link between the real and the monetary sectors of the economy, and to spell out the transmission mechanism which was lacking in the neo-classical compartmentalisation of the two sectors.

Given the common ingredients in the analytical constructs of the two books, especially their general refrain regarding the primary impulse of cyclical fluctuations originating in the investment goods sector, there is little wonder that the basic message of the two theories are broadly similar. However, for a full appraisal of the contribution and relevance of Keynes, it will be improper to gloss over the important differences between the two approaches. Nor is it correct to hold that the *General Theory* contains all the important theoretical innovations of the earlier work, or that the rest of the *Treatise*'s analysis is largely superfluous, if not completely erroneous.

There is, in the first place, a major difference in the mode of analysis adopted in the two cases. In the *General Theory*, Keynes uses the method of short-run equilibrium analysis and draws the conclusion that underemployment equilibrium will be the rule rather than the exception in mature capitalist economies. In the

---

[12] Ibid., p. 204.

[13] J.R. Hicks, 'Mr. Keynes and the Classics: A Suggested Interpretation', *Econometrica*, Vol. 5, 1937.

Treatise also, Keynes' major thesis is that unregulated capitalist societies cannot but be plagued by problems of unemployment and inflation. However, the model used in the *Treatise* is one of disequilibrium dynamics, and the equilibrium which Keynes takes here as the point of reference (or more accurately, as the point of departure) is a full-employment one. Indeed, though the dynamic and sequential analysis in the *Treatise* is far from well rounded and needs to be tightened up at various points, one can trace to it quite a few elements of the disequilibrium systems that have gained prominence in recent years.

Second, Keynes' perception, in respect of the sources of disequilibrium in a mature capitalist economy, is much broader in the *Treatise* than in the *General Theory*. Apart from disturbances originating in the prospective yield or the state of long-run expectations, in the *Treatise* Keynes locates two other factors contributing to disturbances, though ironically their relative importance has turned out to be exactly the reverse of his ordering in 1930. In his exposition of the 'fundamental equations', especially in the parable of the banana economy,[14] Keynes appears to have placed a good deal of emphasis on changes in consumption propensities as a possible source of disequilibrium. However, this factor is not regarded as a significant source of disturbance in either the *General Theory* or the post-Keynesian literature. The other factor, namely, changes in efficiency earnings of labour due to technical improvements, or variations in the bargaining strength of trade unions, is indeed regarded as giving rise to Income Inflation and Deflation.[15] But Keynes does not assign any important role to this factor and concentrates on wage adjustments in response to prolonged overemployment and un-employment of labour.[16] These problems are completely ignored in the *General Theory*, but are examined in some detail in *How to Pay for the War*.[17] In the latter, disequilibrium, originating in the labour market, is perceived to be an important feature of mature capitalist countries—a perception which in fact has resulted in the voluminous post-Keynesian literature on wage dynamics, cost-push and related subjects.

[14] *Treatise, op. cit.*, Vol. I, Ch. 12.
[15] Ibid., p. 155.
[16] A theme we shall return to shortly.
[17] J.M. Keynes (1939), 'How to Pay for the War', in Keynes, *Collected Works*, Vol. XXII, London, 1978.

Finally, in the formal models of both the *Treatise* and the *General Theory*, monetary factors impinge on output, prices and other variables through the interest rate mechanism. But while the significance of these factors is somewhat played down in the later work, they assume an important role in the *Treatise*, both in causing fluctuations and during the process of adjustment of the economy. A related difference between the two Keynesian models lies, first, in the menu of assets competing with shares (or with capital goods indirectly) for a place in the portfolio of economic units; and second, in the treatment of the banking system in the scheme of integration between the real and the monetary sectors. In the *General Theory*, investment is supposed to be financed through the issue of bonds, and the theory of liquidity preference relates the rate of interest, or bond prices, to the demand for holding money balances. The asset holder in the *Treatise* chooses between shares on the one hand and income, business and savings deposits on the other, so that 'the price level of investment is the resultant of the sentiment of the public and the behaviour of the banking system.'[18] The analytical framework of the financial sector of the *Treatise* thus appears to be broader than that of the *General Theory*: in the former, not only is banks' ability to fix *both* the supply of money and the rate of interest explicitly recognised, but the close connection between expectations, the demand for various kinds of bank deposits, and the investment demand is also brought to the fore. This connection, it is of some interest to note, becomes tenuous in the *General Theory* model comprising the liquidity preference and the marginal efficiency of capital, and is finally lost in the IS-LM and the other neo-Keynesian formulations.

Adjustment and Equilibrium

It should, by now, be clear that the *Treatise* cannot be regarded as simply a transitory stage in the development of Keynes' analytical framework. In fact, the *General Theory* suffers from the disadvantage of being written under the shadow of one overwhelming experience of Western countries: not much attention could be paid in this work to income or profit inflation, changes in the bargaining strength of labour, the inter-class distribution of income and other

---

[18] J.M. Keynes, *Treatise, op. cit.*, Vol. I, p. 143.

factors relating to the long-run behaviour of the economy. By contrast, the *Treatise* approach is more general and anticipates most of the major post-Second World War developments in monetary theories, both Keynesian and neo-classical.

Prices and Profits—The Widow's Cruse Theory

In order to appreciate the relevance and importance of Keynes' contribution, it may be helpful at this stage to give an outline of the economic process as visualised in the *Treatise* and the *General Theory*. A convenient point of departure for this purpose is an economy forced out of the long-run full-employment path due, say, to a fall in prospective yield, or other factors. In the *Treatise*, the first impact of such a shock is a decline in prices and profits in the investment goods sector, which, with a positive marginal propensity to consume of the capitalists, reduces the demand, prices and profits in the consumption goods sector as well.[19] It is in this context that Keynes[20] put forth the widow's cruse or the Danaid jar theory of profits. This forms the core of the Kaldor model of income distribution,[21] and underlines the role of spending propensities of different classes in determining the income shares. However, Keynes' widow's cruse theory, unlike the Kaldor model, does not imply a shift of resources between the consumption and the investment goods sectors; nor does it claim to explain the *equilibrium* distribution of income. The theory seeks to analyse the generation of profits at the first stage of the dynamic process initiated by a change in the prices of investment goods relatively to their costs of production, though the multiplier mechanism magnifying the initial impact through expenditure and re-expenditure out of profits (with no change in output), is indeed taken note of.

Quantity Adjustments

Once profits or losses have originated in the system, producers try to change their scale of operation. While the *General Theory* is

[19] J.R. Hicks, 'A Note on *Treatise*', in *Critical Essays in Monetary Theory*, Oxford, 1967.
[20] *Treatise, op. cit.*
[21] N. Kaldor, 'Alternative Theories of Distribution', *Review of Economic Studies*, Vol. 61, 1955–56.

concerned almost exclusively with the short-run equilibrium levels of output and employment which the economy tends to, Keynes' earlier work focuses more on the speed, duration and possible convergence (or divergence) in the process of adjustment. Following the *Treatise*, it is possible to distinguish between two sets of factors governing the speed of quantity adjustment in a situation of disequilibrium. The first relates to the producers' plans in the face of profits and losses, and the other to the constraint operating on the execution of the plans themselves.

It is noted, for example, that in a situation of disequilibrium, 'at first entrepreneurs may continue to offer employment at the old terms, even though it involves them in losses, partly because they are tied up with long period contracts with the factors of production which they cannot quickly get out of, and partly because it will be worthwhile, so long as they hope and believe that the period of loss will be fairly short, to avoid the expenses of closing and starting up again.'[22] It may be observed that such hopes and beliefs, if widely shared, will considerably slow down the speed of decline in output and employment, since the maintenance of the scale of operation of a firm arrests the decline in demand for the wares of other firms. The *Treatise* approach can, thus, account for the widely observed phenomenon of labour hoarding resulting in the pro-cyclical pattern of labour productivity—a phenomenon which would appear outlandish in the *General Theory* world.

Again, in the *Treatise* Keynes analyses, in some detail, the crucial role of working capital (goods-in-process) and liquid capital (stocks of goods readily available for final use) in generating cyclical changes and governing the process of output adjustment, through both the demand and the supply sides. Keynes[23] not only emphasises the part played by inventory investment in the generation of effective demand[24], but also suggests the limit to the short-run expansion of output set by the stock of working capital.[25]

---

[22] J.M. Keynes, *Treatise, op. cit.*, Vol. I, pp. 206–07.

[23] Ibid., p. 304.

[24] Giving rise to Metzler-type inventory cycles. See L.A. Metzler, 'The Nature and Stability of Inventory Cycles', *Review of Economics and Statistics*, Vol. 23, 1941.

[25] Hicks discusses at length the implications of the presence or absence of stocks for the working of the multiplier process. Indeed, the major conclusions of Hicks, in respect of both the depressive effect of surplus stocks and their necessity for the expansion of output, can be found, contrary to Hicks' contention, in the *Treatise*. See J.R. Hicks, *The Crisis of Keynesian Economics*, London, 1974.

Industry is extraordinarily sensitive to any excess or deficiency, even a slight one, in the flow of available output ready to be fed into the productive process. If there is a deficiency, full employment is impossible at the existing level of real wages; if there is an excess, equally though for quite a different reason full employment is impossible at the existing level of real wages. In the event of a deficiency the means for full employment is lacking; in the event of an excess the incentive is lacking.[26]

One of the puzzling features of the *General Theory*—a feature which Hicks also takes note of—is that, practically no role is assigned in this framework[27] to working and liquid capital. The solution to the puzzle lies, perhaps, with Keynes' concern in this work with underemployment 'equilibrium'; the leads and lags in the adjustment process, that are so important in the *Treatise*, may then be regarded as of minor importance. It is also curious that the *General Theory*-type underemployment 'equilibrium' does not arise in the *Treatise*, even as a transitory phase in the process of adjustment, especially when Keynes[28] considers quantity changes explicitly. The reason may perhaps be traced to the absence, in the *Treatise*, of marginal analysis, which Keynes employs so effectively at almost every stage in the *General Theory*.[29]

There are, indeed, passages in the *Treatise* where Keynes comes close to deriving the *General Theory*-type results. Analysing the depressionary forces due to a thrift campaign in the 'banana economy', Keynes notes that there may be a position of 'equilibrium' when the downward process 'peters out as a result of growing

---

[26] J.M. Keynes, *Treatise, op. cit.*, Vol. II, p. 146.
[27] J.R. Hicks, *The Crisis, op. cit.*, p. 12, fn. 2.
[28] J.M. Keynes, *Treatise, op. cit.*
[29] The definition of full employment is given in terms of the equality (in absolute terms), of the marginal utility from wages and the marginal disutility from work; producers are in equilibrium when prices equal marginal costs; the multiplier—the marginal impact of autonomous investment on income—is the reciprocal of the marginal propensity to save; the rate of interest equals the marginal efficiency of capital on the one hand, and the liquidity preference at the margin on the other; the optimum holding of assets is characterised by the equality of their marginal returns, or rather, of the net advantages of holding them. Here, Keynes is employing marginal analysis with a vengeance.

poverty'.[30] All the ingredients for deriving underemployment equilibrium are, in fact, present in the *Treatise*, though Keynes chooses to suggest only its possibility rather than derive it formally.

Wage Adjustments and Unemployment

The equilibrium in the *General Theory* rests, among other things, on the empirical premise that involuntary unemployment does not, by itself, cause *falling* wages.[31] Wages in the *Treatise* are also assumed to be sticky, but they do adjust and the degree of adjustment depends upon both the *extent* and the *duration* of unemployment. While analysing the different stages in the contractionary process following a rise in the Bank Rate, Keynes suggests: 'Finally, under the pressure of growing unemployment, the rate of earnings—though perhaps only at long last—will fall.'[32] It is emphasised, however, that the economy has to put up with 'protracted period of unemployment and business losses which ensues before money earnings per unit of output are adjusted to new equilibrium'.[33] Even though the adjustment process is long-drawn out, it does, indeed, tend towards the full employment equilibrium with lower wages and prices: 'It is only when what I have called consummation of the process has been achieved, namely, the reduction of the rate of efficiency earnings, that a true equilibrium will be reestablished'.[34]

It is also of some interest to record, that the discussion on the wage-price-output adjustment in the *Treatise* identifies a number

---

[30] J.M. Keynes, *Treatise, op. cit.*, Vol. I, p. 179. This goes against the Patinkin contention that Keynes fails to realise the possibility of an equilibrium at a lower level of income, following the thrift campaign. (See D. Patinkin, 'The Process of Writing the General Theory: A Critical Survey', in D. Patinkin and J.C. Leith, eds., *Keynes, Cambridge and the General Theory*, London, 1977.) In the chapter, 'An Exercise in the Pure Theory of the Credit Cycle', Keynes also refers to 'an equilibrium between prices and costs of production [where the economy] . . . is still characterised by unemployment' (*Treatise, op. cit.*, Vol. I, p. 305). This, however, is different from the *General Theory*-type equilibrium and is presumably attained through decumulation of capital.

[31] Underemployment equilibrium, *a la General Theory*, is perfectly consistent with a situation where money images decline in response to a fall in the level of employment.

[32] J.M. Keynes, *Treatise, op. cit.*, Vol. I, p. 207.

[33] Ibid., p. 272.

[34] Ibid., p. 208.

of elements which are regarded as post-Keynesian rather than Keynesian. An expansionary process, it is recognised, may carry the economy beyond the full employment level as 'certain entrepreneurs may now be willing to increase their output even if it means making larger offer than before to the factors of production because they foresee profits'.[35] Such trespass is strictly prohibited in both the *General Theory* and the new-Keynesian models of trade cycles. However, this is not illegitimate under disequilibrium dynamics, where asymmetric expectations of producers and workers in respect of money wages and prices, or inter-temporal substitution of leisure for labour *a la* Lucas,[36] may raise employment above its long-run equilibrium level. Again, in the *Treatise*, Keynes allows for, though he does not go into the details of, wage inflation, operating through the first term of his fundamental equations. This phenomenon is completely left out in the *General Theory*, but once again recognised as an important ingredient of the inflationary process in *How to Pay for the War*. Thus, commenting on the mechanics of the price-wage spiral, Keynes suggests: 'The first step in the spiral's ascent can begin just as well at the wage end, and this, perhaps, is what happens more often'.[37]

Indeed, that Keynesian economics is not simply the economics of underemployment equilibrium is attested by the close attention paid in the *Treatise* to the fact, that under a deflationary or an inflationary process, all wages and prices do not change in the same proportion. Not only does this produce significant distortionary effects, but it makes the way to equilibrium long, winding and tortuous.

> The effect of contraction is not to secure an equal reduction all round, but to concentrate the reduction on those particular factors which are in the weakest bargaining position or have the shortest contracts governing their rate of money-earnings. It may be a very long time before their *relative* rates of efficiency earnings are restored to their (equilibrium) proportions. Nor is this an evil peculiar to depression; there is an analogous mal-distribution of earnings which is equally characteristic of an inflation.[38]

---

[35] Ibid., pp. 263–64.
[36] R.E. Lucas, *Studies in Business Cycle Theory, op. cit.*
[37] J.M. Keynes, 'How to Pay for the War', *op. cit.*
[38] J.M. Keynes, *Treatise, op. cit.*, Vol. I, p. 271.

This approach clearly points to the necessity of disaggregating commodity and factor markets on the basis of the degree of flexibility of prices and quantities, and underlines the inappropriateness of models that focus only on equilibrium, short-run or long-run.

Keynes and the Monetarists

The perception just noted makes the Keynesian approach to the effects of monetary factors quite different from that of the monetarists, or even of the most influential Keynesians. Keynes,[39] to be sure, highlights the motives of economic agents—of consumers, businessmen and others—for holding money balances. It is this strand of the *Treatise* that has been followed up in the *General Theory*, and in the post-Keynesian contributions on the money demand functions.[40] Friedman,[41] in fact, puts forth a system wherein the *General Theory* and the monetarist models of the money market are seen to be identical, and the difference between the two frameworks turns on the rigidity or flexibility of money wages and prices. By Keynes' own admission, in the *General Theory* all the classical propositions come into their own, once the economy has attained full employment. The *Treatise* is more explicit on this point, and provides a sketch of long-run full employment equilibrium, where the quantity theory conclusions remain valid:

> Or putting it the other way round, given the total quantity of money, only those combinations of the rate of earnings, the volume of output and the price level of securities are feasible which lead to the aggregate requirements of money being equal to the given total. This means, indeed, that in equilibrium . . . there is a unique relationship between the quantity of money and the price-levels of consumption goods and of output as a

---

[39] *Treatise, op. cit.*

[40] See, for example, W.J. Baumol, 'The Transactions Demand for Cash: An Inventory Theoretic Approach', *Quarterly Journal of Economics*, Vol. 66, 1952; J. Tobin, 'Liquidity Preference as Behaviour Towards Risk', *Review of Economic Studies*, Vol. 25, 1958; M. Friedman, 'The Quantity Theory of Money—A Restatement', in M Friedman, ed., *Studies in the Quantity Theory of Money*, Chicago 1956; and, M. Friedman, *The Optimum Quantity of Money*, Chicago, 1969.

[41] 'A Theoretical Framework for Monetary Analysis, *op. cit.*.

whole, of such a character that if the quantity of money were double the price levels will be double also.[42]

However, one can discern in the *Treatise* two types of money demand functions—one, the relation that obtains when prices, output and employment are at their long-run equilibrium levels; and the other, the demand for various types of deposits when adjustments in different markets are in progress. So far as the equilibrium relation is concerned, Keynes of the *Treatise*, as we have just noted, is a monetarist *par excellence*. But for explaining phenomena like credit cycles,[43] (*Treatise*), or the behaviour of prices in the short or medium run equilibria, he rejects the quantity theory approach, or even the money demand functions obtaining in long-run equilibrium. The quantity equation, Keynes holds, 'entirely obscures disturbances—which in practice are one of the most important types of disturbances—arising out of a change in the proportions in which deposits are held for different purposes distinguished above as Savings, Business and Income'.[44]

Indeed, in spite of Keynes' apparent acceptance of the long-run quantity theory results, it is impossible to overlook the basic difference between Friedman and Keynes, not only of the *General Theory*, but also of the *Treatise* vintage. While Friedman assumes the money demand function to be basically stable, Keynes harps on the close connection between investment propensities and the 'bear position', and the consequent volatile nature of financial and saving deposits. Lacking the faculty (of the three weird sisters of *Macbeth*) 'to look into the seeds of time and say which grain will grow and which will not', the asset holders are liable to switch from securities to saving deposits, or vice versa, at even transient or random changes in the economic system. Moreover, in the Keynesian framework, at every change in investment and/or saving propensities, there will be an immediate impact on the level of money prices, and the quantity theory 'is intractable for the task of analysing disturbances in the price-level' due to these changes.[45] Last but not the least, the transmission mechanism in the *Treatise*, unlike that of Friedman, hinges crucially on the consensus and the

---

[42] J.M. Keynes, *Treatise, op. cit.*, vol. I, pp. 146–47.
[43] Ibid., p. 222.
[44] Ibid., p. 233.
[45] Ibid.

division of opinion; on the length of contracts between producers and the owners of factors; and on the relative degree of flexibility of various prices and money wages. It is no wonder, then, that in spite of the similarity in the nature of long-run equilibrium in the two systems, the *Treatise* reading of the behaviour of the capitalist economy is so different from that of Friedman: the emphasis in the *Treatise* is not so much on equilibrium, but on the long-drawn process of adjustment attended with 'the protracted period of unemployment and business losses'[46]—a theme elaborated at length in the *General Theory*.

An Overview

Unemployment and the consequent waste of resources are the major themes of the *General Theory* as also of the *Treatise*. The core of the analytical framework developed in the two books for explaining this malady of capitalist societies consists in the saving-investment mechanism intertwined with the asset demand for money. In this framework, expectations play a crucial role in shaping and shifting the investment and the money demand functions, thus subjecting the economy to bouts of booms and depressions. There are, to be sure, differences between the two books which need to be taken note of for an appreciation of the development of Keynes' ideas and perception regarding the functioning and future of Western capitalism. Thus, while the *Treatise* system tends towards full employment equilibrium in the long-run, the *General Theory* points clearly to the possibility, in fact, to the inevitability, of secular stagnation in unregulated capitalist economies. It is easy, however, to overemphasise this difference: even in the *Treatise*, Keynes notes explicitly that the duration of unemployment and the time required for recovery, generally extends 'for a period of years',[47] so that the long-run equilibrium configuration, though analytically interesting, is of little use for explaining the behaviour of capitalist economies, or for formulating policies.

The other difference between the two books, relates to the relative importance attached to monetary and fiscal instruments for controlling business cycles. While the *Treatise* model underlines the importance of monetary policies for countering both

[46] Ibid., p. 272.
[47] Ibid., pp. 271–72.

inflation and depression, the *General Theory* is marked by 'elasticity pessimism',[48] and hence favours fiscal intervention by the government for controlling aggregate demand.

It should, however, be emphasised that even in the earlier book, Keynes, in contrast to the then prevailing neo-classical doctrine, was convinced of the primacy of investment, rather than of saving, as sources of economic growth and fluctuations. Noting that the 'increment of wealth' can come 'wholly out of increased activity and not out of diminished consumption,'[49] Keynes goes on to assert: 'Not only may thrift exist without enterprise, it positively discourages the recovery of enterprise and sets a vicious circle by its adverse effect on profits. If Enterprise is afoot, wealth accumulates whatever may be happening to Thrift; and if Enterprise is asleep, wealth decays whatever Thrift may be doing'.[50] It will thus be entirely in the spirit of both the *General Theory* and the *Treatise* to advocate direct and indirect measures for promoting investment.

The basic message of the Keynesian system is thus quite clear: left to themselves, capitalist economies have an inherent tendency towards stagnation and business cycles. But Keynes believes that his diagnosis points, unambiguously, to the corrective measures necessary for steering the economy clear of the two evils of unemployment and inflation. In fact, once the economy has come to enjoy full employment equilibrium, Keynes goes on to add, all the tenets of neo-classical economics regain their validity and the future of capitalism need cause no worry. This optimism has, alas, turned out to be none too well founded, and the present generation of economists are baffled at the macro-economic behaviour of capitalist nations, characterised by prolonged inflation along with unemployment and balance of payments problems.

The drawback of Keynes' analysis in this regard, may perhaps be traced to his belief that the character of the capitalist society can remain unaffected when governments try to maintain full employment and control the overall behaviour of the economy. It has to be conceded that Keynes could not foresee the emergence of new forces in the process of bargaining or setting of prices—of

---

[48] When investment is relatively inelastic to change in interest rates, and the demand for money is highly interest-elastic, variations in money supply will not have much of an impact on investment, and hence, on effective demand.

[49] J.M. Keynes, *Treatise, op. cit.*, Vol. II, p. 150.

[50] Ibid., pp. 148–49.

commodities, labour, or currencies. But we need to keep in view the fact that not only does the response, of economic agents or groups, to some phenomenon depend crucially upon the economic organisations in which the agents operate, but what is more important, these organisations and rules of the game themselves also tend to change over time as people experiment and learn from experience. Indeed, it may not be too far-fetched to hold that the present failure of Keynesian policies stems, partly at least, from their early success in maintaining an unprecedented scale and growth of economic activity over a considerable period of time, during which the bargaining and price-setting process itself has changed in both domestic and international markets. Economists, we are reminded once again, are hardly in a position to play the role of soothsayers, or formulate laws valid for all time to come![51]

There is, however, one area of Keynesian economics which has proved more enduring than its specific results or policy conclusions. In his analysis of the widow's cruse theory, of the paradox of thrift, of sectional bargaining and wage-setting in the labour market, and, above all, of investment decisions, Keynes underlines the distinction between the individual and the group experience, and the resulting isolation paradoxes in macro-economics. The importance of this Keynesian theme is repeatedly brought home in the modern world by the actions of oligopolistic industries (including oil cartels), of labour unions, of various pressure groups, and of trading communities and nations. The solution to the problems consequent upon the separate pursuit of their goals by various economic agents and groups must, perforce, be Keynesian, namely, some form of collective action at the national and international level. The required scale of planning would not, perhaps, have found favour with Keynes, given his liberal-democratic approach.[52] However, his ideas point, inevitably, to such a remedy for the current ills of the world economy.

---

[51] Indeed, the examples of both Marx and Keynes appear to lend force to such a conclusion.

[52] Keynes, we may note, did want the IMF to act as a supra-national central bank with powers to create 'bancor' which was to serve as the international currency.

3
The Resurgence of Political Economy
KRISHNA BHARADWAJ

In the period since the 1960s, we have experienced a remarkable resurgence of interest in classical and Marxian political economy. This has been evident, on the one hand, in a continuing critical confrontation with the mainstream neo-classical theory and, on the other, in attempts at evolving approaches to economic problems, extending in new directions the surplus-based framework of political economy. Theoretical debates and advances have moved mainly on three terrains. In the first place, they occur in the elucidation and reconstruction of the basic structure underlying classical and Marxian political economy, which has made possible a clearer and more cogent perception of the analytical development of political economy as a theoretical system. Thus, we are now better aware of the peculiarity of concepts and propositions developed by classical economists, the forms which logical problems assumed and were sought to be resolved, with varying degrees of success, by these theorists. This has also provided a fresh perspective to view the radical extensions and reformulations of the rudimentary theory of the earlier classical writers by Marx, who posed new theoretical problems and added entirely new dimensions. No doubt, this has evoked strong controversies in political economy, but active debates are a proof of a theoretical system being alive, kicking and growing. Secondly, the established neo-classical theory which has continued to dominate economic theory (despite occasional exposures of its weaknesses) since the 1870s, is being critically scrutinised, both with regard to its logical coherence, as also its ability to handle and interpret the real world experiences of economies. Thirdly, many attempts are underway to the analysis of accumulation, within the rubric of what may be broadly termed surplus-based analysis, taking inspiration from Marx and other Marxist writers like Lenin, Rosa Luxemburg and Kalecki. The range of these problems is diverse, spanning issues concerned with the dynamics of the capitalist and socialist systems, as well as the experiences of the developing economies, in their national and international setting. New conceptual developments and approaches have significantly emerged, particularly in the analysis of accumulation processes in developing economies.

The present paper can have no pretensions to covering the vast ground. Instead, we have restricted ourselves mainly to reviewing the 'revival' of the classical approach, particularly focusing on value and distribution, so as to bring out the distinctiveness of its approach and some of its critical and reconstructive implications. Our concentration on this narrow issue of distribution and value may appear unduly restrictive. However, the reasons for such a choice are the following: considering the extant economic theories, we notice that the explanation of capitalist value (and distribution) lies invariably at their base; in the sense that, it is only after clarifying this ground that further explanations of accumulation, or technical change, or international trade, etc., are attempted, consistent with the foundation. This appears the sequence in analysis in almost all theoretical works, whether in political economy (Ricardo, Marx), or in neo-classical writings (Marshall, Wicksell, Walras, Bohm-Bawerk, Fisher). In fact, the broad divide between theories could, therefore, be suggested as originating precisely in their differing explanations of distribution and the correlated schema of price determination. It will be even seen that the weaknesses in the underlying distribution theory are further projected—and even accentuated—in the theoretical analysis of accumulation and other analytical domains, say, of technical change. Secondly, viewing the history of economic theories, we notice that the prime-mover that propelled them in new directions, or, which led to refutation of older frameworks, has been the explanation of capitalist profits. Explicitly or implicitly, it has been the floundering rock on which theories have been overturned. Ricardo began his investigation, in part, dissatisfied with Smith's explanation of profits as determined by 'competition of capitals';[1] Marx criticised Ricardo for his neglect of 'constant capital' and his tendency to equate 'surplus value' with profits. Nevertheless, common to them was the approach to the theory of distribution,

---

[1] See D. Ricardo in P. Sraffa (ed.), *Principles of Political Economy*, Vol. I, Cambridge, 1951.

which Marx developed in the advanced form of interdependent commodity production, formulating rigorously the notion of 'prices of production'. It was, again, the not-entirely-successful resolution of the 'transformation problem' by Marx that was used by his critics to fault the surplus-based explanation of profit, and which then led to the abandonment of the entire approach, apparently on this analytical ground. Recent attacks on neo-classical theory have been levelled against their theory of distribution. It would seem, therefore, that the viability and logical consistency of the theory of profit has played a crucial historical role in the survival or rejection of a theory, although this is not a singular ground. We focus, therefore, on the theory of distribution (profit) and the related value theory, as a dividing line to discriminate theories.

This paper has three parts: In Part I, we present very briefly, the nature of the recent resurgence of classical political economy as an alternative analytical system, with a distinctive structure of its own. Included also, is a rough outline of the fluctuating fortunes of theories, and our view that the surplus-based approach of Marx has possibilities of fruitful extensions, both in terms of developing a logically coherent body of theory, and of handling in a better fashion, the changing historical conditions within which economies develop.

Part II carries forward the idea that a consistent explanation of distribution is central to a logically sustainable analysis of accumulation and views, in that light, the 'first crisis' faced by the mainstream theory—the Keynesian challenge—which questioned its result that full employment equilibrium in a capitalist economy is established as an outcome of the unfettered play of competitive market forces. It is further argued in this section, that the way to the 'neo-classical synthesis'—the 'counterrevolution'—was paved by a central weakness of the Keynesian critique in essentially retaining the neo-classical theory of resource allocation, even while seeking to alter radically the theory of output and employment determination. It is suggested that the surplus-based approach may provide a more suitable base, as may be seen in Kalecki.

In Part III, the greater versatility of the Marxian surplus approach to accommodate 'historical changes' are illustrated with reference to his analysis of technical change. Here, a comparative study of Schumpeter and Marx is instructive. Both writers acknowledged technological innovations as an important element in capitalist dynamics, but analysed the problem within radically different theoretical frames—Schumpeter primarily operating within the Austrian theory. The consequent differences in their perceptions of profits, and in their analysis of the mechanism of innovations and their repercussions, are indicated.

I

The post-1960s' resurgence of political economy—what has been termed as the revival of the surplus approach—emerges both as a challenge to the established neo-classical theory, as well as a reconstructive effort to delineate, in clear and rigorous terms, the underlying structure of the classical value and distribution theory on which is ultimately founded the analysis of accumulation and capitalist dynamics. Considerable discussions have occurred in the wake of Piero Sraffa's work, prompting a rereading of the classical theory, while, in the field of 'macroeconomics', Kalecki has inspired work on the dynamics of accumulation in capitalist, socialist and 'mixed' economies. Considerable research—with regard to developing economies, on conditions of production and exchange, on questions of surplus generation, distribution and accumulation, and on problems relating to their historical transition—is growing at a striking pace. Problems relating to trade and financial relations in the international economy are being analysed outside the conventional grooves of 'free trade vulgaris' and 'optimal allocation'. In this paper, for reasons mentioned earlier, we focus on the developments in the theory of distribution.

The attempt in the concerned critical literature has been to view the supply and demand based equilibrium theory, and the surplus-based classical theory, as alternative structures.[2] The latter developed significantly in the hands of Smith and Ricardo, and was critically evaluated and extended in many directions by Marx. This critical extension occurred not only in terms of generating new concepts, but also in embedding political economy into a comprehensive philosophical system, within which to delineate the course

---

[2] See, P. Sraffa, *Production of Commodities by Means of Commodities*, Cambridge, 1960; M. Dobb, *Theories of Value and Distribution*, Cambridge, 1973; L.L. Pasinetti, *Lectures on the Theory of Production*, London, 1977; Krishna Bharadwaj, *Classical Political Economy and the Rise to Dominance of Supply and Demand Theories*, Calcutta, 1978.

of social history. This has involved not only reformulating problems, but also adding altogether new dimensions, particularly in the analysis of capitalist accumulation.

The Fluctuating Fortunes of Theories

It is interesting to note the fluctuating fortunes of the two streams of theory. As noted, the critical element was the theory of profit, concerned as all these economists were, primarily, with capitalist economies. 'Scientific Political Economy', to use Marx's words, developed through criticisms, re-interpretations, and extensions from Petty in England, and the physiocrats in France.[3] Smith and Ricardo evolved the rudimentary frame for the analysis of capitalist value and distribution centred on the notion of surplus. At a time when opposition to the Ricardian theory was already mounting, Marx extended the surplus approach comprehensively, to root the capitalist categories explicitly in historical conditions, and expound the 'laws of motion' of capitalism, as a historical stage in society's development.[4] In the subsequent seventies, an alternative theoretical structure was getting erected by Jevons, Marshall, Walras, et al.[5] In professional circles, the surplus approach was gradually submerged. On the continent, Bohm-Bawerk mounted a direct attack on Marx, choosing 'the transformation problem' as the battle-ground. In England, Marshall, claiming descendency from Ricardo, subverted the classical approach, seeking to establish Ricardo's 'cost of production' theory as but a partial, primitive form of his own, more rigorous, supply and demand based equilibrium theory.[6] In England, Marx was pushed into oblivion through benign indifference. The immediate reaction of Marxists was to resort to a distinction between 'qualitative' and 'quantitative' value problems, to push aside the difficulty posed by the transformation problem, or to concentrate mainly on historico-philosophical issues connected with Marx's method,[7] leaving the field of

---

[3] Karl Marx, *Theories of Surplus Value*, Moscow, 1963.
[4] See M. Dobb, *op. cit.*
[5] See Krishna Bharadwaj, *Classical Political Economy*, *op. cit.*
[6] See Krishna Bharadwaj, 'The Subversion of Classical Analysis: Alfred Marshall's Early Writing on Value', *Cambridge Journal of Economics*, September, 1978.
[7] See Rudolf Hilferding, 'Bohm-Bawerk's Criticism of Marx', in Sweezy (ed.), *Karl Marx and the Close of his System*, New York, 1949.

professional economic theory to the complete sway of neo-classical theory. The latter, despite occasional questioning arising from specific analytical difficulties like increasing returns, non-competitive market structures, etc., reigned supreme until the first challenge was posed by the Keynesian theory, born out of the traumatic experience of the Great Depression. The Keynesian critique, while stimulating new areas of research by posing problems in an unorthodox fashion, brought the macro-functioning of the economy under focus. It challenged the traditional view that aggregative behaviour of the economy could be considered a simple addition of individual decisions. As we shall see later, the critique was soon re-absorbed into the neo-classical mainstream. While the underlying price theory was not very clear, (as can be seen from the debates on the search for microfoundations of macro theory), Keynes' critique left in place—and, only marginally sought to modify—the neo-classical theory of distribution.

A parallel but independent analysis of capitalist accumulation appeared in Kalecki's writing, the starting point of which was the Marxian schemes of reproduction. Currently, the ongoing efforts within the framework of surplus theory appear to be to graft the positive elements of Keynesian theory pertaining to the theory of effective demand on to the surplus approach, to attempt an explanation of output/employment on the basis of that principle, both for the long as well as the short period.[8]

The capital theory debate that was stimulated by Piero Sraffa's *Production of Commodities*, struck, once again, at the neo-classical theory of profit. The debates that continue have demonstrated the internal inconsistency that arises in presuming a well-behaved demand function for capital (which requires the inverse relation between capital per person and the rate of profits). Although the immediate destructive impact of the debate has been on the aggregate production function, the source of difficulty lies much deeper, as it questions the presumption of 'factor substitution' working to restore the theoretical demand and supply relations, that neo-classical theory requires for establishing uniqueness and stability of equilibrium. Further, while the immediate impact is on the theory of profit, in so far as the principle of factor substitution is

---

[8] See Joan Robinson, *The Accumulation of Capital*, London, 1956; P. Garegnani, 'Two Routes to Effective Demand,' in J.A. Kregal, ed., *Distribution, Effective Demand and International Economic Relations*, London, 1983.

used in other theoretical results, such as those pertaining to the growth or international trade, the capital theory debate has wider repercussions on many aspects of neo-classical theory.

The same capital theory critique has also enlivened interest in the labour theory of value and the interpretation of the 'transformation problem'. What appears clearer now is the problem of transformation in Marx—of 'transforming' surplus value into profits and 'labour values' into prices—which reflects the logical difficulty that a labour measure faces in the presence of 'constant capital' in deriving, consistently, the rate of profit from the rate of exploitation. Once the nature of the difficulty, arising in the presence of constant capital, is understood, a solution to the transformation problem can be consistently presented, as is done implicitly in Piero Sraffa's *Production of Commodities*, or explicitly in Garegnani[9] or Pasinetti.[10] While a number of solutions to the transformation problem have been proposed earlier, and a debate about its meaning and significance has gone on over a long period,[11] the advantage of this approach to the transformation problem is that it clarifies the source, the context and the nature of the logical problem, and illuminates the implications of its 'solvability', namely, that its successful resolution establishes the consistency of the explanation of the rate of profit within Marx's surplus theory. Thus, a clear elaboration of the 'capital theoretic problematic' within the two frameworks achieves simultaneously a twin objective: a powerful critique of the neo-classical theory of profit, as also a more coherent reinstatement of the surplus-based explanation of profits. Thus, the tables are turned against the earlier triumph of the neo-classicists, like Bohm-Bawerk, who sought to banish the Marxian theory on the basis of the logical weaknesses attributed to the labour theory of value, particularly in the context of the explanation of profits.

[9] Ibid.
[10] L.L. Pasinetti, *Structural Change and Economic Growth*, Cambridge, 1981.
[11] See L. Von Bortkiewicz, 'Value and Price in the Marxian System', *International Economic Papers*, No. 2. New York, 1907; P. Sweezy, *The Theory of Capitalist Development*, New York, 1942; F. Seton, 'The Transformation Problem', *Reverse of Economic Studies*, Vol. 24, 1957; M. Morishima, *Marx's Economics: A Dual Theory of Value and Growth*, Cambridge, 1973; I. Steedman, *Marx after Sraffa*, London, 1977; L.L. Pasinetti, *Theory of Production*, *op. cit.*; P. Garegnani, *Marx e gli Economisti Classici*, Torino, 1981.

The Core of the Surplus-based Theory of Distribution and Value

Looking at the various explanations of distribution attempted within the surplus theories, we can identify a simple structural core in the theory. This core appears clearly in the reproduction scheme of Marx defining prices of production. As the data of the system, we have social output levels (Adam Smith's 'effectual demand'), and the dominant methods of production, as well as wages which are regulated by social and economic forces best studied separately from those affecting the social product. Given the wage, the rate of profit and prices of production are obtained simultaneously, competition implying a uniform rate of profit for the system. In the core, defined by given social product and methods of production, distributive shares, other than wages, emerge as the difference between the given social product and the given necessary consumption (or, as 'surplus'). Such an approach to distribution has certain features which we may note as follows:

1. Determination of wages outside the 'core', expressed as 'given' wage (which is not the same as 'fixed'), allows a wide spectrum of social and historical factors to enter its determination.
2. Likewise, the 'given' level of social output does not connote fixity or stationarity. It serves only to underline that there are complex historical forces affecting composition and level of output (including the pace of accumulation). The notion of 'effectual demand' in Smith corresponds to this.
3. The notion of a 'given' dominant method of production for each product does not necessarily imply that there is only one method uniquely adopted in use, or that fixed co-efficients are presumed, so that unit costs are invariant to scale of output. A distinction was made by Marx and other classical writers between 'known' or 'observed' techniques—that is, those that are and could be in use and 'new' techniques. The 'dominant' method among those in use may itself be variously defined as the one most widely used, that is, as producing the major share of output), or as the one in which new investments are embodied, or as the 'average' method, (that is, the input co-efficients signify the statistically averaged input requirements). Given the spectrum of

techniques actually in use at any instance of time, it is to be noted that not every change in technique adopted by an individual producer would warrant a change in the 'dominant' technique used for calculation of prices, if the 'dominant technique' is defined in the former two senses.
4. The fact that the core is so 'given' for the purpose of price determination does not rule out from theoretical discourse the analysis of interaction among these components. Indeed, Marx was explicitly concerned with such interactions between, say, the level of output and changes in methods of production, or the speed of accumulation and the wage rate, etc. However, no rigid functional links were *a priori* forged between, say, changes in output and unit cost of production, or changes in labour productivity and wages, as is found in the marginalist analysis. Such theoretical relations become essential for the latter theory so as to ensure the 'well-behaved-ness' of demand and supply relations, consequently generating the right kind of quantity-price responses, as would be required to consistently explain determination of relative prices of commodities and factors in equilibrium. No such prerequisite exists in the classical theory.

The structure of the surplus-based theory thus has an openness, allowing for the introduction of specific historical factors and particularities of social relations. The openness also allows taking cognisance of the macro-level forces directly. This is so, paradoxically, because of the limited characterisation that is *a priori* postulated in the theory of price determination and the more limited role attributed to prices. Prices, in the classical theory, are the consistency conditions for exchange which are compatible with the stipulated mode of production, appropriation and distribution of the surplus. There is a 'separation' of the determination of quantities, which are influenced by a number of economic, social and historical factors, separately from that of prices. In contrast, the marginalist theory of prices is more ambitious, as it tries to determine *simultaneously* within a single framework of relations, all quantities and prices—that is, commodity outputs, prices and factor rewards—taking as data, tastes of consumers, resource endowments and technical conditions of production.

Certain commonplace misgivings must be removed before we

proceed. The association of classical theory with Say's Law underlined by Keynes, is not a necessary one. While Ricardo supported Say's Law, taking savings as identical with investment, he did not deduce full employment as a *result* of the equality. Nor did he suggest, as does the marginalist theory, that this equality would be brought through the equilibrating role of the rate of interest. Under-utilisation of capacity and labour is fully compatible with the 'natural prices' or 'prices of production' in Marx. In fact, the persistence of the 'reserve army of labour' was explicitly discussed by Marx as a feature of the capitalist economy. Further, the use of prices of production does not bind the analyst to the assumption of self-reproducibility. No presumption is made regarding either 'realisation' of values, or of the subsequent use of the surplus. Marx was one of the first thinkers to envisage a 'realisation crisis' as a logical outcome of capitalist accumulation. Further, neither perfect foresight nor lack of uncertainty are presumed in the construction of prices of production.[12]

It would be possible to generalise the surplus-based distribution scheme, taking as given, social output and the methods of production and rules stipulating the distribution of surplus among the classes of surplus sharers. The uniformity of wage, or of profit, is a stipulation with regard to a specific mode of production, and need not be universalised. Smith himself considered a vector of wages and a vector of profit rates (rather than a single and uniform wage and profit) as a possible depiction of the situation where there were persistent and stable profit and wage differentials. It is possible, also, to incorporate similarly sectoral differences in the degree of monopoly, if the latter could be independently identified. (An attempt to incorporate structural patterns and differences in commodity growth rates etc., for example, appears in Pasinetti.)[13]

The Crisis in Marxian Theory

The ongoing debates, as mentioned earlier, have also brought forth a revival of controversies over the labour theory of value,

[12] P. Garegnani, 'Notes on Consumption, Investment and Effective Demand', Part I, *Cambridge Journal of Economics*, December, 1978; P. Garegnani, 'Notes on Consumption, Investment and Effective Demand', Part II, *Cambridge Journal of Economics*, March, 1979.

[13] L.L. Pasinetti, *Structural Change, op. cit.*

which is viewed in certain quarters as an evidence of the 'crisis' threatening Marxian theory. We shall not enter into the much-tangled controversies, and make only brief comments on the nature of the issues and the status of the labour theory of value in the context of the theory of profit. Marx's intention was to demonstrate that, despite the Rule of Property, Bentham, and Equality in capitalist exchange, profit originated in surplus value generated by labour-power in production. It is appropriated by the capitalist who has command over the use-value of that labour power, which secures for itself only the historically determined wage as its value in exchange. In a simple labour value regime, where commodities exchange in prices proportionate to labour values, Marx (and Ricardo), could demonstrate consistently their propositions on profits. Namely, that profit is a surplus limited by conditions of production, given the historically determined value of wages (that is, 'necessary labour'), and there prevails the antagonistic 'inner relations' between wages and profits. These were important for Marx to deduce the 'laws' of capitalist dynamics—the tendencies and counter-tendencies that the system generates as accumulation proceeds. Marx, therefore, proceeded to establish these results, first in labour terms, and then sought to 'transform' them into the scheme of 'prices', while fully aware, from the outset, that capitalist exchange occurs at prices of production and not at labour values. In fact, it is a definite advance of Marx that he clearly enunciated the notion of prices of production in a multi-commodity, general-interdependent scheme, and attempted to draw rigorously the implications of systematically relating prices and values, and recognised it as a problem associated with 'constant capital'. Ricardo, despite his elaborate discussion of the composition of capital, had *essentially* obtained the rate of profits in the simpler case of all capital reducible to wages.

That Marx's procedure of transformation was partial (the means of production were, themselves, not 'transformed' as Marx himself mentioned), and that his *definition* of the rate of profit as $\dfrac{S}{C+V}$ is inconsistent, has by now been demonstrated.[14] However, the formal results now available on the transformation problem do

---

[14] See P. Garegnani, 'Notes on Consumption', Part I, *op. cit.*; I. Steedman, *op. cit.*

suggest solutions, linking directly in some cases and implicitly in others, the rate of surplus value and the rate of profits.[15] One of the results that emerges is that the rate of profits is positive if the rate of surplus value is positive and the two vary directly. This was called the *Fundamental Theorem* by Morishima.[16] While the result, by itself, is not an adequate proof of causation, it does establish that, if independent reasons could be found for positivity of the rate of surplus value, one could infer the basis for profits in exploitation. And, indeed, such an independent explanation is to be found in Marx when he painstakingly presents the historical circumstances that transform the production relations in society, with labour-power 'becoming a commodity'. It is the nature of the capitalist relations that commodity production is generalised and exchange becomes impersonal, 'free as well as equivalent', while the labourer emerges as 'free' in the dual sense: freed from his means of production and sustenance, and free to offer his services as a commodity. The 'labour power' is, however, a peculiar commodity which resides in the person of the labourer, and is 'non-capitalistically produced' by him. Its value is, therefore, determined historically.

It is evident, however, that to demonstrate that the capitalist *system* generates exploitation, we do not require a *Labour Theory* of value. That is, we do not necessarily have to assert that exchange takes place at prices proportional to labour values. What is necessary is to realise that there are historically compelling circumstances, because of which there arises the phenomenon of unpaid labour, namely, labour, 'freed' of both the means of production and of sustenance, sells his labour-power as a commodity to the capitalist, who thereby gains right over the produce of the labour so purchased. The content and meaning of the 'transformation' problem was precisely to establish that the nature of profits does not alter *only* because the prices of production at which exchange takes place would deviate from labour values, and that the theory of profit does not alter in essence.

We may, however, bear in mind the analytical-historical reasons for Marx's procedure—of resorting to the analysis in labour value terms, prior to the consideration of prices of production. It was clear from what transpired after Ricardo, that the Ricardian

---

[15] See P. Garegnani, *Marx e gli Economisti Classici, op. cit.*
[16] M. Morishima, *op. cit.*

theory was meeting hostility, and Marx noticed the decline of scientific political economy. The so-called Ricardians themselves, while asserting the simplistic labour theory of value in uncompromising terms, self-contradictorily abandoned its connection with distribution, and, consequently, effectively discarded the Ricardian theory of distribution.[17] Bailey's influence[18] in rejecting the concept of absolute value, and focusing on 'relative' value as the only valid value concept, was also creeping in. Marx, in his *Theories of Surplus Value*, demonstrates his acute awareness of the state of theory. If Marx feared losing sight of the 'inner connections' by moving to 'exchange value' or 'prices of production' directly, he had sufficient reasons to do so, as the generalisation from labour theory to prices was precisely where the major scuttling had occurred. The Ricardians themselves had yielded to the criticisms that the 'inverse relation' between wages and the rate of profits would no more be valid, if 'exchange values' were to deviate from labour values. They had lapsed repeatedly into the fallacy of 'adding up' which Ricardo had vigorously opposed in Smith. At the same time, the labour theory, severed of its connection with distribution, had been rendered a vacuous assertion. It was to the credit of Marx that he attempted to provide a socio-historical rationale for the theory, and used it to focus attention on the labour process, while attempting to meet its technical limitation through 'transforming', and thus re-establishing, its theoretical results in terms of prices of production. Ricardo's involved procedures of dealing simultaneously with 'values' as absolute labour values *and* as 'exchangeable value' in his theory of profit, had generated considerable confusion. It was an important analytical step forward by Marx to define precisely 'prices of production', and to attempt to relate rigorously labour values and prices.

Further, we must also note that, while the labour *theory* of value is not an essential prerequisite for the determination of profit on the basis of the surplus principle, the theory played an important role in providing certain insights into interpreting contemporary experience of advancing capitalism. As Marx recognised, under competition, producers of commodities had no power of extracting

[17] See Krishna Bharadwaj, 'Ricardian Theory and Ricardianism', *Contributions to Political Economy*, 1983.
[18] Samuel Bailey, *A Critical Dissertation on the Nature, Measure and Causes of Value*, London, 1825.

surplus in exchange—the situation being one of 'equivalent exchange'. And yet, capitalist production was spurred by the objective of maximising profits. The capitalists' struggle to so maximise could be seen operating on the production floor where, through using their control over the labour process, they were capable of implementing their strategies. Marx's graphic description of the way this control was sought to be exercised, and his perceptive analysis of the changes in these strategies, using the notions of absolute and relative surplus value, substantiate this. It was here that the 'use value of labour', 'the value of labour-power' and 'surplus labour' were the immediate concrete concerns of the capitalist. Surplus value, in a sense, is the micro-foundation of profits which emerge at the macro-level. The micro-behaviour of the capitalist could be seen in his attempt to maximise 'surplus value'. On the other hand, the surplus value was only an *ex ante*, potential form of profits. For, it is profits, ultimately, that are actually *realised* through the macro-functioning of the economy.

II

After 1945, Keynes' innovations had become orthodox in their turn; now governments had to admit they were concerned with maintaining the level of employment; but in respect to economic theory the old orthodoxy closed in again.[19]

The Keynesian Revolution, soon after its inception, was tempered into orthodoxy. Recent critiques of neo-classical synthesis,[20] have sought to establish that the counter-revolution was facilitated by Keynes' own partial critique of marginalist theory, particularly its theory of distribution. This development is briefly presented to illustrate the cardinal importance of the theory of distribution at the base of a consistent theory of accumulation, and also, to show how, with the rejection of the marginalist explanation of distribution, its theory of output and employment too cannot be sustained as they face the same difficulty as that in the theory of distribution.

The counter-arguments to the *General Theory* took shape soon, in the wake of its publication, initiated by Hick's early article,

[19] Joan Robinson, *Economic Heresies*, London, 1971.
[20] For example, P. Garegnani, 'Notes on Consumption', Parts I and II, *op. cit.*

'Keynes and the Classics', of 1936.[21] The 'neo-classical synthesis' which developed subsequently, attempted, basically, to establish Keynes' *General Theory*[22] as only a particular case of the Walrasian equilibrium. In a generalised interdependent system within the neo-classical framework, involving demand and supply relations for commodities, money and assets, the Keynesian result of 'under-employment equilibrium' was seen to emerge as a special result of identifying one or other specific assumption as 'crucial', which converted certain functions into constants, or attached extreme values—of zero or infinity—to particular price elasticities, or put restrictions on forms assumed by certain functions within a specified range.[23]

It was initially conceded that Keynes' strong point was the policy inferences. He was praised for his masterly intuition that allowed him to recognise the vital significance of these rigidities and imperfections of the system, and the mode of its functioning. However, in recent times, even this 'strength' of Keynesian analysis has been questioned, as the limits of 'fiscalism' have been exposed, by the complexity of domestic and international economic management in the capitalist countries.

The critiques of this neo-classical synthesis that have been offered in recent years have themselves differed, depending upon the basic framework of value and distribution theory they have adopted. One group of critiques view the limitation of this early synthesis in its eliminating those very insights of Keynes, which, when incorporated, would enrich the neo-classical theory.[24] Or, in short, they argue that the Keynesian problematic demands a reformulation of the Walrasian theory, and a further enunciation and analysis of the sources and processes of disequilibria. Others, however, reject the neo-classical theory of distribution and see a more useful possibility of grafting the Keynesian vision and his theory of output

---

[21] J.R. Hicks, 'Mr. Keynes and the Classics', *Econometrica*, April, 1936.

[22] J.M. Keynes, *The General Theory of Employment, Interest and Money*, London, 1936.

[23] See, for example, F. Modigliani, 'Liquidity Preference and the Theory of Interest and Money', *Econometrica*, January, 1944.

[24] See, among others, R. Clower, 'The Keynesian Counter-Revolution: A Theoretical Appraisal', in T. Brehling and F.H. Hahn, eds., *The Theory of Interest Rates*, London, 1965; A. Leijonhufvud, *On Keynesian Economics and the Economics of Keynes*, New York, 1968; E. Malinvaud, *The Theory of Unemployment Reconsidered*, Oxford, 1977.

determination on another theoretical structure, deriving from the classical theory.[25] It is among the latter, that we see the efforts to integrate the Keynesian output and employment determination (via multiplier), onto a surplus structure.

The sifting out of elements of Keynesian analysis for such a reconstruction requires locating the seeds of compromise in Keynes that led to the neo-classical synthesis. Countering the traditional argument that changes in wages would lead to full employment, Keynes, as is well known, accepted 'the first postulate' (wages must equal the marginal product of labour at a given level of employment), but rejected the second (utility of the wage is equal to the marginal disutility of labour at a given amount of employment). However, the condition that the demand for labour is elastic with respect to the real wage, needs, in traditional neo-classical theory, to be further supported by the simultaneous requirement that interest successfully equilibrates savings and investments, if competitive forces have to establish full employment in equilibrium. It was this equilibrating role of interest that Keynes rejected. Having done so, he needed an alternative explanation of interest rate determination. This he constructed by proposing that the rate of interest is determined proximately by monetary factors—that is, in terms of the demand for and supply of stocks of money. Thus, the rate of interest equilibrated *not* the demand for and supply of *savings*, but the demand to hold money and the exogenously determined supply of money.

However, the theory of interest rate in the orthodox theory, is a part and parcel of their long-run theory of distribution, and is built upon the marginalist hypothesis of substitution of factors of production. The theory hypothesised as resulting from this substitution, an inverse relation between the volume of planned investment and the rate of interest—a result questioned by the recent capital theory debate. Keynes, while rejecting part of the marginalist explanation of the rate of interest, continued to ascribe to their view of distribution, partly reflected in his acceptance of the marginal efficiency of capital schedule, relying on the inverse relation between investment demand and the rate of interest. This kept the way open for the eventual re-absorption of the Keynesian theoretical model into the neo-classical orthodoxy. (There have been

---

[25] L.L. Pasinetti, *Structural Change*, *op. cit.*; Joan Robinson, *Accumulation of Capital*, *op. cit.*; P. Garegnani, 'Two Routes to Effective Demand', *op. cit.*

other grounds too, well known by now, to also challenge the interest elasticity of the marginal efficiency schedule.)

Keynes' own critique of orthodoxy had relied upon two major arguments: One was to establish, with the use of the consumption function, that a decline in money wage could not influence real wages and employment, *except through* its effects on investment, the latter, thus, being the key element. He had then argued that liquidity preference or the future course of expected rates of interest would inhibit the fall of the rate of interest to an order sufficient to stimulate investment to match up to the full employment savings. Secondly, he had emphasised the volatile character of expectations, rendering future profitability and investment uncertain and susceptible to fluctuations. Thus, Keynes stressed the need for quick adaptability of interest rates, but, at the same time, pointed out the obstacles to it. The Keynesian critique thus seemed particularly effective for short-run situations. And, in fact, his theory came to be more and more confined to short period situations.[26]

Consequently, the neo-classical theorists could adopt a long period reformulation of Keynes where the system could still hover around the full employment situation. In fact, invoking the aid of the fiscal hand, much of the growth theory assumed full employment to prevail. The Keynesian obstacles to the system attaining full employment were interpreted as imperfections and rigidities in the system, which may warrant the active intervention of the visible hand of the State.

To conclude: The neo-classical synthesists only had to exploit the negative interest elasticity of investment which Keynes conceded, and tame the expectations suitably, or bring them within the web of rationality. However, as Marx had observed long ago—an observation sustained by historical experience—capitalist societies are marked by continued persistence of the reserve army of the unemployed (to which Marx had also joined the phenomenon of 'excess capacities', particularly in the monopoly phase). Indeed, there persists an effective demand problem, (that is, the insufficiency of aggregate demand to absorb the output produced by the *normal* use of capacity) in the short-run as well as the long-run; in the former case, we refer to the utilisation of existing capacity, while

---

[26] See P. Garegnani, ibid.

in the latter, we refer to the creation of additional capacity. Attempts towards the analysis of accumulation stimulated by the Marxist approach recognise the 'effective demand' problem in both the short-run and the long-run context. Kalecki's work, inspired by Marx's schemes of production, has indicated the possibilities of building up an alternative macro analysis of accumulation.

Along another route, the possibility of developing a theory of accumulation within the surplus approach, borrowing the positive elements from Keynes, have been suggested in some recent works.[27] A main positive element from Keynes is his significant idea that it is not the rate of interest but the level of income that ensures equality between savings and investment. The building blocks for the short-run theory, where production capacity is already in place, exist already in Keynes, particularly with his depiction of the income generation process, with the level of investment as given or as an independent variable. The long-period theory, Garegnani suggests, could be developed on the basis of supplementary analysis of:

1. The determinants of the long run levels of investment.
2. The relation between income and consumption.
3. The generation of savings through changes in productive capacity.

These, no doubt, are relations which are influenced by the specific historical conditions of an economy. The need is to build analytical models that give due regard to the important specificities, while sufficiently simple and logically compact to yield meaningful insights. That the surplus framework could afford more openness in theory to enable it to specify and incorporate such conditions, is demonstrated by Marx's own attempts to analyse the dynamics of capitalism for his contemporary situation.

III

Marx and Schumpeter on Technical Change

Technological dynamism, as a strident force of capitalism, was stressed by Marx as well as Schumpeter. Both came to place

---

[27] See, for example, ibid.

emphasis on historical change and the *process* of capitalist development with cycles as an inevitable, integral part of that development. However, they used radically different interpretations of the capitalist system. Apparent similarity at certain points of analysis between the two—especially with relation to technical change—is not surprising: Schumpeter was greatly influenced by Marx, in the negative sense. As Joan Robinson puts it, his intellectual development was 'a life long struggle to escape from Marx'. In the process, he did recognise some of the positive methodological features of Marx, but differed radically, both in his 'vision' and his theoretical system. While recognising the importance of historical factors, he preserved his allegiance to the formal structure of Walrasian-Austrian theory of value and distribution, particularly the formal theory of stationary state, although disputing specific propositions within it. The synthesis between his history and theory remained uncomfortable: while he displayed historical knowledge descriptively, his theoretical system could hardly keep in step. On the other hand, the attraction of pure formalism inclined him to propose, sometimes, that the core of economic theory—the logic of the circular flow, his own variant—was applicable to all societies, from primitive, medieval, capitalist to socialist ones. His early theorising of imperialism as an atavistic activity ran as a single thread from the Roman empire to the twentieth century.

Schumpeter was among the staunch proponents of 'methodological individualism'. While he maintained that the disturbances to the capitalist system were caused predominantly by external factors, he singled out one endemic, endogenous factor which internally produced regular disturbances. This latter idea of an endogenous cause driving the system is evidently borrowed from Marx, as there is an explicit reference to Marx in this connection.[28] This factor was the entrepreneurial activity of the *individual*. Schumpeter, as a true methodological individualist, analysed the repercussions of this individual's activity on the totality. The dynamics of the macro system were to be analysed as a sum total of these activities. Schumpeter, as is well known, was critical of the use of aggregates in Keynes.[29] As we shall see, such an approach

[28] See, J.A. Schumpeter, *The Theory of Economic Development*, New York, 1961, p. 60.
[29] J.A. Schumpeter, *Business Cycles: A Theoretical, Historical and Statistical Analysis of the Capitalist Process*, New York, 1964 (abridged), p. 21.

rendered his massive study of business cycles descriptive and statistical, lacking in rigorous determination, either of the state of the economy at any time, or of its movement in terms of aggregates of output, employment or income.

Schumpeter's analysis was woven around two central themes: First, a view that 'profits' are entirely to be ascribed to 'leadership' as against 'ownership'. He explicitly took the position that a cardinal fallacy of classical writers, particularly Marx, was to link profits with ownership.[30] Secondly, the view that capitalism is essentially a robust system, subject, inevitably, to cyclical movements caused predominantly by external factors, but also by the 'internal' factor of entrepreneurial activity.[31] (*Business Cycles*, p. 53; *The Theory of Economic Development*, p. 63). In his *Capitalism, Socialism and Democracy*, he was to see the capitalist system riding on the tide of success towards a doom, brought about precisely by the destruction of the entrepreneurial spirit, with the growth of anti-capitalist culture. It was, again, in the realm of ideas, of attitudes and human proclivities that the causes for the doom lay.[32]

Centred as the analysis of technical change was on entrepreneurial (innovational) activity as giving rise to profits, there was no room to bring in the capital-labour relation which was the focus of Marx's treatment of technical change. Schumpeter supported his view of profits as originating in 'innovations' by generating a complete set of mutually sustaining *definitions* to yield 'the Schumpeterian System', the principal aim of which was to establish that leadership—and, that alone—explained the rise of profits.

The Circular Flow and the Zero Rate of Profit

Schumpeter begins with the notion of the 'circular flow'—a 'capitalist' system in perfect equilibrium. He attributes considerable significance to the idea of circular flow, which he ascribes to the physiocrats and the classical writers as much as to Walras and Bohm-Bawerk, without distinguishing among the different perceptions of the economy they had.[33] His own definition of the capitalist

---

[30] Ibid., pp. 78–79.

[31] Ibid., p. 53; *Theory of Economic Development, op. cit.*, p. 63.

[32] J.A. Schumpeter, *Capitalism, Socialism and Democracy*, London, 1966, pp. 121–63.

[33] J.A. Schumpeter, *Theory of Economic Development, op. cit.*, p. 18.

system as 'a commercially organised state, in which private property, division of labour and free competition prevail', is a non-discriminatingly wide rubric as commerce, property and division of labour have characterised a large variety of societies in history. Conspicuous by its absence in this definition of the capitalist society, is the specificity of the capital-labour relation which stands at the centre of Marx's perspective on capitalism.

Schumpeter relies on Walras and Bohm-Bawerk to define the valuation–distribution process in the circular flow, with the difference that, by assumption for Schumpeter, there are no capitalists and no profits in the circular flow. Production is fully adjusted to demand, the optimum technique is adopted once and for all, and there is no scope for change in the system which keeps repetitiously reproducing itself. A major difference in Schumpeter's analysis of circular flow from that of the physiocrats, is his one-way characterisation of the economic process, based on the idea of hierarchy of commodities, from primary factors to final consumption goods, and his adoption of the corresponding Austrian explanation, as well as of value and distribution.

In such a circular flow, Schumpeter argues, there is no 'surplus product' and no 'profits', all value being competitively imputed to land and labour as rents and wages respectively, these being the two primary factors. This principle of imputation under competition, for Schumpeter, is the *proof* of zero profits. For, the process of imputation will not suffer surplus over and above wages and rents. However, this reasoning reverses the causal relations. Close students of Wicksell and Walras—and, for that matter, Marx and Sraffa—would realise that *it is when the rate of profit is taken to be zero*, that value can be imputed back entirely into wages and rents in an interdependent commodity system as, for example, under the simple commodity production, but this would also be the case under which the labour theory holds.

Schumpeter, while following the Bohm-Bawerkian hierarchical structure of commodities, criticises Bohm-Bawerk's explanation of profit resting on the basis of 'the element of abstinence' or 'the necessity for waiting'. Schumpeter distinguishes between (a) the process of 'creating a productive apparatus', as happens, say, when a roundabout method of production, seen as a case of innovation, is adopted, and (b) the process of operating it, once created and incorporated within the circular flow. He denies that abstinence or savings can have any role in the latter situation in generating profits, which he associates exclusively with the former process of innovation. 'There can be no question of abstinence in the sense of nonconsumption of the sources of return, because by *our assumption* there are no other sources of return other than labour and land.'[34] Since consumption is fully adapted to the present and future flow of goods and optimally arranged, Schumpeter argues, there is no motive left for underestimating future products, and no 'waiting', consequently. This argument, by itself, however, cannot rule out a positive rate of profit, for it is only tantamount to saying—and here, certainly Schumpeter has a point—that there could have been underestimation of future consumption *if* there were a positive rate of profit (interest) given exogenously, and that when the rate is zero, there could still be an equilibrium at that zero rate. However, Schumpeter regards this as a *proof* for the absence of time preference, and hence, for the prevalence of zero rate of profit. His *proof* for zero rate of interest, indeed, has to rely on the principle of imputation, already referred to, where the principle is assumed rather than explained.

On the same ground of already established equilibrium in the circular flow, Schumpeter abandons the idea that there exist 'advances' in production. 'Workers and landlords always exchange their productive services for present consumption goods only, whether the former are employed directly or indirectly in the production of consumption goods.'[35] However, as Wicksell envisaged, in a simultaneous instantaneous production model of general equilibrium where there could not, or need not, be 'advances' in the sense of historical stages (and intermediate goods as well as final goods would be produced continuously and simultaneously), there could yet be a positive rate of profit and 'accumulation' of profits. On the other hand, a self-reproducing (as distinguished from a self-replacing) system could be in equilibrium without generating any surplus product and with no profits. Again, it is the *assumption* of the zero rate of profit that appears crucial to Schumpeter's argument.

Thus, Schumpeter abandons, along with the notion of profits, the notion of capitalists as possessors of means of production and also the idea of capital as accumulated stocks of goods in circular

[34] Ibid., p. 38, emphasis added.
[35] Ibid., p. 43.

flow. 'If the possessors of produced means of production were called "capitalists", then they could only be producers, differing in nothing from other producers, and could no more than the others sell their products above the costs given by wages and rents.'[36] Implicitly then, Schumpeter is confirming himself to a situation of simple commodity production where the category of 'capitalists', and consequently, 'profits', vanishes. Arguing likewise, Schumpeter finds no room in his circular flow for credit, and money therein plays no other role but the one of facilitating the circulation of commodities.[37]

Innovations: The Source of Profits

Schumpeter then introduces 'innovations' in the circular flow. What is striking is that while there have always been innovations in history, Schumpeter's 'innovations' seem to be the powerful intervention that introduces into the circular flow, all the typical capitalist institutions and categories: profits, money, credit. Another set of definitions and categories follow to show that profits are entirely the yield of 'innovation', themselves defined in a special way, by disassociating the innovator from the necessity for prior possession of means of production or 'savings' or, in fact, any conditionality concerning access to credit. Thus, the innovating producer is delinked from any past history of accumulation, and the innovation is paramountly an individual's act. This disassociation from the past is carried even further in defining innovation as 'carrying out new combinations'—concretely meaning introduction of a new good, a new, as yet untried, method of production, access to new markets, to new sources of supply of raw materials, or carrying out of new organisations. And these new combinations, as a rule, are carried out by new firms, using new equipment.[38]

The 'entrepreneur' is the agent who carries out the new combination, and is the one who receives profits generated because of the more productive use of resources. Innovations, not requiring any past possession of means of production, may be introduced by

[36] Ibid., p. 46.
[37] Ibid., p. 53.
[38] J.A. Schumpeter, *Theory of Economic Development*, op. cit., pp. 74–94; *Business Cycles*, op. cit., pp. 59–62.

any entrepreneur from among labourers or landlords. Innovation is purely 'a matter of business behaviour' in a capitalist society. Thus, to Schumpeter: 'Entrepreneurs do not form a social class' and 'their genealogies display more varied origins'.[39] He goes further to suggest that the leadership it demands 'is distributed by a Gaussian Law and not exceptional'. Thus, the entrepreneur of Schumpeter is paradoxically the one whom he divests of means of production, more particularly the possession of prior capital, and entrepreneurship is an individual's achievement, *par excellence*.

Entrepreneurs, thus, need credit (Schumpeter argues even more strongly, 'only the entrepreneurs need credit') to enable them 'to withdraw the producer's goods which he requires from their previous employments, by exercising a demand for them, and thereby to force the economic system into new channels.'[40] Commensurately, the 'capitalist economy' and 'capital' get redefined:

> That form of economic organisation in which the goods necessary for new production are withdrawn from their settled place in the circular flow by the intervention of purchasing power created *ad hoc* is the capitalist economy.... Capital is nothing but the lever by which the entrepreneur subjects to his control the concrete goods which he needs, nothing but a means of diverting the factors of production to new uses or of dictating a new direction to production.[41]

The *function* of capital, thus, consists in procuring for the entrepreneur the means to adopt his innovation. Capital is not goods, but a fund of purchasing power available for specific purpose of transference to entrepreneurs. Here, the access to credit is not posed as a problem. Presumably, free and equal access to all entrepreneurs exists. Further, the entrepreneur assumes no risk—it is entirely the lender's responsibility. 'Innovation', therefore, rests purely on the 'leadership' quality of the innovator. The rate of interest, a purely monetary phenomenon, is determined by the demand by entrepreneurs for 'capital' (as above-defined), and its supply by banks.

[39] Ibid., p. 78; ibid., 79.
[40] *Theory of Economic Development, op. cit.*, p. 106.
[41] Ibid., p. 116.

Entrepreneurial Profits

The only profit in the system Schumpeter recognises, then, is the premium put upon successful innovation in a capitalist economy, which is temporary by nature. It needs to be noted that Schumpeter closely follows Marx's description of the rise of 'super profits' in the wake of new technical advances, enjoyed temporarily by those producers who initiate them, and which are wiped out by the competitive forces, with other producers following suit. This is precisely the way in which the competitive tendency towards the uniform rate of profit asserts itself in Marx. This competitive process of absorbing the innovation may, however, leave its effects on the general rate of wages and profits. The 'super profits' are profits over and above those profits accruable at the uniform common rate of profit in the economy. In Schumpeter, the system, after the burst of entrepreneurial profits, returns to the profitless circular flow. If a chain of innovations is speedily re-absorbed, he envisages even 'profitless prosperities'.

Business Cycles

Schumpeter sketches the evolution of a capitalistic society with innovations perpetually producing the undulating movements of business cycles. These are deemed to be generated internally, through innovations alone. In the Pure Model (operative in the absence of errors and speculative activities), there are two phases—prosperity and recession. In the prosperity phase, the entrepreneurial activity surges ahead to exhaust the opportunities to gain. As borrowing diminishes, earlier firms pay off debts, auto-deflation follows, and with increased output, prices decline. The new equilibrium has greater total output, lower prices, with the same aggregate money incomes. The second approximation is obtained by adding other elements to this pattern, like the secondary wave of induced investments and speculative activities. This leads to the four-phase cycle. Added on to the two phases are 'a pathological phase of depression and of revival'. Depressions are not 'indispensable' in the capitalist process, and occur when the multiple cycles (Kitchin, Juglar and Kondratieff) manage to overlap in their troughs.

Schumpeter's scheme of business cycles is, at best, a descriptive account. His vision of historical change and the 'dynamics' is entirely governed by his view that innovations are the prime movers of the capitalist system. But he does not offer any explanations for the rise of innovations, or the reason for their clustering, rather than their occurring in a continuous stream. While innovations are considered by Schumpeter as 'internal to the economic process', they, in fact, appear as a spontaneous, external factor as their 'source' is in the Gaussian distribution 'of leadership quality'. Apart from the propensity and urge for profit, there is nothing that explains this drive to innovate, and since this urge is ever-present, there is no explanation available for the time pattern of innovations. Evidently, the 'entrepreneur' is not constrained by the means of production in his possession, nor by the limits on the access to the sources of finance. In such a case, there are no obvious constraints working on entrepreneurial activity.

Nor do we obtain rigorous analysis of the nature of innovations, or of their impact on employment, wages, level of profits, absolute mass of profits, level of investments, etc. Schumpeter, as we have noted, did not favour aggregative analysis, and we find no theory of aggregate output and employment even while cyclical variations in these magnitudes are described. Full employment of resources is presumed in the circular flow, and the system returns to a new circular flow after the innovations. Unemployment of resources, particularly labour, receives no attention except as a transitory phenomenon. The only rivalry and conflict of interests that attracts some attention is between the old and new firms; those who innovate and those who adjust. But entrepreneurs are no special class. The 'dynamics' of the system is worked out—rather described—in terms of acts of individuals, while business cycles are to be recognised on the basis of statistical data available on macro magnitudes. As Kuznets and Rostow rightly pointed out, it was hard to put the Schumpeterian 'dynamics' into empirical work, although the sweep of his description continues to impress even now.

While profits are to be seen as temporary returns to individual entrepreneurial activity, we have no clue how the rate of profit or mass of profits is to be theoretically determined. In fact, there is no question of providing a rationale for the tendency towards uniformity of profits, and, more importantly, no reason is given for systematic profit differentials. To Schumpeter, in a situation where the entrepreneurial activity is to be financed by 'capital'—purely *ad hoc* finance created by banks—no such questions appear to be pertinent. The two major concerns for the analysis of capitalist system, the determinants of investment and its level, do not figure in Schumpeter. Along with the level of investment, the issue of the level of employment is bypassed; presumably the system equilibrates at full employment. Thus, the picture of capitalist evolution that we have is one motored by the force of innovations, carried out by individual leaders, spurred by the profit motive. The pattern of this movement is to be discovered from past history. The capitalist system spontaneously moves from one equilibrium situation to another. Innovations are the disequilibrating force and the vehicle of historical change, and the cycles are, thus, an integral part of this evolution.

Recessions in the Pure Model are no more inimical to the system. In fact, those are the periods when the fruits of prosperity are reaped in terms of expanded output, its changed composition and lowered prices. Speculative factors in 'the secondary approximation', monopoly elements and 'trustified capitalism', are 'institutional factors' that are added on to enrich the basic scheme. Depression is viewed only as a 'pathological' case when the Kitchin, Juglar and Kondratieff cycles overlap in their troughs—this, supposedly a fortuitous and rare occurrence.

Technical Change in Marx

In Marx, the process of technical change and the role it played in shaping the growth of the capitalist mode in industrialising Britain is analysed in a markedly different framework. Marx, too, attaches a great importance to the march of productive forces (a point which probably inspired Schumpeter), and recognises that the pursuit of profit motivates the adoption of such changes. He also describes (of which we find an echo in Schumpeter) the temporary super-profits that the producers first initiating a technical improvement derive, until the time that competition induces the leading technique to become the 'dominant' (in the sense discussed earlier in part I). However, he maintains: 'It is not because he is a leader of industry that a man is a capitalist; on the contrary, he is a leader of industry because he is a capitalist. The leadership of industry is an attribute of capital just as in feudal times the functions of the general and judge were attributes of landed property.'[42] The contrast here with Schumpeter is striking: Schumpeter exactly reverses the proposition. Marx analyses these changes in productive forces in close link with his theory of profit. The capitalists' pursuit to maximise profits is reflected in his attempts to extract as much surplus value in production as possible by using his control over the labour process. Historically:

1. Marx traces out how the nature of the labour-process itself changed, qualitatively transforming the capital-labour relation in production, and bringing about changes also in the intra-capitalist relations.
2. Also, at each stage of development of capitalist production, a certain minimum of capital in the hands of, or accessible to, a producer was needed, so that 'the minimum required to metamorphose the producer into a capitalist change with different stages of development of capitalist production and is at given stages different in different spheres of production, according to their special and technical conditions.[43]

This had effects on the structural characteristics of industry, as well as in terms of intra-capitalist competition. The 'creative' individual rising to be an entrepreneur without prior possession of capital would increasingly be a rarity. The access to credit would itself depend upon capital under command of the individual, so that it, too, discriminated in favour of property owners.

The Process of Capitalist Development in Marx

Marx deduced certain results regarding the development process. He not only demonstrated the possibilities of cyclical fluctuations due to the disproportionalities and mismatching of the various (commodity, credit and productive capital) circuits, but also indicated long-term tendencies concerning the possibilities of the falling rate of profit, and of the disproportionality and realisation crises. While the capital-labour relation was seen to be affected by the changing technical and organisational forces, the effect of the prevalence of the reserve army of the unemployed and of organised

---

[42] Karl Marx, *Capital*, Vol. I, London, 1867, p. 332.
[43] Ibid., p. 309.

labour on the character and pace of technical change, was also discussed. Thus, at the centre of his analysis was the capital-labour relation and its distributive implications.

Marx analysed the technical changes that took place in England in terms of three stages: Cooperation; division of labour and manufacture; machinery and modern industry. The capitalist process is seen as moving progressively from the dispossession of direct producers of their means of production, to labour-power becoming a commodity, and further, on to the position of increasing subservience of labour to capital. At first, capital subordinates labour on the basis of technical conditions which it finds historically. Even without the alteration in the system of working, the simultaneous employment of a large number of labourers affects a revolution in the material conditions of the labour process, under cooperation. It increases productivity through economy in the use of overheads and the common means of production. It not only increases individual productivity, but makes attainable such tasks as are possible only by collective manpower. However, the social productiveness of cooperative labour now appears as productivity of capital. Since, to bring about this cooperation a minimum of capital is required, gradually the labourer becomes absorbed into the production process as a seller of his labour power. His productive achievements are possible only when he joins capital which is no more his.

Manufacture introduces further division of labour inside the production unit, just as social division of labour occurs with specialisation across industry. Processes are partialised and 'a productive mechanism' is created, the parts of which are human beings. This intensive specialisation implies that labour not only has to sell his labour-power, but its functions can be exercised only in an environment that exists in the working of the capitalist. There is, thus, increasing dependence on the capitalist for the realisation of his own labour-power. Simultaneously, the interdependence in capitalist production also increases, so that the seeds of 'capitalist anarchy' are sown in this mutual interdependence. The technical conditions progressively adopted under manufacture also make it a necessity to have 'increased number of labourers under the control of one capitalist', and hence increases the minimum capital required in the hands of the capitalist. Further, technical intensification occurs under the machinery and modern industry phase, where the minimum required capital increases even further. Along with this arises the significant role of finance and of access to credit institutions. The progressive expanse of productive forces unleashed through the ownership and control of capital, generates, internally, a tendency towards the rise of monopolies, destroying competition while the 'inner antagonistic relations' of capital and labour sharpen, bursting the seams of the system.

Changing Capital-Labour Relations

The changing capital-labour relations are reflected in various strategies adopted by capitalists to extract surplus value, which have diverse consequences for the labourers during the various stages of industry. In the initial phase, the strategy appears to have been one of increasing the length of the working day, utilising the weaker sections of the labouring population (children and women) at a time when the 'reserve army of labour' was swelling in numbers. However, this exploitation reached its limits when it was considered wiser to delimit the working day. The legislative acts to that effect were results of both, the struggle of the working class, as well as the realisation that productivity-increases via technical improvements (increasing relative surplus value) were superior as a method of surplus extraction to the previous methods. (An interesting observation of Marx is that, given the fact that no individual capitalist would have liked to take the lead in curtailing the working day which had reached unproductive proportions, the move had to be brought through a legislative enactment.) Marx also comments extensively on the changes in the composition and volume of employment, and on the changes that occurred in the level of wages as also in the wage systems in various phases of the capitalist development. An important element that entered capitalists' choice to adopt mechanisation was anticipations regarding the strength of the reserve army of labour, and the level of working class militancy and organisation.

At the level of macro-relations, Marx analysed the effects of technical developments on the increasing 'organic composition of capital', increasing social division of labour imposing increasingly stringent conditions of proportionality among industries; the effects on the general rate of profits of technical improvements, cheapening wage goods on the one hand and increasing organic composition of capital on the other. On the demand side, Marx analysed the effects of relative immiseration of labour on realisation of profits. In other words, attempts were made by Marx to analyse the interconnections between technical change and the process of accumulation working primarily through the changing production and distributive relations. He analysed these effects on the macro-system by noting the tendencies and countertendencies that were generated by increasing organic composition of capital, cheapening of wage goods, changing class-relations and their distributive implications, the 'anarchy' as well as the growing monopoly dominance in intra-capitalist relations. All these sharpened the internal contradictions of the system, giving rise to cyclical fluctuations and threatening the long-term prospects.

History and Formal Theory in Marx

What is remarkable in Marx is the ingenious way in which he was able to integrate the historical experiences of the specific epoch in capitalist development with his formal analysis. His analysis, at places, was incomplete, and not all his specific results/prognostications have been proved correct. Yet, his is perhaps the best example in economic theory of an attempt to integrate historical changes with an abstract theoretical analysis of the accumulation process of an economy. While analysing tendencies and countertendencies at the level of the macro-system by using the conceptual tools of surplus value (relative and absolute), Marx was able to delve deeper into the production sphere, and describe the dynamics of capital-labour relation within the labour process where the capitalist was in control, and provide a micro/macro-dimension to his analysis. The openness of his theory of distribution (profit) allowed him to grapple with historico-specific features that entered into the determination of technical methods, the wage level and the expanding universe of commodities. Schumpeter, on the other hand, with his Austrian (modified in his own way) theoretical framework for value and distribution, failed to integrate history and technical change into his formal analysis of capitalist societies. Nor could he deduce rigorously the dynamic consequences of technical change.

To conclude: In this chapter, an attempt was made to focus on the recent resurgence of political economy, which has led the debates in theory to concentrate on alternative structures of theories, particularly the theories of value and distribution which form the base to further analyse the dynamic problems of accumulation. Our view is that the more open structure of the classical political economy, particularly as extended and reconstructed in Marx, allows the possibility of integrating historical changes with logical abstraction, and leads to a more meaningful and richer analysis of output, employment, technical change—in short, of the dynamics of accumulation.

4

Joseph Alois Schumpeter: A Centennial Appraisal

P.R. BRAHMANANDA

The Three Centenaries

1983–84 happened to be the birth centenary year of both Keynes and Schumpeter, and the death centenary year of Karl Marx. Keynes' and Schumpeter's birth dates were separated by four months. Schumpeter died in 1950 and Keynes four years earlier. Keynes claimed in his letter to Bernard Shaw, that his *General Theory* would be 'knocking down the Ricardian foundations of Marxian economics'. Schumpeter's theory of development, first set out in 1911, sought to present for the dynamics of the capitalist process, a vision, the implication of which was the uprooting of the Marxian foundations of the theory of the course of capitalism. The works of Keynes and Schumpeter, taken separately, represented a creative response seeking, in effect, to negate the scholastic achievement of Marx on the life path of economic systems.

In an obituary reference on Schumpeter in the *Economic Journal*, Austin Robinson made a historic prediction that Schumpeter's ideas would have an enduring influence long after all the highly published seminal ideas then in circulation had disappeared. It is well-known that in some respects, Keynes' rise in fame in international circles, particularly after the 1930s, put Schumpeter's achievements under shade. The English translation by R. Opie of Schumpeter's book on Development appeared in 1934, when the world economy was confronted by one of the greatest depressions, and attention had shifted to short period problems of restoration of stability and full employment. In fact, the entire inter-War period, from 1919 to 1939, was characterised by considerable instability in economic life in all leading countries. In such periods, economic attention naturally gets concentrated on highly contemporaneous, and even transient, issues. Schumpeter's two-volume study on Business Cycles, a supplement to *The Theory of Economic Development*, appeared in 1939, when the Second World War had just begun. It is unfortunate that Schumpeter missed the plane of fame twice during his lifetime.

Unlike Keynes, Schumpeter was too detached a scholar, and with so little passion for the propagation of his own ideas as to have trained a school of close-knit disciples. Schumpeter was no 'operator' even in the highest sense of the term as Keynes was, according to as close an observer of Keynes' correspondence and writings as Elizabeth Johnson. Schumpeter seems to have helped a number of distinguished scholars, the foremost among them being Leontief who migrated to the USA and settled down there. At Harvard, Schumpeter had in his class brilliant students like Paul Samuelson, William Fellner, Paul Sweezy, J. Tobin, R. Goodwin, to mention only a few out of a galaxy. But none of the above can be stated to have been his followers in the sense that Joan Robinson, Austin Robinson, Harrod and R. F. Kahn have been to Keynes, though Goodwin has recently presented a mathematical model of dynamics based partly on Schumpeter's ideas. Kalecki also shows an influence of Schumpeter's innovation theory. Schumpeter's personality shunned the presentation of his own ideas before his students. (In an academic semester programme which is course-ridden, why should students bother about what their teacher might have written, if these ideas are not in the courses; and where are the colleagues who, even if slightly famous, bother about each other's writings?)

The Books

Schumpeter's major connected writings are:

1. *Theory of Economic Development* (1911).
2. *Business Cycles*, Vols. I and II (1939).
3. *Capitalism, Socialism and Democracy* (Portion reprinted as *Can Capitalism Survive?*) (1942)
4. *History of Economic Analysis* (1954).

There are also some other books/monographs like *Imperialism and the Social Classes, The Tax State, Economic Doctrine and*

Method, Ten Great Economists and *Essays*. Schumpeter wrote a number of papers in German. An edited version of all his writings does not appear to have been contemplated, even by Harvard University.

The Theory of Economic Development was first published when Schumpeter was just 28 years old. It is among the most recognisedly creative contributions by any economist at that age. Judging from the English translation, one cannot but be amazed at the young scholar's mastery of the then existing literature in economics. The synthetic presentation of the reference-frame of the circular flow, which contained the essence, from his angle, of the contributions of Quesnay, Cournot, Thunen and Walras; the analysis of the various phases of the innovation-imitation process; the emphasis on the distinctive role of banks as creators of credit; the rationale of money as finance; the new perception regarding capital as the power to realign productive resources; the monetary angle on the rate of interest; the theory of the origin of profits and of the relationship between profit and interest; the linking of the innovation theory with the theory of business cycles; and the numerous theoretical insights interspersed at various places in the book—all these certainly mark the *Theory of Economic Development* as a highly original, seminal classic, indispensable to anyone who seeks to master economics. Though the work was done under the supervision of Bohm-Bawerk, his formidable mentor, *The Theory of Economic Development* is a breakaway from Bohm-Bawerk's own mature positions, particularly on the origin of savings, the nature of static equilibrium and the emergence of interest.

Some of the ideas in the above book seem to have been popular in the late 1920s in England, since both Robertson and Keynes were aware of portions of Schumpeter's theory. It seems Schumpeter himself was working on a treatise on money at the same time that Keynes' publication came out. One could understand the similarities between the approaches of Schumpeter and Keynes at that stage. Schumpeter had tried to break out of the rigid frame of the quantity theory of money, and had tried to link money and finance in a context of the existence of forced savings potential. At this point, if we identify new investment with innovations, the process of excess of investment over savings has a productivity-improvement component and an output-increment component, as a result of which, the rigours of actual forced savings are considerably tempered. The chances were that the Schumpeterian process had a greater chance of getting through under certain assumptions. Keynes' approach in the *Treatise*, could be attacked on the score that since it came into conflict with the real implication of marginal productivity theory, it could not have a long-run significance. Such a criticism could not be levelled against Schumpeter's own approach.

Whatever the similarity between Schumpeter and Keynes on the mechanisms discussed in the *Treatise*, Schumpeter, of course, could not and did not, have much sympathy with Keynes in the latter's analytical glorification in the *General Theory* of the depression psychosis. Schumpeter's own perceptions of a depression were different. Keynes' vision of a capitalistic system wallowing in prolonged slump equilibrium with a perfectly elastic liquidity preference curve and an interest-inelastic, weak, investment demand schedule, could certainly not have appealed to Schumpeter. Schumpeter also did not accept the implications of the *General Theory's* argument for monetary and fiscal intervention by the authorities. Schumpeter believed then, that the dynamics of the capitalistic process could not but lead to a further bout of innovations. (It was Robertson who continuously nagged Keynes for neglecting the important role of autonomous investment which could be independent of both the current state of income and even of interest.) Schumpeter criticised Keynes very severely for the latter's thesis on 'euthanasia of the *rentier*'. There were class differences between the two. Keynes was a bourgeoisie intellectual whereas Schumpeter was certainly an aristocrat's aristocrat. Strictly speaking, Schumpeter did not consider innovators as his heroes at all; their role, he compared, to that of robbers! But he looked at the economic effects of the processes, not at the moral values of the personalities involved.

In his *Business Cycles*, Schumpeter permitted speculative influences to be superimposed on the innovation process. This could, of course, introduce minor complications to the pure innovation-imitation process. The slump would perhaps be more prolonged as a result, and the boom nipped in the bud too soon. Schumpeter appears to have also played with the thought of permitting some unemployment in the initial frame though it would not be of the Keynesian type. In *Business Cycles* Schumpeter was kinder to non-competitive forms, particularly monopolies. This was on account of the link between research expenses and development (in a sense, multinationals also could be brought in here). The institutional forms would have to change to suit the development urgent in the system. *Business Cycles* substitutes steady growth in place of 'development's circular flow;' the notion of neighbourhood of equilibrium plays an important role as a reference frame. Schumpeter incorporates the Kondratief long-wave hypothesis and builds an integral relation among Kitchins (forty months), Juglars (six to nine years) and Kondratiefs (fifty years). He bravely puts together statistical data to test his own hypotheses.

Business Cycles has been a failure. The methods which Schumpeter adopted to test his theory and the data chosen by him have been questioned. His attitude towards 'depressions' has not been accepted. But surprisingly, though the old fashioned Juglars (and Kitchins) seem to have temporarily gone out, the long-wave hypothesis has returned. It has become a major topic of contemporary discussion. Frankly, Schumpeter was right in forecasting a recovery from the Great Depression of the thirties; currently, too, the capitalist economies seem to be recovering from what Hicks has termed as another Great Depression. Ultimately, Marx's forebodings on the future of capitalism as also the Ricardo-inspired predictions of the Club of Rome, are negated if the long-wave hypothesis, the Kondratief cycle, is seen to be grounded on firm rock. Sweezy's classroom triumph over Schumpeter is short-lived.

In *Capitalism, Socialism and Democracy*, which, unfortunately for him, has had the widest public reception of all his writings, Schumpeter seems to have been rather casual in his diagnosis of contemporary process. The critique of the Marxian theory certainly stands out, but Schumpeter's own conclusion that capitalism will tend to wither away on account of its very successes, transforming the glamorous innovation process into a mechanical, bureaucratic routine, seems to be slippery. Like all economists who are out of depth in non-economic matters, and particularly in the sphere of political predictions, Schumpeter too had no strong foundations for his views on the future of capitalism. His observation that labourism would have a prolonged reign and socialist ideas would gain ascendency, has not come through: nor is his view that intellectuals would lose commitment to the achievement potentials of capitalism borne out; rebellion is building up even among economists against high rates of taxation. Schumpeter's prophecy that the post-war world would forever be 'a Tax cum Inflation State', fortunately, is empirically getting falsified. History seems to be turning. In most Western economies, and even in Germany itself, there has been a revival of conservation and it is Keynesianism that has faded, and not Schumpeterianism. In a recent paper, Samuelson makes a remark that Schumpeter, during his last phase, seems to have been depressed by the triumph of the Soviet Union in the Second World War. Samuelson hunches that Schumpeter had, perhaps, a wee-bit sympathy for market fascism as against Soviet Communism. Samuelson, of course, had opted for Keynes against Schumpeter. A point for Schumpeter is, that countries have gone out of market fascism but no communist country has so far come out of the tunnel. Schumpeter was no populist, and in making one's judgement on Schumpeter's personality in the light of Samuelson's remark, may I humbly advise scholars to wait for a full definitive biography of Schumpeter, whenever it comes.

We now come to the great *History of Economic Analysis* posthumously published, thanks to the devoted labours of his wife. Portions of the *History* had appeared in *Ten Great Economists*, but the *History*, as it emerges, cannot be dispensed with by any worthwhile economist. Schumpeter's magnificent generosity to young scholars from whatever land, race or religion, is clear on every page. Along with Viner, (Haberler and Leontief), Schumpeter truly had an international temperament. He would never grudge originality on the score that the author's earlier works were not well-known, or that he belonged to a country or race other than his own. These qualities, alas, have almost disappeared in modern-day economics which has now become a conglomeration of informal cliques, clubs and groups. Economists are divided by nationality, ideology and race. The Nobel Prize seems to have added its own quota to the narrowness of the familial horizon of economists.

The *History of Economic Analysis*, is an incomplete palace of massive proportions. It deals with the institutional background of economists, their philosophical presuppositions, their economic ideas, and their concepts and theories. It brings developments to the end of the Second World War and has minute analysis of certain controversies. In particular, we may refer to the Say's Law, capital theory (and production function) controversies where Schumpeter misses almost nothing. The *History* shows Schumpeter's admiration for the Walrasian version of the economic process in terms of the magnificent vision of general equilibrium. It is also very sympathetic to Marshall, but is rather highly critical of Ricardo and of the English classical school.

Schumpeter's approach like that of Samuelson, Solow and Blaug (in *Economic Theory in Retrospect*) is that the subject of economics had a linear development culminating in the theory of general equilibrium with its dependence upon the marginalist method. One may rightly challenge this approach. The worldwide revival of the classical theory of value was not anticipated by him; with this revival, new strands have appeared which would have surprised Schumpeter. The theoretically intrinsic separation of value and distribution; the scope for factor-intensity reversals; re-switching; the re-entry of reproduction models without role of demand; the popularity of the notion of a commodity rate of profits; the destruction of the link between resource-scarcities and price signals, the latter deemed now to be *random* ratios; the neutrality of money and of fiscal interventions under rational expectations—all these cannot be projected from a study of Schumpeter's *History*. Schumpeter blamed Ricardo for his preoccupation with problems of England; but to moderns, Ricardo reappears as the fount of new classical economics. Read as deeply as you may of Schumpeter's *History*, but you won't perceive the seed of the 'Sraffa Revolution' in it! But then Schumpeter would have welcomed the new drifts, for he believed in opening and not closing the doors of knowledge (witness the welcome he gave to Econometrics, in contrast to Keynes' attitude regarding the same).

Insights

Young Schumpeter, it is said, had three ambitions. To be the greatest horse-rider, to be the greatest lover and to be the greatest economist. He was a scholarly prodigy, a dazzlingly original mind, a generous teacher to outstanding students, a sympathetic peer biographer to the great economists, a massive thinker of depth and sweep, and of great proportions. His family life at an early age was marked by sadness. He never rode a horse. He had himself surrendered to Walras the epithet of the greatest economist of all time, and during his own lifetime saw Keynes gathering all the honours, and even from Harvard for what, he, Schumpeter, must have internally felt, transient and populist public positions. To himself, his life and work must have been a tragedy; what he generously, spontaneously, gave to other economists, he never got in return, and he must have been too proud to seek acclaim from those around him. We see him riding economics like a Colossus, but alone. The Muse of Economics must have admired him; that is why she kept him for herself, not surrendering him to the capricious damsel of pedestalled fame.

Many of Schumpeter's original insights missed the scholars, often even those around him. Very few were aware or had the boldness to point out to the other Cambridge, that the theory of short-period forced savings which Keynes had presented in the *Treatise* by means of the mechanism of investment exceeding savings, had its early origin in Schumpeter's own theory nearly two decades earlier. Very few knew that it was Schumpeter who had outlined investment, generating productivity changes, by means of the instrumentality of a recombination of the means of production made possible through bank loans. The mechanism of forced savings bridged the gap between *ex-ante* investment and *ex-ante* savings. In the 1934 English translation, Schumpeter gave a handsome acknowledgement to the work of Robertson in his 'Banking Policy and the Price Level'. Unlike Hayek of the early 1930s, Schumpeter long ago had asserted that the innovation-forced savings would tend to lead to such improvements in productivity as would make the whole process self-financing. There could be no abortions in such a process. Keynes himself, in his *Treatise*, expressed his acceptance of the Schumpeterian theory of trade cycle but did not acknowledge the relation between the fundamental equations of the *Treatise* and Schumpeter's theory of the process of financial implications of innovation. Again, most economists hailed the *General Theory's* originality in the pioneering of the monetary theory of the rate of interest, without being aware that it was Schumpeter who pioneered it, though in a different context, in his *Theory of Economic Development*. A perusal of Schumpeter's *Theory of Economic Development* makes it clear that, perhaps, his was the first of the models which worked out the implications, particularly in the understanding of the circular flow of economic activity. The separation of the circular flow from the development process requires the application of the rational expectations concept to the former. Further, Schumpeter was the earliest to distinguish between risk and uncertainty (between insurable risks and non-insurable uncertainties). The dynamic process of a modern economy was clearly put in the mould of a circular flow process of potential steady growth. In *Business Cycles*, Schumpeter had all the ingredients of steady growth theory, but only as a scaffolding to superimpose upon it the development process.

In his *Business Cycles*, as in the early *Theory of Economic Development*, Schumpeter postulates a more or less fully committed economy, in terms of employable labour and produced materials as the basic norm. But this leaves room for a measure of unemployment, which could not be absorbed in the initial stage because of supply scarcities. In *Business Cycles*, the measure of unemployment permitted is wider in content, and can be considered to be a precursor to the concept of natural rate of unemployment which is prominent in recent discussions. The natural rate is a wider notion than frictional unemployment as visualised by Keynes. Strangely enough, it was Robertson who foresaw the need for it in a dynamic analytical frame. (Yet another similarity between Schumpeter and Robertson; the outstanding similarity is that both were scholars of authentic rank so rare among economists!)

On this theme, I would also like to mention that Lucas' perception of cyclical or recessionary unemployment, as a volitionally optimum response of the economy from a dynamic angle, can be compared with Schumpeter's characterisation of depression as a *necessary* phase for the price as well as employment adjustments to work themselves out in the wake of the implications of the innovation boom. At this stage, we may also note, as Robertson did in his *Banking Theory*, and later tried to convince Keynes of the need of institutions like banks, that Schumpeter had provided an integral role to banks, in the mechanism of transfer of command over goods and services from circular flow operators to the new entrepreneurs. Schumpeter's theory provided room for structural changes in the dynamic process going along with changes in the financial process. The inter-link between innovations, process of changes in productivity and the process of financial development has been an important theme in post-Second World War discussions. But, unfortunately, Schumpeter's insights did not seem to have enriched these excursions.

It is widely agreed that the discovery of the productivity growth theme is an important element in the dynamics of development, as in the writings of Abramovitz, Solow, Kendrick, *et al.*, it is a big landmark in our subject. A close perusal of Schumpeter's *Theory of Economic Development* makes it clear that this was *the* theme central to Schumpeter. The whole of the *Theory of Economic Development* was set out as a major challenge to the orthodox and then stratified themes of capital accumulation with accompanying labour growth as *the* causative factor in production growth. Even in early and mid-1950s, accumulation of capital was deemed as a central element in growth analysis (witness the contributions of R.F. Kahn, Joan Robinson, Arthur Lewis, et al.). Schumpeter had long ago perceived that productivity growth was the central element in development and looked at the entire economic process from that angle. In fact, the *Theory of Economic Development* has a long discussion on the imputation of shares in the circular flow model and opts for weights as per distribution shares for aggregate heterogeneous agents of production. Unfortunately, during Schumpeter's lifetime, not much data were available on long-period development. Otherwise, his technique would have shown how powerful and wide-sweeping the contribution of productivity growth was to the process of development.

Fortunately, in most recent years, a number of writers like Rostow, Maddison, J.J. Van Duijn, N.B. Forrester, E. Mandel, G. Mensch, *et al.*, have returned to the interpretation of the capitalistic process in terms of the Kondratief and other long waves. The big changes that one notices in Schumpeter's perception between the *Theory of Economic Development* and *Business Cycles* is his support to the Kondratief long-wave phenomenon. Given the long-wave hypothesis and the Schumpeter-Lucas perceptions on depression, one emerges with a powerful role for autonomous investment as an internal factor within the economic process, lifting the economy out of the slump.

I have given above a glimpse of the powerful contributions of Schumpeter to current day modern economic discussions. That Schumpeter's name is not generally identified with these contributions is a standing indictment on economists in general, particularly in the light of the fact that one of the most authentic accounts of the history of the subject has been composed by Schumpeter. Schumpeter, as is well-known, made little or no reference to his own contributions in his own *History of Economic Analysis*, and in this respect, economists after Schumpeter seem to have been Schumpeterian!

Concepts

Schumpeter's circular flow is different from that of Quesnay, Ramsay and Sraffa. In Quesnay-Ramsay-Sraffa, the circular flow is a *two-way* affair; we may visualise goods as *stocks* proportioned exactly reproducing themselves in the same manner at the end of the year. In George Ramsay and Sraffa, wage-goods are not strictly necessary in the stocks. Consumption goods are also not strictly necessary at the end of the year for generation of values. In Schumpeter, the circular flow is a *one-way* affair, from productive resources to consumption goods, and this is necessary from the point of value generation. In the static circular flow there are no profits; there can be random disturbances between expectations and realisations and perfect synchronisations between plans and performances may not occur. But Schumpeter's circular flow model and the relations therein are not altered thereby (as would be derived as noted already from the application of rational expectations at micro-level). Schumpeter's steady growth is uniformly expanding circular flow at the same rate as the joint-supply of capital and labour. In the circular flow the rate of interest is deemed to be zero. A study of Schumpeter's *Theory* indicates that he was aware of consumption loans but consciously gave importance to production loans. If steady growth as in *Business Cycles* becomes the reference frame, there is room for a positive interest rate relayed to the growth rate; on this is superimposed the effect of innovations. In a developing economy, interest has the following five components: (1) The Bohm-Bawerk component (2) The steady growth component (3) The shift in distribution share component (if we get out of the rut of marginal productivity theory) (4) The incentive component to raise savings independent of (3). Schumpeter differentiates the innovator from the usual entrepreneur/manager. His hypothesis that large and established firms are reluctant to innovate can be related to Kalecki's principle of increasing risk with size (and age). The extension of the concept of money to finance *has* to postulate *sustainable* forced savings. But this can only be, in the absence of a non-marginal productivity theory set up, if a productivity improvement component and output increment component *as a result* can be brought in. The 'Schumpeterian credit inflation' is different from the standard inflation. Schumpeter's concept of capital refers to ability to divert productive resources into new combinations, a coexistence of finance with same *versatility in factors* is implied. Capital thus has both *savings* and physical dimensions. Schumpeter's innovation-traverses permit changes both in relative prices and in the general price level. If capital is interpreted purely in a *vectorial materialist* sense (as in Von Neumann's, not in Sraffa's model, according to Le), there is no scope for Schumpeter's *Theory of Economic Development*. (There is a view held by my distinguished colleague Dr. Ranganath Bharadwaj, that a production model can be interpreted only in the vectorial materialist sense. In that case, shifts involve labour redeployment with a measure of losses undreamt in conventional models.) A strong feature of Schumpeter's *Theory* is that it can be used to dynamicise Sraffa's model. The course of the maximum rate of profits can be altered favourably by innovation.

Hypotheses on Development

Let us now turn to some of the basic hypotheses propositions of Schumpeter's Development Theory:

1. In the absence of production growth generating innovations, the economy tends to settle down dynamically in a circular growth-rate of production, equal to the balanced growth-rate of capital and labour. We may say that given the measure of natural unemployment, the potential growth-rate of the economy would tend to be equal to the growth-rate of labour force, and of population.
2. Improvements in per labour productivity obtained by greater capital intensity, *a la* Bohm-Bawerk, would already tend to have been exhausted in the circular flow, so that there is no harm in treating per labour productivity growth rate as corresponding roughly to contributions of innovations to output growth-rate. Even if one disagrees with the above proposition, then one may choose a composite index of factor-quantity growth as representing output growth-rate under expanding circular flow conditions. The difference between long-period average growth-rate, and factor quantity growth-rate, would contribute the measure of the contribution of innovation to output growth-rate.

3. Whatever the variant for sifting the contribution of productivity growth we choose, Schumpeter's theory would be validated if the contribution of productivity growth-rate happens to be at least as significant, if not more, as the contribution of accumulation or of factor quantity growth.
4. The development process will be characterised by an expansion in the number of goods, in the number of the processes of production, in the number of combinations in which factors or inputs are mixed, in the number of firms, in the number of organisational forms at the micro and sectoral levels, etc.
5. The economy will be witnessing changes in relative prices, relative shares of contributions of different industries, etc.
6. The growth-rate of money tends to be not merely in excess of the potential steady growth-rate of output, but would also witness considerable ebbs and flows in the above growth-rate. A steady growth-rate of money is not a characteristic of developing economies.
7. The sources of funding for the expansion process, under development, would have a high and even rising share of contribution from outside of those available through ploughback of profits, and since development implies a rise of new firms as against old firms, the process has to be characterised by the succession of new business leaders over old business leaders. The leaders in profit positions would be constantly changing. The same firms would not forever be growth firms; there would also be shifts in labour dispositions.
8. The organisation of the firms will also be undergoing changes as a creative response to challenges. During the upward phase in development, given the long wave, money rates of interest will be rising as also real rates. This will be in a context in which money supply rates would also be rising. Rising interest rates and rising money supply would tend to go together.
9. Since per capita standards would be rising in the development process because of successful innovations leading to price and income effects, the goods formerly in vogue among the very rich would trickle down for use among even the relatively lowest of income classes. Thus, the standard of living would tend to be going up and up.

10. If we introduce initial conditions of abject poverty with considerable long-period unemployment, open and concealed, a successful development process, as per Schumpeterian lines, should witness a reduction in the ratio of unemployment to labour force and removal of abject poverty. In fact, innovations come here as the chief instrument for the removal of poverty and unemployment; they also make it possible for the savings ratio to move up higher and higher. Since the poverty barrier will be broken, it is possible that innovations will also lead to an upsurge in population growth.

11. Since spontaneous and discontinuous changes are the essence of development process, and the latter requires both the generation of new technology and new organisational ideas and avenues for their implementation, and the changes must appear potentially viable on the net, the system of property ownership, division of labour and general profit-oriented business activity, are pre-conditions for the Schumpeterian development process. The system must also have dynamic flexibility in relative prices and scope for flexibility in relative dispositions of factors of production, including the avenues of mobility of labour.

12. In terms of the above hypotheses, the acceptability of capitalism is conditioned by its ability to successfully carry out innovations, such that the gains of productivity growth are transferred to labour at large in the form of improvements, in the components of good living and in the quality of life. The capitalistic process is, therefore, an instrumentality for the above, not primarily for technological changes by themselves, but for the distribution effects of the same on the masses of the community. The striving for material welfare by the mass of labourers is fulfilled by the results of the innovation process. Whereas the Marxian vision of capitalism getting superseded by socialism depends upon the continuance of absolute and relative privation of the mass of the workers as an instrument for homogeneous class consciousness, the Schumpeterian process removes the circumstances causing continuance of privation. In other words, if sequential material improvements become the hallmark of capitalism, the prospect of a socialistic revolution from the angle of inner mechanism of the system is eroded.

The above twelve results/propositions have abstracted from the Schumpeterian position, powerfully supported by R.M. Goodwin, that development and cycles cannot be separated.

A Critique of the 'Theory of Economic Development'

Schumpeter's *Theory* requires the following assumptions:

1. Property is privately owned/operated.
2. Labour, finance, are mobile; factor-uses can be altered; competitive conditions generally obtain.
3. No excess productive capacity; economy's stocks and inputs/input services are all committed to pre-designed uses.
4. Relative prices and the general price level are two-way flexible.
5. Real wages, property incomes initially are at such a level as to permit scope for forced, albeit temporary, reductions.
6. Existing, established, leading firms are reluctant as compared to new firms, new leaders, in the matter of undertaking innovations; new ideas in production emanate largely exogenously to existing, established enterprises.
7. Bank credit is elastic within limits, and banks do not mind financing new ventures, new lines, etc.

The model requires the existence of some forced savings potential, and a climate in which new production forms and avenues are generated in an atmosphere of potential supply of finance and availability of innovators. Technological changes *per se*, availability of entrepreneurship *per se*, existence of mobilisable forced savings potential through bank credit *per se*, cannot assume the problems of development under capitalism. Most important of all, why should not savings be interest elastic? One supposes that the specific model of Schumpeter is not general enough.

Further, in Schumpeter's model it is only *ex-post* that we know whether the full sequence of innovations has been gone through. What guarantees are there that the three conditions are always synchronously present? These, it may be noted, are three independent conditions.

We now turn to a more fundamental critique of Schumpeter's theory. We have already noted that Schumpeter's reference economy has no excess productive capacity; no excess stocks and no excess labour. (It has only one excess capacity namely, of ability of banks to create credit!) Labour does *not* know that real wage rates will go up eventually after the innovations are completed. In this situation the current flow, and rate of growth, of existing outputs in the form of final goods have to be absolutely *reduced* during the innovation phase. Why should labour under full unemployment conditions agree to reduce its real wage rate? Under a model of rational expectations, such a reduction in the flow of wage-incomes, or a reduction in its rate of growth, cannot be conceived as a normal phenomenon. There can be no forced savings potential in the fashion Schumpeter visualises. Again, what if real wages will not admit of a reduction because of physiological, conventional reasons?

Let us now turn to a second criticism. Schumpeter brings in an assumption that at higher and higher stages, produced goods, land and labour are all versatile. He takes support (later in the English translation) from J.B. Clark's works for this position. Notions of abstract capital, abstract labour and of abstract land lie at the back of this theory. He does not use the concept of 'basic goods' (not necessarily in hierarchical order) as Sraffa does later. It follows that some losses in *outputs* and *values*, though not of the magnitude in the Von Neumann-R. Bharadwaj models, must occur if the shifts of agents have to be successful. Such losses occur with the onset of innovation itself. Why should established firms, etc., submit to this process? A situation of rising credit and money incomes is conducive to prevent such shifts.

Thus, we have two sets of criticisms. There is no forced savings potential; even if it exists banks cannot help to get them mobilised. (The latter problem can be tackled in a model of plough-back, where the latter itself exploits technological opportunities.)

Cannot the process of plough-back of profits in a context of technological changes generated endogenously within leading firms permit development to occur? The process may be slower than in Schumpeter's model but yet may take place. Again, why should banks alone as agents cause forced savings? Actually, a sudden bout of favourable terms of trade; weak trade unionism, with or without a reserve army of labour; dualism in labour markets leading to dual wage systems; opportunities of imperialistic exploitation—all these may release savings. In fact, short-term scope for distributional changes can permit innovations to occur without banks being brought in.

The Indian Case

To what extent can we attribute per capita income growth necessarily to the innovation–imitation process? How much of the per capita income growth may be attributed to (a) rise in capital intensity per worker (b) movements from inside the production possibility frontier (c) reduction in the rate of population growth, and (d) terms of trade gains and such other improvements, and how much can be attributed to the Schumpeterian causes? Is it possible to attribute the rise in per capita savings enabling the rise in capital intensity as itself being due to the per capita income effect of previous innovations? Why should not movements towards the production possibility frontier itself be deemed as aspects of the Schumpeterian development process? Since such movements would have the productivity improvement effect in the end, carrying out of the desired change would not be a smooth affair. Variations in population growth rate themselves may often be attributed to the effects of innovation in a general sense, since an improvement in per capita income makes it possible to grow at higher rate; so if we introduce income-induced health and welfare measures and their consequences. Similarly, reductions in population growth itself may lead to the beneficial effects of improvements in per capita income, causing expectations of rising living standard subject to limitations of family size. Efforts are required to take advantage of potential trade opportunities including those of favourable terms of trade. Elements of Schumpeterian development process may be deemed to be operative here as well. We may, therefore, leave open the issue for a further examination as to whether or not a high proportion of per capita income growth witnessed in most countries could not be attributable directly or indirectly, to the elements of development process as visualised by Schumpeter.

Kaldor has sought to bring under *technical dynamism* the numerous big and small changes carried out successfully by progressive workers, alert managers and entrepreneurs in developing economies, or in not-leading developed economies. The distinction between innovation and the imitation fades out; it is possible to consider the tremendous progress achieved in Japan leading to unheard-of productivity growth rates therein, as explainable in terms of the Schumpeterian process as we abstract from the cyclical components thereof.

There is, however, one difficulty in applying Schumpeterian theory under conditions wherein project choices are governed by non-economic considerations. In the case of the Indian economy, it has been noticed that there is no statistical relation between investments and (a) levels of the surplus rates (b) the incremental output-capital ratio, and (c) the rate of profit. This can be accounted in terms of the predominant role of the state in the determination of the pattern of investment and composition of the projects. The economic process under Indian conditions does not seem to have followed a path of spontaneous investments governed by appraisals of potential economic worthiness of projects and schemes. Nor can we apply the Schumpeterian theory of the link between temporary credit expansion and the carrying out of innovations. Extension of credit has been undertaken in India purely for reasons of increase in the capital investment, with little or no relation between such increases and improvements in factor productivity.

In the Indian economy, input-output costs have risen phenomenally, capital output ratios have also risen phenomenally. The input cost of unit of net output has also risen phenomenally. Inflation has been persisted upon without there being any compensating production and productivity improvements off-setting the inflation. The role of banks in financing the Green Revolution and agricultural improvements, has so far been insignificant. A good deal of bank credit has been absorbed for any non-viable purposes, for actual or potential sick units. Deficit financing has not been resorted to with a view to primarily causing productivity improvements. While, no doubt, a good measure of forced savings has been imposed in the Indian scene, particularly on poor and vulnerable sections, there has been no prospects of productivity improvements ex-post of a sort to justify the forced savings.

Schumpeter adopted the crucial test of improvements in mass consumption or in per capita consumption for judging whether the development process was worthwhile. In the Indian economy, the proportion of population below the poverty line continues to be 50 per cent. The development process does not seem to have satisfied the Schumpeterian test.

In terms of Schumpeterian criterion, one wonders whether the term 'development' can be applied to the Indian experience so far. One would, therefore, be reluctant to test the Schumpeterian theory under Indian conditions. The Indian developmental model had not built any component on factor productivity growth. We seem to have been paying only lip service to the goal of productivity improvement. To what extent the poor results of our development experiences are attributable to the faulty strategy we adopted, and to what extent to leakages in the process, certainly needs to be discussed. However, even assuming that the leakages in the Mahalanobis model had been plugged, there is no room to believe that per capita *consumption* improvements of such sort, as to have reduced the proportion of people below the poverty line by a significant extent, would have taken place. Underlying Schumpeterian theory is the postulate that investment must, ultimately, lead to improvement in consumption standards. This is the corner stone of the Jevons-Menger-Walras-Bohm-Bawerk theory. Unfortunately, as Tugan Baranowski pointed out, there could be conditions under which development of related heavy industries can become an end in itself. There is no empirical justification, that goods in the higher order are necessarily versatile. As Sraffa has demonstrated, the postulate of consumption demand is not a necessary condition for the generation of values. If values represent mutually constant relations and have an internal balance, a model of heavy industry growth including infrastructure requirements thereof, can go on forever with continuous rises in capital-output ratio and no perceptible effects on the ratio of employment, and in the proportion of people below poverty line to labour force. If leakages are plugged, it would mean that no consumption improvements at all would occur! The logical implication of such a model continues to be eternal poverty! I would, therefore, submit that the Indian experience so far cannot, thus, be brought under the rubric of Schumpeterian development theory.

Conclusion

Let us stand apart if it is possible, and appraise the achievements of Schumpeter, Marx and Keynes. Both Marx and Schumpeter had a vision of the economic process through history and of the secular future. Marx was a rebel against classical economists; Schumpeter was a rebel against the classical economists and Marx. Marx used and expounded the kit of tools bequeathed by Quesnay, Ricardo and George Ramsay in order to support his vision; Schumpeter used the conceptual frame of Quesnay, Cournot,

Thunen, Bohm-Bawerk and Walras, and the historical method of Marx, to substantiate his vision. In place of Marx's simple reproduction model, Schumpeter has circular flow; in place of the expanding reproduction model, he has steady growth; in place of the mode of production, he brings in innovation; in place of Marx's thesis of immiseration of the working classes, Schumpeter brings in steady affluence in consumption standards of the worker; and in place of Marx's growing sequence of crises, Schumpeter brings in the sequence of the triple cycle schema, taking the economy forever upward in terms of production possibilities and per capita consumption levels.

The circumstances of the Second World War and the rise of liberalism and socialist ideas put Schumpeter off his poise. He jumped to the generalisation that capitalism would possibly wither away because of its achievements. Note that Marx too had thought that the State would wither way. In this respect, both were mistaken. Marx's hunch on the Socialist Revolution was right for a portion of the world, but perhaps for entirely wrong reasons. Marx glorified saving and accumulation and Schumpeter played up innovation and productivity growth. One portion of the world (the Soviet Bloc) under communism is witnessing saturation of growth because of rising capital-output ratios and natural resources constraints. This, despite very high savings and investment ratios to national income. Another portion of the world, with one part with low savings ratios and another with high savings ratios, seems to be witnessing the possibility of continuous but low growth. The capital-output ratios seem to be within manageable levels.

India, following Marx and the Soviet Bloc, has placed its faith on accumulation and has been threatened with the prospect of a stationary no-growth state with 50 per cent of the population yet below-the-poverty-line. It is too early, as we do not have enough data, to speculate on the future possibilities of China. Though communistic in outer garb, the Chinese seem to be experimenting with more and more capitalistic modes. Is it, then, true to say that had Schumpeter, and not Marx, been the governing deity, the Soviet Bloc and India could have done better? A question like this has to be boldly asked, since without substantial and sustained productivity improvements, there must be no economic future for India. The Western world has gone out of Keynes and is seeking to recapture the springs of productivity growth. In a sense, the poor and the developed countries are linked together in a quest for discovering the secrets of the process of development outlined by Schumpeter nearly seventy-five years ago. Yes, Schumpeter is the economist of the future. It is his vision of development which has to be governing bold-vision of the rulers/planners in the world, if any sort of stationary state is to be escaped. In that sense, Schumpeter's vision may at last triumph over that of Marx and certainly of Keynes.

Appendix

Discussion on Schumpeter's work touches most aspects of economics, including its history. The following notes may be of interest to scholars.

Zero Rate of Interest

1. There is a controversy among theorists, on whether in a stationary state, the rate of interest will be positive or zero. Bohm-Bawerk argues that the rate of interest will be positive under a stationary setting given constant technology. Schumpeter contends that the rate of interest will tend to be zero. Schumpeter has not been supported by some economists on the ground that a positive interest rate would be established even in a stationary state because of the phenomenon of consumption loans; the rate of interest will have to be positive in order to penalise excess, or improvident, consumption. In other words, in order to prevent the emergence of retrogressive economy, interest rate will have to be positive. Bohm-Bawerk's view is that positive time preference *is* a fact of life; present goods, directly or indirectly yielding consumption utility *in the present*, are valued more highly than future goods. Pigou holds the view that there is a tendency to underestimate pitfalls and adversities, as may arise in the future.

2. One could imagine the following reasons for causing a premium in favour of present goods:

(i) The uncertainty about the accrual of future goods by the foregoing of present goods. These uncertainties may be due to both subjective and objective factors; one may also include the uncertain nature of the dates of mortality.

(ii) Positive time preference due to a higher valuation of the current utility of present goods. This can be due to the expectation of improvement in one's status in the future, as a result of which, income would be larger than what it is currently and the marginal consumption utility of income would tend to be lower.

(iii) Positive time preference at micro levels due to irrational reasons as described by Pigou.

Bohm-Bawerk's argument is, that because of time preference, the available volume of present goods for diversion towards the future uses will be scarce, even though by increasing the measure of roundaboutness the (physical) productivity of present goods could be increased. Hayek in 'Pure Theory of Capital' adduces the reason that if interest is zero, a portion of capital would tend to be consumed away.

3. As noted in the text, Schumpeter would seem to assume rational expectations. Given this, there is no question of Pigouvian myopia or Bohm-Bawerkian *agio*. Further, given the existence of banks, there always emerges the possibility of altering the command over present goods, through loans to entrepreneurs who will be exploiting the incremental productivity possibilities. In strict theory, according to Schumpeter, the initial *distribution* of command over present goods is not necessarily sacrosanct. In fact, Schumpeter's theory can explain why savings become larger during the course of economic development.

4. There is, however, the difficulty as pointed out in the writings of Ramsey, Harrod, Goodwin and others, that even if we postulate socialist means of ownership of production, there will be genuine hardships in the unlimited transfer of present goods for transformation into future goods; so too with potentially higher incremental productivity. This is because of the higher marginal utility of current consumption to a large number of people, of whom the poorer sections would be a predominant part. From a planning angle, even granting the potentiality of forcing savings through inflation, forced labour camps, etc., one should not activise such potential to the hilt. The thesis put up in India during the third Plan by Allen Manne and Rudra who incidentally referred to Schumpeter, for maximising the use of forced savings potential had abstained from the issue of higher marginal consumption utility of present goods, there is, or should be, a limit to forced saving; in fact, except under extraordinary circumstances, there should be no forced savings on the absolutely poor.

5. In all these cases, one has to operate under an *as if* hypothesis.

The planners will have to presume that present goods for present consumption from the point of the poor, have *higher* levels of marginal utility than could be imagined in the calculations of investment enthusiasts. At the same time, it is good to point out that Bohm-Bawerk and Schumpeter were concerned with such uses of savings and savings potential, and such forms which add to total productivity of primary sources. On the other hand, in planned systems, forced savings from the poor can be utilised to buttress the consumption of the top salariat, the upper echelons of trade union workers, and the participants in political parties and in various other unproductive ways, many of them often justified as *necessary socialist consumption*. The forced savings emerge in Schumpeter because of the scope of temporary inflation of credit, which will be resorted to, primarily, by innovators engaged in productivity-improving operations. Even then, as noted earlier, there is a long tradition in economics which would *restrict* the use of banking power for purposes of transfer of command over present goods. The classical economists would emphasise the primacy of adequate stocks in the determination of extent of bank credit. As we have seen earlier, economists for different reasons also would like to evolve rules and restrictions on the use of banking power. The Central Bank's traditional role is to keep *down* forced savings; the free play for the rate of interest and the injunction that the authorities should not depress the long-term rate, is also with a view to preventing the emergence of opportunities of forced savings. Schumpeter's model of unrestricted banking power abstracts from the role of Central Banks and other monetary authorities and seems to be more relevant in non-poor societies.

6. The issue is not whether interest *can* be zero, but whether interest should be deemed to be zero. So long as interest is a barrier to both excessive, unproductive consumption and too great a diversion of resources for long period purposes, there is no harm in assuming that while interest may tend to be zero, it should *not* be deemed to be zero. This, in my view, is the best safeguard for the poor under Indian conditions.

Schumpeter on Imperialism

Schumpeter's theory of imperialism set out in 'Imperialism and the Social Classes', has been considered by scholars as the most powerful psychological-sociological alternative to the Marxian theories.

Schumpeter maintains here, that fundamentally capitalism and imperialism are antagonistic to each other, and thus, will not go together. Imperialism is associated with the irrational psychological attributes of aggressive rulers, ruling warrior castes, jingoistic and nationalistic passions of people leading to expansionism—all these are characteristics of a number of pre-capitalistic stages, and may often survive as visages in early phases of a capitalist system. The strong proposition of Schumpeter is that the capitalistic process under conditions of democracy, competition and rising real standards of workers, will tend to give no room for the emergence, or persistence, of imperialism. Business firms and leaders will tend to have their own goals of expansion, unrelated to power-domination over other countries. Schumpeter's work includes large number of examples from history and innumerable insights. Schumpeter does admit that monopolistic tendencies are fostered by protectionism, and that this, in its turn, may lead to imperialistic policies including in finance (after Hilferding). However, he believes in the ultimate domination of capitalistic rationality, and the consequent avoidance of wars and of war-like situations. The emergence of multinationals can be said to break the link between national interest and the interests of firms. A world spanned by interlocking multinationals, may refute the Marxian theory and give support to Schumpeter's emphasis on the capitalistic motivation as an all-embracing factor. Schumpeter's theory may also be interpreted to show that in development under capitalism no single country has dominance. This means, that the collusion of capitalist interests with the interests of the State required for the success of the Marxian theory of imperialism, may not materialise. The oil-price shocks brought about major redistribution in the ownership of liquid reserves, but the process of transition should be deemed peaceful. In the present day world, countries belonging to capitalistic and socialist systems are in rivalry among themselves and between each other. Modes of production are getting mixed, and criss-cross relations among countries is common. There was a time when a Marxian theory based on quest for markets was in vogue. But this has been partly supplanted by a theory based on quest for cheap raw materials and fuels. It is also difficult to distinguish between Schumpeterian, purely militaristic, defence-oriented territorial expansions, with ideology playing a fifth wheel role, and primarily economic-expansion oriented territorial annexations.

Can we consider the Second World War as a case of Marxian theory? Does it not illustrate more accurately, Schumpeter's theory? We must admit that there are several theories of imperialism and Schumpeter's theory can coexist on a level with the Marxian theories. Paul Sweezy included Schumpeter's theory of imperialism in a 'Schumpeterian system', which was comparable in scope, according to him, to Marxian social science.

The Relation Between the Trend and the Cycle

1. In Schumpeter's theory the trend is an imaginary, *ex-post*, concept. Whatever the trend line that one derives *ex-post* is itself *caused* by the cycle and the upward boost it gives to income, savings, per capita income, per capita consumption and interest. The phenomenon known as 'growth' as measured by means of the *ex-post* trend line cannot be conceived in capitalism without the cyclical process. In a world where cycles do not exist, in all probability the trend line would have a lower slope; in other words, the growth rate of per capita income, per capita consumption, savings, as also the level of real rate of interest would be lower. Business cycles are the heart-beats of capitalism and are responsible for the difference in the two trend lines. An economy subjected to business cycles would find the slope of the trend higher than an economy not subjected to business cycles.

2. A question may arise as to what would happen under mature capitalism when, according to Schumpeter's *Capitalism, Socialism and Democracy*, innovation-decisions tend to get bureaucratised. Transfers of resources occur through fiats or through secular inflationary processes, with the public sector undertaking the initiative, high and rising rates of taxation would have eroded the significance of the entrepreneurial drive. If we assume the innovations are specific to the private investment process, with the banks providing the monetary wherewithal for recombinations, etc., the innovations made to order under socialism, emerging after bureaucratised capitalism, would be manifesting a *lower* trend line in growth than would have been in the case under the former, full-fledged, robust capitalism. There is an additional point that where the public sector takes the initiative, the proportion of unproductive expenditures would be high and rising, banks also serving the above purpose; genuine innovation-loans are less than those used

for all sorts of non-viable purposes. The fundamental rationale of *economy* generally tends to have less scope in a socialist system. It would follow from this, that from the point of view of the mass or ordinary workers, the trend line in consumption would perhaps be higher under full-fledged, robust capitalism than under populist socialism. Perhaps socialism may be characterised by a greater measure of equality, but the *level* at which the distribution is measured would tend to be higher under capitalism than under socialism. In other words, from the point of view of *absolute* income and consumption of the bottom groups, capitalism, particularly when supported by redistributive welfare measures, may tend to show better results than socialism. The Schumpeterian capitalist model as applied to the United States, U.K., West Germany and Japan should be compared to the socialist model of the Soviet Bloc.

Criticisms of the Business Cycle Theory of Schumpeter

Schumpeter's *Business Cycles* theory has been criticised on a number of scores:

1. No satisfactory explanation of the triple-cycle scheme and of the integral nature of the different lengths of the Kitchins, the Juglars and the Kondratiefs.
2. Turning points not exactly identified.
3. The hypotheses of the bunching of innovations at the time of the depressions not argued out.
4. No distinction between experiences of lead countries and of follower countries.
5. Not clear why Schumpeter does not take recourse to Keynes' refutation of Say's Law, and thus avail himself of the multiplier-accelerator mechanism.
6. The empirical link between banks and innovations not always and everywhere supported.
7. The phenomenon of building cycles not integrated with the scheme.
8. The *inevitability* of the cyclical nature of development not proved; why should not steady improvements in techniques occur along with accumulation of an expanding scale?

9. The interlink between value implications of the triple-scheme and the development process not worked out.
10. The model depends too much on flex-prices and flex-price levels.

Rigorous empirical testing is not possible, and should not be expected, when there are so few triple-cycles in history. Schumpeter's conception of economic dynamics involved statistics, theory and history; the last implies a measure of uniqueness for each cycle. In recent years, considerable empirical evidence has come around to vindicate Schumpeter's link between depression and revival of autonomous investment. Schumpeter left open the issue of the macro-scale at which his theory has to be referred. Why should the nation be the sole reference frame? One supposes that the nature of the hinterland, background, situation would help partly to define whether a change is an innovation or not. Recently, many gaps in Schumpeter's theory concerning relative prices movements are being filled. For example, Rostow considers terms of trade between primary products and manufacturing as important. It is easy to adjust Schumpeter's theory to conditions of secular, uni-directional, price movements. An upward rising price trend independent of the cyclical processes may have to be postulated. All these only mean that Schumpeter's theory is only a starting point and can be extended and generalised further. But which theory of the whole economic process can be said to be strong in perception of *both* woods and trees? Which portion of Marx's scheme of capitalism has stood the test of both theoretical and empirical scrutiny? Has Ricardo been vindicated in his model of the relentless march towards a stationary state? Has Keynes' vision of engineered full employment been vindicated? How much of the present day problems of our globe can be comprehended by Marshall's *Principles of Economics*?

Schumpeter and the Third Decade

Schumpeter believed in the hypothesis that the best creative work of scholars is achieved during the fertile third decade—the sacred decade according to him—of their lives. This hypothesis seems to have a good measure of support in natural sciences, particularly in mathematics. In the field of economics, too, we have many well-known illustrations to support it: Malthus' *First Essay on Population*; Longfield's contributions to distribution; Torrens' hunch on comparative costs; John Stuart Mill's contribution to international trade theory as set out in *Essays on some Unsettled Questions*; Jevons' seminal paper to the British Association on marginal utility and the mathematical method; Menger's contributions to foundations of marginal utility approach; Wieser's conception of opportunity costs; Schumpeter's own *Theory of Economic Development*; Pigou's *Wealth and Welfare*; Robertson's *Industrial Fluctuations*; Frank Ramsey's work on saving; Haberler's statement of trade theory in terms of opportunity cost; Viner's work on the transfer problem; contributions of Sraffa, Chamberlin and Joan Robinson to the theory of value under non-competitive markets; Kantarovich's work on linear programming; Kahn's work on short-period economies; Samuelson's *Foundations*; Solow's contribution to growth theory; Arrow's *Social Choice and Individual Values*; Bhagwati's work on immiserising growth and on optimum subsidies; A.K. Sen's perception of technique choices as an issue in welfare economics; Chakravarty's generalisation of development as an investment-choice affair; B.V. Krishnamurthi's expansion of pricing under planning to the domain of increasing returns; K.S. Krishnaswami's unpublished work on distribution of factor-share, 'Keynesian Revolution', experimenting with simultaneous equations frame, and the unpublished similar work in Keynesian theory around the same time by R.H. Honaver at Bombay, would all perhaps come under the category of subjectively, and perhaps also objectively, original *and* important theoretical contributions by scholars below or close to the age of 30. There are, of course, conspicuous exceptions like those of Adam Smith, Ricardo, Marx, Cournot, Walras, Thunen, Marshall, Bohm-Bawerk, Wicksell, Cassell, Keynes, Hicks, etc. There is hope for the ageing. High originality at the same level often may not be sustained throughout one's life. Secondly, scholars may change their views or positions as they become mature. In economics it is very rare, that fundamental and new contributions to different branches go on appearing throughout the scholar's life work. In Schumpeter's own mind, theory, range and vision, all are important. Schumpeter produced before he was thirty, a major theory in the new area of development, an in-depth treatment of the role of money in social product and a comprehensive survey of the whole domain of economics. He took great pains to emphasise the potentialities in young minds for breaking fresh ground, and even went out of his way to hunt out and encourage talent, with no biases regarding the soil from which it comes. Insularity, parochialism, cliquishness, all may succeed for a time under the shadow of one or more great names, but in course of time talent will shun, and shy away from, such places. No scholarly habitant can be so enduring to afford to be always self-centred. (Look how creative work in the West itself shifted from centre to centre—Lausanne, Manchester, Cambridge (U.K.), Vienna, Stockholm, London, Oxford, Cambridge (U.S.), New Haven, Chicago at one stage or other has been fluttering its flag high. Centres don't make great minds; great minds make great centres. Harvard was great because it had giants like Taussig, Schumpeter, Leontief, Hansen and others, who, in turn, helped to nurture scholars like Samuelson, Metzler, Tobin, Sweezy, Goodwin and others. That is, of course, the job of universities in developing countries. To attract, to keep, to nurture *and not to rule*, creative minds; to cultivate and build an environment which grows such minds. Fortunate is a country if it also instills in their minds an attitude of compassionate, one might say, even an aristocrat's camaraderie with the masses of the poor.)

Schumpeter's Greats

Students of history of economic analysis have been perturbed by Schumpeter's choice of Quesnay, Thunen, Cournot and Walras as the four great economists. Goodwin, a close student of Schumpeter, has expressed the view that Schumpeter's admiration for Walras was exaggerated. However, Samuelson has defended Schumpeter's choice. It may be noted that Schumpeter excluded Adam Smith, Malthus, Ricardo, Jevons, Menger, Bohm-Bawerk, Wicksell and Cassell from the above list. All four great economists are non-Englishmen. (Samuelson says that Marshall was the fifth economist; but there is no mention of this in Schumpeter's writings.) Secondly, contemporaneously, and even for some time after his life, each of the four had not received due appreciation from the profession. Was Schumpeter prejudiced in his appraisals? Let us take Quesnay. A close perusal of Adam Smith, Ricardo and Marx would reveal how deeply they had been influenced by Quesnay.

The role of stocks in production, the circular flow, the distinction between circulating and fixed capital, the concept of a natural order, the role of prices as a signal for allocation of resources, and the unproductive effect of government operations—all these ideas can be deemed to have been absorbed by Smith from Quesnay and Turgot. Schumpeter had anticipated the pioneering significance of *Tableau Economique* as the precursor of the input-output system. Schumpeter under-played the influence of Ricardo because of Ricardo's preoccupation with the problems of Great Britain and also because of his long-term analytical bias in favour of diminishing returns, a bias he, Schumpeter himself, strongly rejected. He admired Marx as a social scientist but had nothing to do with his economics. Marx, according to Schumpeter, missed the powerful role of development in expanding levels of mass consumption and in achieving the miracle of sustained, substantial reduction of absolute poverty. Capitalism, according to Schumpeter, *is* a success story and from the point of the workers, there would be no *internal* economic forces making for a revolution. Marx had excluded the powerful role of innovations in improving the productivity levels in consumption goods purchased by the workers. While Schumpeter admired Bohm-Bawerk and Jevons, he seems to have relegated marginalism to the static sphere. His own interest was in dynamics. His admiration for Thunen was on the basis of the latter's contribution to the theory of distribution, and his admiration was all the more greater because Thunen worked all by himself. Schumpeter's admiration for Cournot was essentially because of the technical apparatus which he employed to understand the diverse market forms. His great euphoria for Walras is essentially because of the latter's *vision* of general equilibrium. One notices that in Quesnay, Cournot, Thunen and Walras there is a great emphasis on interdependence. Is it not correct to say that behind the input-output coefficients we perceive Quesnay, behind the theory of value under alternative market forms we perceive Cournot, behind the theory of distribution we perceive Thunen, and behind the general theory of value and distribution we perceive Walras. As pointed out in the text, it is true that Schumpeter played down the English classical contributions. This is because they had a bias in favour of stocks, history and the past, and in favour of known techniques and coefficients. All classical models would tend to land themselves in a stationary state in view of the hidden premise of the exhaustible nature of non-renewable resources. (Strangely, Goodwin too seems to have opted for the classical vision of a potential catastrophe with all his admiration for Schumpeter.)

Schumpeter's theory of dynamic economic process has to be contrasted with the Walrasian model of a static system in general equilibrium. Schumpeter's breakthrough is in rejecting the actual applicability of the above system to the dynamic process. Schumpeter is a rebel against not merely Ricardo and Marx *but Walras* also. He postulates the source of dynamism as internal to the economic system. Under vigorous capitalistic conditions as defined by him, the source of energy disturbs the tendency of an actual system to settle down to a static state. The source itself would be created and recreated, again and again, like Phoenix. The vigorous system could therefore *never* be observed in static form. Unlike either theorist of dynamics who would treat *portions* of actual economic categories as the resultants of economic changes, Schumpeter treated almost the *whole* of the fundamental economic categories as a creature of the dynamic process. In this sense, the Schumpeterian paradigm refers to economic society in continuous development and in incessant ferment. The development angle colours the economic perspective and policies in such countries. We are unconsciously adopting the Schumpeterian angle when we are distinguishing between a developing and a developed economy. In fact, if we take the Schumpeterian clue, we look at every economic phenomenon differently from that to which we are accustomed from the Marshall-Walras angle. In this sense, the transition from underdevelopment to development *is* a traverse from Ricardo to Schumpeter jumping over Walras. But the Classical and Schumpeterian views will *always* diverge, and one's perception of the economic problem depends upon whether one goes with the Classical or the Schumpeterian vision. If one takes the former road, the great lights will be Quesnay, Malthus, Ricardo, George Ramsay, Sraffa and so on. (Marx belongs to social sciences in general.) Where does Schumpeter belong? I think his *Theory of Development* belongs to the *future* of the classical line. For he represents the triumph of leaping hope over gaping doom.

5

Schumpeter: The Inconsistencies of a Prescient Ideologue

AMIYA KUMAR BAGCHI

Schumpeter has been one of the most self-aware, and one of the most successfully self-concealing, economists of this century. Trying to trace the origins of 'Imperialism as a catch phrase' in England, in the speeches of Benjamin Disraeli, Schumpeter wrote: 'After the split over the question of repealing the Corn Laws in the year 1846, the Conservative Party in England, reconstituted around Stanley, Bentinck, and Disraeli, was in an extremely difficult situation. During long years of unbroken dominance, ever since the Napoleonic wars, it had at bottom lacked a single positive plank in its platform. Its entire programme may be summarised in the word "No!"'[1] Much of Schumpeter's analytical work, and even a considerable part of his work in the history of economic thought, can be seen simply as a reaction to what he took to be current fashions. He then successfully fooled a large number of economists into believing that he had a positive system of explanation or recommendations to offer. With a man who wrote so much on such a diverse range of subjects, it is not easy to establish this precisely. But if we begin to look carefully at any of his books before his *Business Cycles*,[2] with this particular thought in mind, we shall not find it very difficult to pin him down.

Like most German and Austrian social scientists of his generation, Schumpeter was reacting to the influence of Marx and the

I am indebted to Krishna Bharadwaj and Luca Meldolesi for helpful comments.

[1] J.A. Schumpeter, *Imperialism, Social Classes*, New York, 1966, pp. 7–8. The *and* which is often put in citations to join 'Imperialism', and 'Social Classes' is not there in the title of the essay. The two are separate essays which are only loosely related to each other.

[2] Vols. 1 and 2, New York, 1939.

Marxists on the intellectual and the political processes. The key concept of the entrepreneurial function of the capitalist, in his *Theory of Economic Development*, was taken over by Schumpeter from Marx. This was acknowledged by him in the book,[3] although his later references to Marx's contribution to the recognition of the specific role of the entrepreneur, are almost uniformly negative.[4] But having borrowed the concept of the entrepreneur, the analytical use Schumpeter made of it was surprisingly meagre. He gave a description of the circular process of a stationary equilibrium, with its much-debated (and analytically trivial) property of a zero rate of interest, and then introduced the entrepreneur as the *deus ex machina* which disturbed that stationary equilibrium, and a credit system which sustained that disturbance. The surprising element in all this, for all the fame that the book acquired, is the meagreness of the analysis that supported Schumpeter's contentions. For all the role his entrepreneur performed, he could be the other name for a series of natural disasters or of bumper harvests.

Through all the apparent changes his system underwent in his hands, Schumpeter remained ideologically committed to the conception of a capitalist system which is governed by the actions of individuals, or individual firms, and in which government intervention can only create avoidable complications, if nothing worse. His methodology—which took maximising individuals as the units of analysis—often ran counter to his insights regarding the rise of giant corporations in the modern capitalist system. But he was shrewd enough to anticipate some of these problems and provide for them.

Take, for example, his notion of 'equilibrium' as the starting point of all economic analysis:

> We can be sure that we understand the nature of economic phenomena only if it is possible to deduce prices and quantities from the data by means of those relations [that are comprehended by the Walrasian system—A.B.] and to prove that no

---

[3] For documentation of Marx's priority and Schumpeter's acknowledgement, see my *Merchants and Colonialism*, Centre for Studies in Social Sciences, Calcutta, Occasional Paper No. 38, 1981.

[4] See J.A. Schumpeter, *History of Economic Analysis*, New York, 1968, pp. 462, 556, 646, 896. Marx is criticised here for not recognising the special personal role of the entrepreneur.

other set of prices and physical quantities is compatible with both the data and the relations. The proof that this is so is the magna charta of economic theory as an autonomous science, assuring that its subject matter is a cosmos and not a chaos.[5]

Schumpeter distinguished his concept of disequilibrium from what he considered to be Keynes' concept of aggregative equilibrium. While grudgingly admitting that the latter 'might be useful for some purpose', he went on to dispute its utility for analysing business cycle phenomena. At the centre of the business cycle phenomena in Schumpeter's schema, stands the individual entrepreneur as he occupies the centre-stage of economic development itself. It is his doings that move the technological frontier and justify the earning of profit. Schumpeter measures his effectiveness by the frequency and magnitudes of disequilibria that are created by his activities. The economic system is simply composed of the sum total of activities of individual entrepreneurs. There are unintended consequences of individual action, but those unintended consequences had best be left to history to take care of. Mere governments, or, even less, policy-mongerers such as Keynes, cannot be entrusted with the task of tinkering with economic processes unleashed by entrepreneurial behaviour.

Schumpeter was sophisticated enough to recognise that it is not just entrepreneurial action that can cause disequilibrium or stickiness in the Walrasian system. Imperfect competition, and by implication, regulatory action[6] by public authorities, could also cause stickiness in the system. By the time he came to write *Capitalism, Socialism and Democracy*,[7] Schumpeter had assimilated imperfect competition in the very logic of entrepreneurial behaviour in an economy dominated by giant firms. In this way, he proved to be a true precursor of the Chicago School, and in some ways outdistanced them. For while the Chicago School economists were, at first, mostly busy whittling down the importance of the static deadweight loss caused by monopoly, Schumpeter made monopoly a positive asset for a dynamic capitalism. (In this, of course, he has been followed by economists, who tried to show

---

[5] J.A. Schumpeter, *Business Cycles: A Theoretical, Historical and Statistical Analysis of the Capitalist Process*, Vol. I, New York, 1939, p. 41.
[6] Cf. Schumpeter, *Business Cycles*, op. cit., Vol. I, p. 52.
[7] London, 1947.

that the exorbitant prices charged by giant drug companies were entirely justified by their record of innovation.)

Schumpeter also saw that continual disturbances to the economic system through innovation or changes in data, would set up expectations in the actors' minds regarding further changes, and might threaten the equilibrating tendency he needed to provide the rationale for treating the Walrasian system as the 'theoretical norm'. So, he more or less anticipated the device of rational expectations[8]:

> The first thing to be noticed about expectation is . . . that in many cases it materially facilitates both the movement toward, and the preservation of, equilibrium, sometimes to the point of preventing disequilibria that would without it arise from the working of the Walras system . . . . The effects of technological lags, for instance, will be reduced if the change—in adaptation to which they occur—has been expected, and the Hog Cycle, as far as it is really—we shall see reason to doubt it—due to inability to foresee the mass effect of 'improvident' reaction to a favourable fodder-pork ratio, would entirely disappear if the time range of farmers' expectations increased. Speculation of the type described by classical theory—buying in advance of a rise in price that is foreseen, selling in advance of a fall—works the same way. In such cases expectations may open up a short-cut toward a definitive (though possibly different) equilibrium state.

Schumpeter is often credited with the elaboration of the construct of a pure credit economy. It is possible that in this area he made an advance over the analysis in Marx's *Capital*, Vol. II. But what he did not really do was to show that once unleashed, this pure credit economy would serve the purposes of his entrepreneurs, and would not lead a life of its own. The gambling aspect of the working of the capital market in modern capitalism stressed by Keynes in his *General Theory*, was not something that could be

---

[8] Schumpeter, *Business Cycles*, op. cit., Vol. I, pp. 53–54. Even the example Schumpeter gives, the Cobweb Cycle, is the case John Muth chose in order to formulate the apparatus of 'rational expectations' see J.F. Muth: 'Rational Expectations and the Theory of Price Movements', *Econometrica*, Vol. 29, No. 3, July, 1961.

assimilated to the Schumpeterian scheme. His entrepreneurs would create the institutions needed for their aggrandisement, but could not be ensured by them. Schumpeter never showed how this was to be accomplished without some action of coordination—in fact, without the intervention of a monetary or fiscal authority. Of course, this intervention might be ineffective or counter-productive in many cases. But Schumpeter normally would refuse to consider the desirability of such action under any circumstances.

One of the Schumpeterian themes which gained some currency in recent years was that of the so-called Kondratieff, or long cycles. Economists and historians as disparate in their methodologies as Fernand Braudel, Christopher Freeman, Richard Goodwin and Ernest Mandel have been fascinated by the idea. In fact, all these different analysts have constructed their own stories and they often have little resemblance to Schumpeter's construct(s). The idea of a purely technology-driven long cycle has been viewed with scepticism by some of the most careful students of technology and its relation to past economic developments in advanced capitalist countries.[9] We do not want to take up these issues here. But we want to note two points in this connection. Firstly, methodologically, the Kondratieff long waves suited Schumpeter's general aim of avoiding uncomfortable questions such as changes in class relations within capitalist societies, changes in relations between the metropolitan countries and their colonies, and the senescence of capitalist institutions. Secondly, the construct of technological long waves or, for that matter, the Schumpeterian theory of innovations, has little light to throw on how innovations may be diffused to the Third World countries, what might impede their absorption or adaptation, and what enables some countries to catch up while others lag behind. Beyond the glorification of the capitalist entrepreneur, there is no theory in these areas which we can pull down from the Schumpeterian shelf.

It may be claimed that as a believer in methodological individualism and as an avowed opponent of aggregative system-building, Schumpeter's achievement should be judged in terms of

---

[9] See, for example, N. Rosenberg and C. Frischtak, 'Technological Innovation and Long Waves', *Cambridge Journal of Economics*, Vol. 8, No. 1, March, 1984; and S.N. Solomou, 'Long Term Growth Phase: Long Waves, Long Swings and Traverses—A Case Study of Britain, France, Germany and America since c.1850', Ph.D. thesis, University of Cambridge, 1983.

the explication of individual entrepreneurs' motives, rather than in terms of his success in building up a mutually consistent system of economic relations. But here again, Schumpeter contradicts himself all the time. In his *Theory of Economic Development*,[10] he sees the entrepreneur as a person who correctly foresees the results of his actions in a very uncertain future. In his later work, he recognises the difficulty of this position, and admits that entrepreneurs may be quite irrational or over-optimistic in judging the future, and it is only in the outcome and in the aggregate that innovation may be privately profitable.[11] (Schumpeter may claim to be the originator of the Friedman-Savage theory, which postulates the generation of an unequal distribution by the willingness of individuals to put a higher value on the small chance of a very large gain, than on a large chance of a small gain or even loss.) Schumpeter nowhere tries to establish how or what class of individually irrational moves become translated into socially profitable actions, or even how the sum of individual gains or losses comes out to mean a positive profit for the capitalist class as a whole.

On the other hand, Schumpeter, with his near-contemporary Max Weber, always treats the capitalist class as possessing particularly rational characteristics, in respect of both individual intention and social outcome. His work on *Imperialism* is nothing but a special plea to explain away the First World War, and imperialism in the era of capitalism, as an atavistic aberration.

Let us look at the title of Schumpeter's essay: 'Sociology of Imperialisms'. Schumpeter is, here, in the distinguished tradition of popularisers of history and sociology—from H.G. Wells to Johan Galtung. He treats the imperialism of the Assyrians and the imperialism of absolute monarchies of Europe in the eighteenth century with equal facility and equal lack of depth. Not for him the distinction between colonialism imposed by the conquering bourgeoisie and the expansionist policies of earlier empires, or the distinction between capitalist colonialism and capitalist imperialism.[12]

---

[10] Cambridge, 1934, p. 85.

[11] See, Schumpeter, *Capitalism, Socialism and Democracy, op. cit.*, pp. 73–4. See, for a lucid discussion of Schumpeter's ambiguity on this point, J. Elster, *Explaining Technical Change*, Cambridge, 1983, pp. 113–20.

[12] This latter distinction was, of course, made sharply for the first time by V.I. Lenin, whose *Imperialism* was published in the same year (1917) as Schumpeter's essay. But the distinction had, implicitly, been already adumbrated in the work of J.A. Hobson and R. Hilferding, of whose work Schumpeter was aware. See, for an

Schumpeter's key characterisation of imperialism was summarised in the following passage[13]:

> Imperialism is . . . atavistic in character. It falls into that large group of surviving features from earlier ages that play such an important part in every concrete social situation. In other words, it is an element that stems from the living conditions, not of the present, but of the past—or, put in terms of the economic interpretation of history, from past rather than present relations of production . . . . It is from absolute autocracy that the present age has taken over what imperialist tendencies it displays. And the imperialism of absolute monarchy flourished before the Industrial Revolution that created the modern world, or rather, before the consequences of that revolution began to be felt in all their aspects.

Schumpeter then goes lyrical about the culture the Industrial Revolution created—not only the bourgeoisie, but the working class, the intellectuals (which are as a 'class' created by capitalism), the coupon-clipping *rentiers*, and even the peasants become imbued with a spirit of rationalism:

> They were moved from the old world, engaged in building a new one for themselves—a specialised, mechanised world. Thus they were all inevitably democratised, individualised, and rationalised . . . . We see this process of rationalisation at work even in the case of the strongest impulses. We observe it, for example, in the facts of procreation. We must therefore anticipate finding it in the case of the imperialist impulse as well; we must expect to see this impulse, which rests on the primitive contingencies of physical combat, gradually disappear, washed away by new exigencies of daily life. There is another factor too. The competitive system absorbs the full energies of most of the people at all economic levels. Constant application, attention, and concentration of energy are the conditions of survival within

---

elaboration of the distinction, my paper, 'Towards a Correct Reading of Lenin's Theory of Imperialism', *Economic and Political Weekly*, Review of Political Economy, 30 July 1983, reprinted in P. Patnaik, ed., *Lenin and Imperialism*, Delhi, 1986.

[13] Schumpeter, *Imperialism, Social Classes, op. cit.*, p. 66.

it, primarily in the specific economic professions, but also in other activities organised on their model. There is much less excess energy to be vented in war and conquest than in any precapitalist society. What excess energy there is flows largely into industry itself, accounts for its shining figures—the type of the captain of industry—and for the rest is applied to art, science, and the social struggle.[14]

This lyrical account, of course, runs counter to the feat of the ruling classes of the first industrialising nation, in creating the biggest empire the world had ever seen in a practically unbroken series of wars, from 1756 down to the 1890s. There was hardly a decade in which some army or the other under British command was not fighting a war in some part of the globe. Schumpeter conjures this all away as just defensive action.[15] In doing so, he also displays the typically Eurocentric (racist?) propensity of most European social scientists of the day. The Boer War gets a mention as a departure from England's pacific past, but not the Zulu Wars, the Ashanti Wars, or the series of wars which led to the conquest of India. Schumpeter manages another conjuring act when it comes to the USA: any imperialist inclinations are ascribed to the retrograde values of European immigrants, and the conquest of Cuba, or the frequent landing of US Marines in defence of US property in Central and Latin America, are quietly overlooked.

At this point of his development, capitalism for Schumpeter still meant mainly competitive capitalism. He certainly knew the work of Marx on the growth of monopoly, and the work of Hilferding in pinpointing the special role of monopoly capital in fostering imperialism. But he dismissed all this as a phase of export monopolism, which was unfortunate, but which would be challenged by the people against whose interest the cartels and the monopolies work.[16] To the extent that this part of Schumpeter's work has any interest, it had all been anticipated by Hobson. But Hobson's book was, after all, published long before the First World War, and Schumpeter's was written in the middle of the biggest imperialist war the world had witnessed till then.

Thus, until the end of the First World War, most of what

[14] Ibid., pp. 68–69.
[15] Ibid., pp. 15–22.
[16] Ibid., pp. 74–98.

Schumpeter had written was either unoriginal, or trivial, or false. The triviality arose from his inability either to fully master, or to escape from, the general equilibrium system of Leon Walras which he so admired; the falsity sprang from his conscious reaction against the Marxist corpus, which he challenged only with spurious logic and dubious history.

It is only with the 1920s, and more definitely with his stay in the USA, that the specifically Schumpeterian contribution to the understanding of monopoly capitalism begins. This, incidentally, is an ironical counter-example against his pet hypothesis about the peak achievements made in the glorious third decade of a man's life. Marx and the Marxists had already written extensively on the processes of centralisation and concentration of capital. What Schumpeter did was to give reasons other than economies of scale in production and finance for the rise of modern monopolies. In common with his earlier conflation of phases of capitalist colonialism and capitalist imperialism, Schumpeter sometimes clubbed the chartered monopolies of the Mercantilist period with the modern monopolies based on economies of scale in production, marketing, finance, research and risk-bearing. But barring this problem, there is no doubt that Schumpeter understood much better than most of his contemporaries the transaction costs and risk-bearing aspects of monopoly.[17] For example, while cataloguing the reasons for the emergence of the earlier legally established private monopolies such as the East India Company, Schumpeter wrote:

> Poverty is a bad customer, and normal risks of doing business are greatly increased in an environment where the wealth from which demand is to proceed has not only to be attracted but created. In business as elsewhere, forward strategy very often requires defensive tactics as a complement, though most economists of all ages stubbornly refuse to see this. But under conditions in which long-run advance was inevitably slow, each stage had to be safeguarded with particular care in order to gain means and time for advancing beyond it. It is quite natural that the observing historian should be much more impressed by the practices and policies that aimed at positive restriction, which

---

[17] For the most thorough exploration of these aspects of monopoly, vertical and horizontal integration, and hierarchical control, see O.E. Williamson, *Markets and Hierarchies: Analysis and Antitrust Implications*, New York, 1975.

dominate the scene at every point of time, than by the picture of the process over time. But it is true nevertheless that even an ideally rational government, actuated by the sole motive of fostering industrial development, would have had to grant privileges of monopoly in many cases in which enterprise would not have been possible at all without it, and that, in others, it would have had to permit monopolistic practice on the part of the businessmen concerned. This holds, of course, with added force for those countries that had been ravaged by war, such as Germany, where only prospects of abnormal gain could call forth entrepreneurial effort from a population immersed in misery and despair.[18]

Schumpeter was, of course, aware of the less reputable reasons (such as hope of personal gain on the part of the crowned heads), for creating monopolies, and knew that all the reasons did not apply to all the monopolies. I am, here, merely trying to select those aspects of his work which can claim an originality of a useful kind. The two chapters on 'The Process of Creative Destruction' (carried on by the monopolies) and 'Monopolistic Practices' in his *Capitalism, Socialism and Democracy*, must rank among the best pieces of rationale (or apologia) for monopolies and monopolistic practices that have ever been penned by an economist. They also contain the major Schumpeterian hypotheses regarding the relation of market structure and innovation.[19] I am not going to discuss here the merits of his hypotheses. One aspect which is worth noticing is that in this part of his work, the notion of competition Schumpeter was using was closely akin to that implicit in the work of Adam Smith, Ricardo and Marx, and had very little to do with the notion of pure competition in Walras or Menger. Again, we find the typical Schumpeterian hiatus between the theory he admired and his own analytical practice.

In *Capitalism, Socialism and Democracy* he advanced his theory of democracy which he defined as follows: 'The democratic method is that institutional arrangement for arriving at political decisions in which individuals acquire the power to decide by means of a

---

[18] Schumpeter, *History of Economic Analysis*, op. cit.., p. 15.
[19] For a discussion of the Schumpeterian hypotheses and their empirical testing, see M.I. Kamien and N.L. Schwartz, *Market Structure and Innovation*, Cambridge, 1982, Chapters 2 and 3.

competitive struggle for the people's vote.'[20] This theory has been developed by other writers such as Downs, as the economic theory of democracy.[21] Again, I am not concerned here with the usefulness of this particular theory. What is interesting is that there is no discussion of the impact of the prevailing monopolistic structure in the capitalism Schumpeter was portraying, on the competitive process in the political sphere. Nor is there any discussion of the external relations, including possibilities of armed conflict, in a capitalist world dominated by national and supranational monopolies.

Again, in *Capitalism, Socialism and Democracy*, Schumpeter presents the picture of a capitalism which would collapse, not because of any inherent economic contradictions, but because of the erosion of the strata of rulers naturally fitted for ruling, who were derived from the pre-capitalist past of the advanced capitalist countries, and because of the opposition of the intellectuals to the system. How would the argument about the erosion of the protecting strata apply to the USA, which had no pre-capitalist ruling class to start with? Notice the stark contrast between this view of Schumpeter with the view he had advanced in *Imperialism, Social Classes* on the baneful effect of values, culture and residual strata derived from the past of the European capitalist countries. As Albert Hirschman has reminded us recently,[22] the feudal-shackles thesis about the development of capitalism is often turned on its head and becomes the feudal-blessings thesis. But it is rare to find this inversion in such a naked manner in the same writer.

Of course, the point can be made that Schumpeter simply changed his mind. But did he change his mind because he realised the untenability of his earlier views? There seems to be little evidence that this was so. The many inconsistencies, the omissions, and the plain disregard of facts in much of Schumpeter's work can be explained if we regard him as a deeply conservative hedgehog, who reacted to whatever he considered to be the fashionable, progressive views of his day. Since his environment changed from

[20] *Capitalism, Socialism and Democracy, op. cit.*, Chapter 12.
[21] For a summary of the literature, see D.C. Mueller, *Public Choice*, Cambridge, 1981, Chapter 6.
[22] A.O. Hirschman, 'Rival Interpretations of Market Society: Civilizing, Destructive or Feeble?', *The Journal of Economic Literature*, Vol. XX, No.4, December, 1982.

Europe to the USA, and the era changed from the time of war-like preparations by the Prussian and Austro-Hungarian empires to the period of the New Deal, the anti-trust campaigns of Thurman Arnold and the goings on of the American wheeler-dealer politicians (note Schumpeter's implicit distaste for the content of the slogans peddled by politicians in a democracy), our reactive hedgehog also changed the direction of his spikes. These changes have given the world the impression that Schumpeter had a number of new ideas on many things old and new, contrary to the facts of the case. Viewed in this light, Schumpeter's idea that intellectuals would undermine the moral authority of the capitalist state takes on a rather sinister hue. It can be taken as a warning against the intellectuals as a group, or more innocently, can be likened to the cackling of geese in the capital of Rome.

I will conclude this very rapid sketch by giving a list of obvious contradictions in Schumpeter's work, both as regards his evaluation of different fields of schools of economics, and as regards his assessment of the real world:

Inconsistencies between Schumpeter's evaluation and his own practice or achievement:

1. Schumpeter held the view that the third decade was the most productive as far as the work of any important economist is concerned. He probably assessed his own achievement in the same way. In fact, most of his achievements can be dated from the fourth to the sixth decades of his life.
2. Schumpeter regarded 'pure' economic analysis as the only part worth exploring in detail in a history of economic thought. (The only exception to this, his evaluation of Marx, makes sense only because he rightly saw him as the most dangerous enemy of capitalism the world had ever produced.) His own contribution to pure economic analysis, in this sense, was practically negligible. His contribution lay in the field of organisation theory, or in the analysis of incentives to invest, and not in his construction of any internally consistent body of pure economic theory.
3. Schumpeter regarded the Walrasian system as the height of scientific achievement in economics. In fact, his own work was a negation of the Walrasian system, but he was never

able to get rid of the obstacles his admiration for this alien system posed for him. His failure to analyse the problem of effective demand may conceivably be traced to this factor.
4. Schumpeter had a poor opinion of the Ricardian system. Yet, one of the more interesting features of his work, his notion of competition, resembles the concept of the classical economists, rather than the neo-classical definition of pure competition as a market consisting of price-takers.

Inconsistencies between Schumpeter's vision and the present or the past he was trying to analyse:

1. Schumpeter thought that imperialism was an atavistic phenomenon after the Industrial Revolution had taken place, but he could not explain how the British created the biggest empire of all time in history, nor, how the USA, which had no pre-capitalist past, practised such imperialistic aggression in Central America, the Caribbean, Latin America and the Philippines.
2. Schumpeter regarded profit-seeking by individuals as very often irrational, and yet thought capitalism was a rational system. He never established in macro-economic or macro-political terms, how individual irrationality is transformed into aggregative or social rationality.
3. Schumpeter regarded modern capitalism as consisting of monopolies, and modern democracy as the product of competition for votes. He somehow never connected the two phenomena, although to somebody who was aware of the work of Robert Michels and Gaetano Mosca, the connection should have been fairly obvious.
4. From an uncritical admiration of England as a country least burdened with pre-capitalist entanglements, he shifted to a position where he saw the feudal past of England as providing the much-needed ruling classes trained for ruling, that a fully capitalist society lacks. He managed this feat by taking two very partial views of British history, and by never comparing the decision-making processes in industry and government.

There is no point in lengthening this list. Schumpeter should be evaluated as the person he was, namely, a Viennese bourgeois, evolving a powerful ideology for the ruling classes of the country he had chosen as his own.

For theories of technical progress in the advanced capitalist countries, and their diffusion in other countries, or adaptation of frontier technologies in the latter, we have to erect structures of our own. The explanation of global recession will, similarly, have to be sought in types of interdependence which Schumpeter would have declared to be inadmissible *ab initio*. There is no point in continuing to worship false prophets, although we will have to go on studying them.

6

On Political Explanation in Marxism

SUDIPTA KAVIRAJ

Marxist political analysis[1] seems forever threatened by two opposed types of imminent collapse—into determinism or pluralism. Critics of Marxism usually claim that it must necessarily reduce political

Author's Note: The argument this paper offers is necessarily incomplete. It deals with three central political ideas of Marxist theory: relative autonomy, determination and structures of various kinds. But these ideas, of course, depend on logical support from a host of other concepts in historical materialism. Traditional ways of reading their meaning may have been unsuggestive, but they certainly had the advantage of internal coherence. Any re-reading of their meaning, it follows, would have to redefine not only these three ideas, but all other implicated ones. Althusser's attempt to rework the meaning of some of these—particularly, causality and determination—led, necessarily, to a general reworking of explanatory concepts. Obviously, this rule also applies to the exercise presented in this paper, and because it cannot show how the surrounding concepts can be consistently reworked, it remains flawed. I have, however, tried the following method in presenting the argument here. In the course of my own argument on the three main concepts, I have tried to indicate points at which supporting demonstrations are required, though these are not provided here, obviously. For example, both the reductionist and the redescriptive notions of an explanation involve some idea of a 'last instance' of explanation, a kind of 'rock bottom', after which, to call for more explanation would be meaningless. At a later point, it appears essential to me to disentangle two very different sets of meanings with which some Marxist propositions are used, because one set can lead to systematically misleading presentations, or even explanatory mistakes. For phrases, which can only be defended if they are seen as relating to consequences, are often apparently made about origins of social actions. Questions like these are merely indicated here.

[1] Recently, several forms of this move have been tried out. One of the most influential was Althusser's views about structural causality and overdetermination, a theory discussed below. The other significant move is presented in G.A. Cohen's *Karl Marx's Theory of History: A Defence*, Oxford, 1978. Some of the issues arising out of this work were discussed in reviews by Elster and a reply by Cohen in *Political Studies*, 1980, I. A more pessimistic view is held out in Terrell Carver, *Marx's Social Theory*, Oxford, 1983, who regards the thesis of determination in the last instance as nothing more than a research hypothesis. This seems to me to

occurrences into mere reflexes or corollaries[2] of economic events, and thus cannot say anything interesting or helpful about the way politics goes on.

This objection is made up of two distinct ideas. The first is (*i*) that a systematic reduction of political facts to any other order of facts, is, in principle, wrong, and explanatorily unhelpful. Its corollary is that although political occurrence can have significant interconnections with occurrences of other kinds, these are not of a sort which can justify an *a priori* assumption of a single form of ordered relationship. The second proposition is that (*ii*) political analysis by Marxists must necessarily result in a reduction into the economy. To state this more fully: for an analysis to be Marxist, it must use some critically important concepts, and the logic of these

---

weaken the proposition too much, while the real need is for a reworking of its common reading. A similar statement is found in Ralph Miliband, *Marxism and Politics*, Oxford, 1977, p. 8. 'There remains', according to Miliband, 'in Marxism an insistence on the "primacy" of the "economic base" which must not be understated. This "primacy" is usually taken by Marxists, following Engels, as meaning that the "economic base" is decisive, or determining, "in the last instance". But it is much more apposite and meaningful to treat the "economic base" as a starting point, as a matter of the *first* instance.' This, of course, is possible; and Miliband's interpretation makes it more likely by suggesting that 'Marx's own cast of mind was strongly anti-determinist.' On this reading, the matter becomes identical with treating the thesis as a research hypothesis, in Carver's terms. (Terrell Carver *Marx's Social Theory*, Oxford, 1983.) But there seems to be one in appositeness to this procedure. Statements about the last instance, right or wrong, are presumably about the way things happen in history; the first instance proposition, must, however, be a matter of explanation, of how these things are sought to be understood. Surely, in the first case, there is a latent expectation of symmetry between the structure of the historical process and the structure of the explanatory form. But it seems difficult to take the second (the first instance proposition) as about the historical process.

[2] I have used these terms here advisedly. Of course, causes have consequences, not corollaries. But this is to indicate an oddity that lies inside deterministic Marxism. Political events may indeed be seen as being caused by economic ones; but this, taken in a strict sense leads to paradoxes. 'Hard' uses of the base-superstructure idea tend to see political events as something close to corollaries. For economic causes have economic effects too, and political consequences must be seen as being more secondary in some sense. Strictly speaking, therefore, deterministic Marxism contains an ambiguity about the relation between the economic and the political behind its appearance of decisiveness and clarity. Ironically, however, this apparent clarity is the main reason behind its appeal. What appears clear when it is allowed to talk in metaphor, appears much less so when a clear logical account is asked for.

concepts is such that the analysis must become reductionist as a necessary result of their use. These concepts, therefore, have the dual effect of rendering the analysis both Marxist and determinist. These offending concepts are well known—determination, structures, contradictions, and their various conceptual aliases. I shall refer to this cluster of ideas as the *structure-related* concepts of Marxist theory.

If this is a correct way of analysing the critical objection, then Marxists can answer this in two very different ways. A first response would contest statement (*i*) and accept statement (*ii*). In that case, instead of being seen as a weakness, reduction could be seen as a critical strength. It could then be claimed that like natural science, Marxism reduces the apparent disorder of the world of social facts into the convenience of a few general theorems. Marx's propositions would, then, be a sort of equivalent in social thought of the unified field theory. This is a response sometimes adopted by Marxists—erroneously, in my view. To satisfactorily defend determinism as a model of social or cultural explanation is an impossible undertaking. On this view of the relation between the economic and the political, rather more than a narrow problem is at stake; the intellectual enterprise of treating a class of facts as political facts, preparatory to calling for a separate order of explanations for them, would then be condemned to redundancy. The Marxists' position would be very paradoxical indeed. For they would be saying in that case, that explanation of politics would be covered by the general thesis that politics does not need separate explanations.[3] The reductive case fails to make a case at all about how politics can be explained. It is no theory of politics, not even a bad one, as much as a statement that no theory is needed, is not a statement of a theory.

If, on the other hand, a Marxist does try to establish relative autonomy of the political level, and asserts that political events do

[3] All this still does not open up the endlessly contentious question, what kind of creatures are what we term 'the economic, the political', etc.? Surely, this is not a trivial question. The entire philosophic tradition of Marxism is implicitly divided on this question. Some regard the concept of totality in Marxism as a structure stretched over planes and levels; others, like Korsch and Lukacs deny that the dialectical category of totality can be so split, except according to the shifting contingencies of argument. Despite Lukacs's well-known hostility to Weber, his view on this question seems fairly close to Weber's discussions in *Methodology of the Social Sciences*, New York, 1949.

have a logic which is not reducible into a corollary of the economic process, this must, it is argued, lead him to two falsehoods. Either he is reduced to making question-begging statements at crucial turns of his demonstration, hinting at reciprocal causation, which means that if he were really honest and not conceptually pre-committed, he would have confessed that he did not find any form of primacy or causality. He may have simply noted a 'structure' or a 'figure'; but simply to note a structure is not to establish causality. Alternatively, he would be led by his evidence so far away from his preferred model that he would turn into a pluralist with a bad conscience. Anyone who would deny that any kind of primacy can be ascribed to any level of social reality, or that such primacies are local and contingent, is a pluralist. But this pluralist would be in a very false position, for he would have pre-committed himself to a theory of primacy.

A Marxist is, thus, given the generous choice between a falsity of his empirical judgements, or a falsity in the use of his concepts. I wish to argue that the critical case may not be as decisive as it appears. Such conundra arise because of a misunderstanding of the conceptual logic of Marxism. I shall first examine some conceptual strategies by which Marxists have tried to escape a collapse into determinism, and then suggest some ways in which one can choose between them, effect a partial reconstruction, and, finally, render the entire structure of concepts logically coherent.

Some Remarks on Marx's Language

A kind of non-determinism of intentions in Marxist political theory is not difficult to establish hermeneutically, that is, in terms of the intended meanings of authors. Marxists normally take this particular route in their response to charges of determinism. Engels had written enough letters in his old age, when he was trying to protect Marxism from admirers who suspected that it had revelatory powers over history, to establish that this was their hermeneutic intent. Or, perhaps, what Engels intended then, they had intended earlier. Individual arguments, as structuralists often say, must be seen in context, as part of a structure of either a general discourse or of a particular controversy. What a particular idea means depends as much on its etymology as on what it is supposed to say or do to opposing ideas. One useful test of meaning of theoretical statements is to study its opponents, a reconstruction of what it wished to say to them, rather than what its later adherents made of it in history. Paradoxically, in interpretation of polemical ideas, the character of the theory X wished to shoot down, constitutes a formal component of the context that determines the conceptual point of X's own doctrine.

To understand each particular brand of Marxism, therefore, one must understand its favourite enemy. A crucial element in the understanding of Gramsci is obviously an understanding of Bukharin, or, at least, what seemed to Gramsci to be the point of Bukharin's work. This spares us some agonising over Marx's logical sanity when, for instance, we come across statements with contradictory emphases. Some of Marx's statements on politics are evidently voluntaristic in their emphasis and stress that it is men who make history; some others are deterministic, and emphasise the limits under which they are obliged to make it. A simple solution to such elementary mysteries is to stick to Gramsci's judgement, that Marx was not trying to set up a theory which was voluntaristic or determinist in the usual sense, but to break the plane of that kind of discourse. His endeavour was to discover a level of coherent discourse which would be free from these persistent, and in his view, sterile, dichotomies.

But in order to say this one needs to clarify a point about the use of philosophical language in Marx. All discourse has to use pre-given constituted language, and cannot create an entire vocabulary all at once. Original thinkers are, thus, placed in a situation of paradox. They must use old concepts if they are to be understood by their audience; but they must press these concepts to express ideas that are new. Thus, the concepts and their precise denotations exist in a kind of tension.[4] These concepts are the traditional vehicles of ideas which they now wish to displace. All original thinkers are, therefore, condemned to write in conceptual language which does injustice to the content of their thought. Sometimes authors try to underline the newness of content by explicitly putting together concepts which, under the pre-given rules of constituted discourse, could not conceivably be used jointly. By saying startling things, by saying things which are contradictions in

---

[4] I do not pretend that this question can be solved in the simplified manner in which it is presented here. Here, only those minimal propositions are presented which are necessary for making my case.

terms, by pre-given rules, they wish to convey that they are suggesting rules that are different. For, in cases of such statements which the rules do not permit, there are two possibilities: the first is that what is stated is a simple error; if not, this may indicate the need for a different set of rules. Apparent linguistic incongruity is meant to alert the reader to the fact that under shocking neologisms, what was being suggested was an unconventional and important thing. It is an incitement to alter fundamental definitions, and through them, gradually, the structure of the discourse itself.

I think this is what can truly be called a 'change of terrain', or breaking the plane of discourse. For every discourse is marked by its fundamental distinctions; those are what make it what it is. Breaking the plane of a discourse is to give it a new set of distinctions. It is usually forgotten, due to the general ahistoricity of discussions on social theory, that the term 'dialectical materialism'/'materialist dialectics' was a phrase of exactly this kind. Marx's theoretical revolution should be seen as a project of presenting the discourse of modern social science with a whole set of new distinctions, of which three are most significant: the distinction in philosophy between idealism and materialism; in theories of science between positivism and hermeneutics; and in politics and social action, between determinism and indeterminism. To say this term, and to mean it seriously, the normal philosophic discourse of the nineteenth century had to become incoherent, that is, get out its distinctions, or cross its normal frontiers. What is meant is not meaningless. It shows, rather, that the language used has become allegorical; it does not mean what it says, or it has invented new ways of saying things; or still further, it stretched the resources of the philosophic language to express thoughts which people did not know could be said with it. After all, ingenuity in its use is the only way a language, and its world of meanings, can be stretched. Marx had to communicate with an audience whose discursive alphabet had been formed in determinate ways. They perhaps would not have understood an argument unless it was stated through a grid of concepts and pre-suppositions, which used dichotomies like materialism/idealism, voluntarism/determinism, subjectivism/objectivism.[5] Marx is evidently interested in over-throwing

---

[5] After he announced his intention of developing a transcending discourse in the *Theses on Feuerbach*, (1845) Marx consistently pursued it. But in later discussions this is implied, rather than stated in such dramatic declarations of intent.

these dichotomies, in making them redundant. Yet, the only way in which he can attempt to do this is by using a language which presupposes them, and treats them as 'natural'. He uses it in a way which communicates with his audience, yet undermines it, much in the way of Wittgenstein's dispensable ladder.

Original thinkers are consequently in perpetual danger of being misunderstood. It is easy to see why this creates possibilities of slippage in interpretation. Those used to living within a constituted discourse, and translating every other into its own terms, can see in this not an invitation to think differently, and to alter fundamental distinctions, but merely positions that are indecisive, middling or contradictory. It is impossible to rigorously substantiate a view, that Marxist philosophy occupies a position midway between idealism and materialism, or a combination of some elements of both. For, both idealism and materialism are theories which have structures which do not allow this kind of a middle term to be coherent.[6]

Critics of Marxism argue that the existence of the letters of the

[6] I think it can be argued that what is true about political statements is also true about doing things in politics. The bureaucratic and occasionally tyrannical deformations of the socialist idea that one finds in the real world, and the usual rationalisations of such systems are results of doing or seeing political life through such fragmented categories. It is particularly due to the fact that the values of equality and liberty are allowed to be seen in zero-sum terms. This relation is implied not only by conventional critics of say Soviet society, but equally by its conventional defenders. Marxists often go into disputes about moral questions, and take up and defend their positions in a language that does not allow them to do it properly, because the theoretical and value syntax of this discourse is different and uncongenial. Consequently, they are obliged to misrepresent their ideal in the very act of defending them. Too often Marxists, in debating moral evaluation of societies, allow themselves to be put a question like: Which do you hold primary: liberty or equality? Which obliges them to answer 'equality'. They ought to say in such cases that the question ought to be reconstituted, and given an historical form. If they answer that question in that form, they make a tactical mistake, giving their critics an ineradicable advantage. Historically, of course, it is clear that the two contending societies are not amenable to such simple moral descriptions. Capitalist societies are not realms of untrammelled freedom; just as there are obvious limits to equality in historical socialist societies. Indeed, the best course in such debates seems to be the one Marx suggests in the *Critique of the Gotha Programme* (1875)—to register the deformities in socialist societies, but retaining an historical optimism about their correction. The defence then has to be done in quite other terms. Instead of pretending, or what is worse, believing that these societies are perfect, one believes that they are historically perfectible.

late Engels is no proof that a non-deterministic political theory is possible, and that it can be coherent within the boundaries of Marxist theory. These may be simply acknowledgements by the ageing Engels that his theory did not work, and attempts to cover its breakdown. Indeed, the more the number of exceptions and attenuations suggested to the main propositions of economic determination, the more conceptually disingenuous the theory becomes. The proof of non-determinism would not lie in the discovery of passages in Marxist texts, but in the logical workings of its concepts. It needs, in other words, logical and not exegetic proof. This is what is attempted in the rest of this paper.

Situations of choice, I shall argue, are not related to structures as exceptions to rules. It is not helpful to suggest that it is in exceptional cases that agency comes into play, by an uncharacteristic generosity of structures that choice becomes possible. Given this view, the whole of concrete history appears as an uninterrupted story of exceptions to this curious rule. It is odd, to say the least, to see the whole of history as a deviation. A rule should not be something that rarely happens. Complete determination of events by economic interests (pretending for the time that 'economic' and 'interests' are unambiguous ideas) rarely happens in real history, but determination as structural limitation happens all the time. That is why we can speak of a 'law' of determination only if it always, in principle, contains non-finalities and space for possible choice.

Marxist historians do not work with simple reductionist models of actual historical explanation. But formal adherence to reductionist propositions and actual non-reductionist analysis introduces a kind of internal incoherence in Marxist theory. Usually, the way to avoid such threatened incoherence is thought to lie through some well-rehearsed evasive action.

Such evasive actions are, of course, well-known. A common one is to appeal to the notion of 'a relative autonomy of politics'. But the real nature of this concept is, in my view, very often misjudged.

There is some evident ambiguity in the ways in which the term is often used. Surely, Marxism is not a narrowly economic theory; it tries to provide a global theory of the historical process, in which economic explanations have a special place. Relative autonomy, it can be argued, is an economist's legitimate phrase to indicate what is, for him, a residue in analytical terms, to signalise formally that he does not feel entitled to expect a simple reduction of the political order of things to easy explicability through analyses of the society's economy. It is a mark of his acceptance of the existence of areas in his global theory of society which his kind of analyses do not explain. That does not mean, however, that this is the only *side* from which social reality can be seen, even by Marxists.

Relative autonomy is, then, a primarily logical concept, not an explanatory concept in the ordinary sense, though one can argue that it is a precondition for the invention of explanatory concepts within Marxist theory. It explains the logical distinctions and hierarchies within Marxism, but nothing directly in the world. It describes the logical status of a class of facts—that they are not reducible to economic causalities. To say about a series of political occurrences that they demonstrate 'the relative autonomy of politics', is not to explain what happened and why it happened. It simply means that one should not expect a complete accounting for them by way of a reference to the economy and its necessary rhythms. Unfortunately, one finds too often that Marxists do take it as an explanatory concept, and believe that instead of calling for explanation, it actually does the explaining. This is to ask a wrong question of the concept, and to expect of it what it cannot do.

In my view, the idea of a relative autonomy of the political is a *logical*, not a substantive political concept. It indicates some logical qualities of the Marxist analysis of society; it does not say anything, as is often erroneously thought, about facts in the political world. Therefore, it is not a concept to be used directly in political analyses; it is, rather, something like a logical container in which political concepts of explanation, once formulated, can be conveniently stored. Relative autonomy is a summary name for processes which are not specified theoretically, but which must be. But to begin this argument, one must go back to the idea of two kinds of concepts in Marx's works.

Filled and Empty Concepts

Social theories are systems in two different senses. First, they are completed structures of propositions, which their authors presumably wished to arrange with internal consistency. Each of them is also, in a sense, an invitation to further elaboration. It is this quality of logical extendability which is suggested when some modern theories are designated as scientific. Some theories have an open conceptual space in and around their major propositions, to be filled in later, subject, of course, to consistency criteria. Scientific theories are open systems in this sense. It is to this corrigible form of openness to which Marxism aspires when it refers to itself as scientific. The author pointing out these areas in the general map, gives them provisional names and places in a definite hierarchy of significance, draws their boundaries, but places nothing or very little inside. These are conceptual vacant lots, empty spaces with names, with no theoretical occupants.

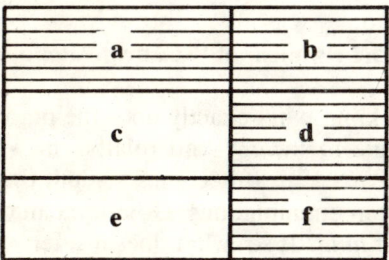

It is, of course, proverbially dangerous to use visual equivalents to logical relations, but the diagram points out roughly what I wish to assert about the internal unevenness in historical materialism. In a theoretical structure of this kind what are specified are not only Rab, but also Rac, even conceivably, Rce; or what are the necessary logical relations between statements that would fall in the areas c and e, even before these statements are, in fact, made. I shall call these 'filled' and 'empty' concepts.[7] The falling rate of profit, to take an example, is a filled concept. It does not merely demarcate the theoretical space this concept has to cover and analytically control, but it also provides detailed moves and arguments by which it can do so. Empty concepts only demarcate an

---

[7] This is similar to the sense in which philosophers use the term. To use an example from Husserl: looking at a row of houses at the end of a field, one can specify the determinate characteristics of the front of the second house from the left; but one's idea of its back must remain empty. One knows that a house must have a back, with specific determinations, but it must remain unspecified.

area within the theory which must be covered if the theory is to be consistent, or live up to the criteria it has set for itself. But they do *not* provide the arguments with which to cover and control it. In a rather loose sense, concepts of the first kind provide answers, the second merely formulate questions (which, if they are taken as explanatory concepts, are mistaken for answers). Relative autonomy, therefore, designates an untheorised, or inadequately theorised logical space, rather than a theory of politics. It indicates the site on which a Marxist political theory would eventually be placed. It is not that theory. But simply the announcement that a theory is necessary here. The accretion of metaphors makes this a particularly important idea to analyse with rigour, for metaphors are, after all, the unlit extremities of arguments.

The Problem of 'Relative Autonomy'

But strictly speaking, what exactly does the phrase mean? It is an autonomy relative *to what*?[8] And relative in what terms? Once such questions are asked, it becomes evident that the meaning of the idea is far from unambiguous. Does it mean relative autonomy in some terms of *time*? If so, what does it refer to? The distinction between possibilities in long and short terms? If this means that relative autonomy exists for part of the time in history, would not it be less confusing to call it a temporary or intermittent autonomy? Or does it mean relative autonomy in terms of the topological metaphor, that is, the 'base', the economy, determines its politics in a relative, not an absolute sense? But, where does the critical line between the relative and the absolute run? Or, is this again a different kind of reference to time? Does it mean that it does so for the 'normal' times, but not in abnormal times? Can time be distinguished after Hobbes's beautifully judged phrase, as 'high' and

---

[8] Althusser pursued some of these ambiguities in the 'Appendix' to 'Contradiction and Overdetermination', *For Marx*, London, 1969, pp. 117–28.

[9] This refers to that wonderful passage at the start of *Behemoth*, in which, instead of introducing a metaphor of fast and slow, which is inherently confusing when used about time, Hobbes uses the deliberately inappropriate metaphor of high and low. The first is confusing because time, or time consciousness, can be said to be fast or slow. Use of the other metaphor, since time cannot be naturally high or low, alerts one to the metaphorical status of the reasoning. One wishes all metaphors in social discourse were used with such discretion, so scrupulously, or that such little danger signals were built into all of them.

'low'?[9] In low times, the economy determines the political (absolutely?) and in high times, it is the other way round. This implies a privileged time, and privileged history makers who are inhabitants of these time zones (both, of course, determinable retrospectively), but other trespassers are prosecuted. Or, does it mean applying some criterion of significance? That is, in more important things the economy is in control; but politics too has small consolations to restore its pride. On less significant things, it often goes out of the economic prison on parole. Does this not justify suspicions of conceptual disingeniousness? Does this, alternatively, relate to the interesting but muted suggestion in some parts of Hegel's historical philosophy, that the process of history should be seen as a slow rising of humanity to consciousness, to reflexivity, tending to a self-reflexive resolution of the 'problem of history'—a gradual movement to a point of final transparency when what men do and what they think they are doing would become identical? This would imply, of course, that the rhythm and character of what is implied by determination has been changing over time. Through a vestigial extension of this idea into Marxism, one can argue that although the economy determined the polity in the earlier, 'unlit', forms, one should not be surprised if, after a socialist revolution, this gets reversed. This will be very similar to the ideas of the early Lukacs about the identical subject object of history.[10] But can one make sense of these jostling possible meanings of this 'enigmatically transparent'[11] idea, or reduce them into some kind of a reasonably ordered relation?

Political theory was given exactly this kind of logical treatment in Marx's mature works, specially in the high theoretical works like the *Grundrisse* and *Capital I*. Often, Marx refers to political events, occasionally in considerable detail. But it would be inattentive not to notice the discrepancy between the levels of generality on which the economic and the political explanations are placed! Both kinds of exercises do, of course, offer explanations, but the relations between them are asymmetric. The levels of abstraction are quite different. The time scales and rhythms are different, the point at which an object crosses a threshold to become theoretically noticeable are different. *Capital*, for instance, takes an occasional glance at the political regimes under capitalism;

[10] *History and Class Consciousness*, London, 1968.
[11] Althusser's phrase, used about the concept of alienation.

it is ordinarily content to deal with forms of state in very abstract propositions. By contrast, the *Eighteenth Brumaire* does not consider the activities of even moderately ineffectual statesmen beneath its analytical attention. *Capital* seeks to explain the movement of capitalism from epoch to epoch—the *Class Struggle in France* follows the fortunes of French politicians literally from day to day. No doubt, days become epochs if one waits long enough. But unless one places one's faith in an unusually strong version of methodological individualism, one can hardly presume that statements about one would be convertible into reliable statements about the other. There is, thus, a lack of a sense of proportion in the suggestion that the political theory collateral to the socioeconomic explanations of *Capital* can be found in Marx's writings about the historical short-term. It is plausible to suggest that we learn Marxian economics in *Capital*, and political theory from the *Eighteenth Brumaire*. But, in fact, the political analyses we get in one is not on the same scale and, therefore, not strictly comparable to the economics in the other. Of course, these have a vital interconnection in Marx's work, but it must be seen, I suggest, in a more complex fashion.

Autonomy as Exception

There is a general trend in current Marxist thought to look for non-reductive models of historical explanation. But there are logical variations between various non-reductive moves. Traditionally, Marxists often tried to open up some space for a 'play' or indeterminacy within the base-superstructure metaphor, by postulating a notion of weak reciprocity. But reciprocity is a relation, not a quality of which there can be more or less. Sometimes Marxists implied that the movement of politics was random, which would then mean that it will not be amenable to theoretical generalisation. As the purpose of theory is to map regularities, if politics excludes regularities by definition, all that theory can do is to ceremonially dissolve itself. This is not a frivolous suggestion. Marxist political literature shows recurrent examples of this sort. Individual political events are seen as framed in larger scenarios of slow-moving class forces which determine (wholly or positively) economic options and choices of basic social groups. But on the surface, above this deep level, there is the other plane on which everyday politics takes place, which demand detailed interpretation and commentary. Often, one finds an inverse relation between the large and the small analysis. Precisely because the 'large' analysis is done in such deterministic style, the political, as it were, takes its revenge. The 'small' analysis is done through a discourse which rarely refers to political forms which mediate class behaviour into history. Individuals are analysed either psychologically, or through a summary political ethics which can yield instant, and, therefore, necessarily changeable judgements about good and bad, or, progressive and reactionary. There are temporary traitors and heroes, because a twist in the immediate situation can turn one into the other, and they are fitted through their immediate political acts to the supposed longings of social classes.[12] An analysis of this kind, precisely because it has no patience for the problematic middle term, the political formations, oscillates violently between a language of teleological fatality, and a language of abusive psychologism.

A second familiar move is to declare that since Marxist theory is 'dialectical', all laws include the possibility of occasional reversals. This is bound to be unclear, because the initial task of theory was not only to specify regularities of behaviour, but also, preferably, specify conditions under which it can take particular turns. To say that something is probable, but the opposite of this is also equally probable, and not being able to specify conditions under which each is so, must reduce a theory's explanatory power. This is what Marx criticised younger Hegelians for: 'Yes becoming no, no becoming yes, and both yes and no becoming yes and no'.[13] But in more recent Marxist theory, some other interesting moves towards non-reductionism have been tried out. I should like to analyse one of them briefly.

Autonomy as Overdetermination

One of the most influential among these is Althusser's avoidance of determination. He observes the logical disingenuousness of the

---

[12] As an Indian, I find one example irresistible. After Indian Independence, Soviet Marxists dismissed Nehru as an agent of imperialism and a representative of a comprador bourgeoisie. After a few years, he came to be celebrated as a heroic builder of non-capitalist society, a change unrelated to any major alterations of policy on Nehru's part. It was a purely conceptual revolution.

[13] Marx, *Poverty of Philosophy*, Moscow, 1973.

idea of an extenuating long term.[14] If law X is to hold over the long term, but the opposite of X can hold in the short run, this causes obvious difficulties, because the long term is composed of short ones. And this kind of relation can hardly obtain, unless it is stated why short runs of the non-X types cannot occur all the while, or methodologically, non-individualistic conditions are specified. Althusser tries to avoid these logical traps, yet retain the quality of non-determinism which they impart to Marxist historical explanation. The two related concepts which enable us to do this in his thinking, are 'over-determination' and 'structural causality'. Even though the long term argument is a time argument, the last instance one is about the logical specification of causality. It is an idea of causality which has many layers, as it were. On some levels, the account closing falls due in a short period, and an economic level on which it takes a long time. Other levels of the social totality are allowed some room for play, subject, of course, to their coming back home at nightfall. But to analyse this literature is to witness the richness of metaphors, rather than a comparable richness of strictly conceptual moves.

The two concepts of contradiction and determination are integrally related; from different directions, they refer to the same qualities in historical events. The purpose of the concept of contradiction, like that of determination, is to show constraints on behaviour, to reveal underlying patterns, to reduce randomness, and exclude possibilities. In Marxist analyses, one must, of course, register the compulsions of 'pure' contradictions, like the one between the bourgeoisie and the proletariat. But in their pure form, these contradictions are merely heuristic devices, close to Weber's ideal types.[15] In history, one never comes across pure contradictions standing singly. Although it is analytically proper to characterise modes of production or social forms by their contradictions, actual conjunctures show the existence of many contradictions, not just the central one. No society is 'pure' in this sense. In fact, the notion of a conjuncture graphically suggests the plurality of contradictions at a point of time. I think Althusser's argument implies a subtle reworking of some concepts in Marxist social

---

[14] *For Marx*, op. cit., 117ff.

[15] Max Weber, *Methodology of the Social Sciences*, op. cit., pp. 41–46 and 92ff, which makes the suggestion that 'Marxian laws are ideal-typical'.

theory. Distinctions between central and incidental are not in terms of their significance; for, even the smallest element of the conjuncture is necessary for it to have the effect it actually does. In making a conjuncture what it is, therefore, the primary and secondary contradictions are all equally necessary. They are meant to do quite different chores in the conceptual division of labour within the theory.

Significantly, there is a certain monochromic quality in Althusser's picture of contradictions, which is deliberate. Althusser is not introducing, as Gramsci and Sartre or Lukacs would in similar circumstances, other planes which intersect or qualify objective contradictions: interpretative or perceptual elements. Althusser's analysis is self-consciously distinct. All the complexities that Althusser carefully unravels exist on a single plane—the plane of objective contradictions, unmediated by interpretative aspects of meaning. An event happens all between contradictions. Both its structured and unstructured qualities can be deduced from the way structures are related. Any absence of rigidity or teleology occurs not because objectivities are crossed out or mitigated by other things, but due to the relations that obtain between these objectivities themselves. If contradictions are taken to be equivalent to structures (this diverges from Althusser's more scrupulous usage which reserves the term structure, only for the *global* structure, the structure in the 'structure-in-dominance'), each conjuncture is then a total effect of these. Structures that are analytically distinguishable always act in history through their conjoint effects. In history, there are no dark, lonely alleys in which groups or societies can be set upon by single, overwhelming structures. That is why there is not much point, in concrete historical explanations, in distinguishing between institutional structures like governments, and abstract ones like classes. Both types are historically present, although Althusserians would surely admit that the sense in which they are 'present' must differ. When a structuralist Marxist speaks of 'the structure', the structure in this solemn singular is the combination, the conjunctural unity of all those structures that are analytically separable. (Which, in structuralist terms, does not mean that they exist singly, like people in a crowded underground, each with a newspaper to his nose. Rather, no existence is part of their being; since in structuralism the character of an object is determined not by what it is in itself, but by the relations it has with objects in its surrounding world.)[16]

Each contradiction determines, has a logic of pressure on agents, and the actions they initiate and unintentionally cause. The totality of these effects gathered together in a conceptual unity, is the structure-in-dominance.[17] It is to this, in Althusser's view, that an adequate causality can be attributed. It is this structure which can fully explain an historical incident. Again, there is a subtle shift of implication. Traditional Marxism presupposed a traditional notion of what happened in an explanation, based on a strict distinction between explanation and description. For that tradition, therefore, to explain X was to refer it to Y. It would be inconceivable to refer X to X, and call it an 'explanation'. That would be disconcertingly similar to saying X is what it is because of the way it is.[18] But in Althusser's theory, to say this is not necessarily trite, or to beg the question. In words without a theatrical make-up, when we say something has been 'explained' in history, we simply indicate this whole complex of things. Theories of science, of course, have a very long tradition which asserts that a scientific explanation is a *reduction*—it referred an occurrence to another level of facts. To put it in a different, but related form, it reduced the chaos of

---

[16] Althusser, 'On the Materialist Dialectics', *For Marx, op. cit.*
[17] Ibid., p. 202.
[18] This involves an interesting problem, but one too large to be taken up here. The language of the 'last instance' implies a reference to an idea which is more often discussed in non-Marxist literature. Can one say, with some kind of explanation, that one has reached a kind of rock bottom, that this explanation cannot be further explained? Charles Taylor associates this with pre-Galilean science, and demarcates the natural science theories from social science theories of purpose by this division. Natural science explanations always leave room for further possible explanations of the same phenomenon, by reference to a finer, or still more basic, element. What distinguishes explanations by purpose is that after such an explanation is given, it leaves no room for anything more to be said. The two notions of explanation underlying the two types of Marxist theory, ironically make very similar claims to the effect that nothing can be said after these. But they do it in very different ways. The last instance idea, obviously, hints at this; but because it believes social reality can be divided between levels, and because, in its view, no more fundamental level can be discovered than the economic level. Althusser's redescriptivism also implies that there cannot be a more basic explanation, because a condition for an explanation must be a complete account. And if it is complete, nothing could be added to it. See the discussion in Charles Taylor, *Explanation of Behaviour*, London, 1964, pp. 21–25.

concrete phenomena to the comparative manageability of general laws. Traditional Marxism exhibited fairly strong influence of the idea of explanation as a reduction. (Of course, there reduction does not have any derogatory implication. On the contrary, it suggests precision, economy, order and other similar scientific virtues.) Althusser's suggestion that causality is 'structural', or that it can be attributed only to the 'structure-in-dominance', obviously marks a sharp departure from the notion of explanation as reduction. It asserts, on the contrary, that in historical analysis, a reduction, even in terms of the acknowledged central contradictions of a social form, is misleading. Modes of production are abstract analytical constructs, they map basic and minimal regularities, but they never have the richness of determinations of the concrete, to use a Hegelian phrase. To explain the concrete cannot be done by way of these. Reduction attenuates complexity. So, although there is an obvious Cartesian streak in Althusser's epistemology, central assertions about historical explanations in Althusser are, surprisingly similar to a Diltheyan construction, which presupposes a distinction in logical form in explanation in natural and historical sciences. Structure-in-dominance, if taken seriously, brings his theory of historical explanation quite close to some hermeneutic doctrines of history, despite the Cartesianism of his language. Structure-in-dominance is a structuralist's equivalent of situational uniqueness.

Althusser provides a clear account of the redescriptive nature of his category:

> In this complex whole containing many contradictions we cannot 'find' one contradiction that dominates the others as we might 'find' the spectator a head taller than others in the grandstand at the stadium. Domination is not an indifferent fact, it is a fact essential to complexity itself. That is why complexity implies domination as one of its essentials: it is inscribed in its structure. So to claim that this unit is not and cannot be the unity of a simple, original and universal essence, is not, as those who dream of that ideological concept foreign to Marxism, 'monism', think, to sacrifice unity on the altar of 'pluralism'—it is to claim something quite different; that the unity discussed by Marxism is the unity of the complexity itself, that the mode of

organisation and articulation of this complexity is precisely what constitutes its unity. It is to claim that the complex whole has the unity of a structure articulated in dominance.[19]

This passage is full of interesting theoretical motifs, although it is not always easy to disentangle the conceptually suggestive in Althusser from the meretricious. Part of its attraction lies, perhaps, in this combination. But some of these are worth pursuing at a greater length.

Despite Althusser's declarations of hostility to Hegelianism, his argument shows an interesting similarity to Hegel's on one point: his belief that in explaining historical situations one should not ascribe analytical values *a priori*, but only *after* the event. Unilinear causality of the economy is normally an *a priori* ascription. We do not wait for an event to happen to know how it has been caused or can be explained; in a formal sense, we know in advance, through our commitment to a causality ascribed to the 'economic'. Althusser's approach to historical occurrences is more circumspect. Even among his jostling contradictions, one cannot decide any *a priori* hierarchy. In fact, he goes further to argue that any ascription of priority in a complex whole, which could not, in one's judgement, have been without all of its attendant circumstances, is itself inappropriate. Althusser's theory, therefore, avoids not only any *a priori* primacy, but the idea of primacy itself. And precisely because it avoids the idea of a priority among the circumstances in thinking of historical causation, it becomes similar to an extended (though perhaps not unsuggestive) tautology or redescription. If it means that an historical conjuncture is what it is, because of the specific way its contradictions that constitute it are precisely mixed (that is, overdetermined), what is it saying really? It comes fairly close to saying that the historical situation is what it is (this is to put the language in a 'causal form'), because its elements are what they are, and they are related precisely the way they happen to be. The situation is what it is, because it is what it is. There is of course nothing, in principle, strange about this view of history, but it does require a drastic alteration in the notion of causality underlying most Marxist discourse. It raises the problem of the defining of an explanation in history; it implicitly faces us with the question of a

---

[19] *For Marx*, op. cit., p. 202.

choice between two notions of what an explanation is. Is it primarily a *reduction*: a way of referring the apparent chaos of facts to the clarity of some essential laws and regularities, so that an explanation is 'simpler' in an epistemic sense, than a merely descriptive account of an historical occurrence? Or, is it a name for a redescription which tries precisely to preserve the complexity of the occurrence? Evidently, the two notions of explanations are opposed. In one, there is a clear line of demarcation between explanation and description, and an explanation is seen to be both more significant and economical than a descriptive account. In the other, it is this precise distinction that is formally questioned: an explanation is simply a description that is adequate to the complexity of the occurrence. The two theories arrange epistemic values differently. In one, simplicity is the value explanations would aim at; in the other, complexity. Surely, there are traditions in natural science theory which claim that there cannot be any clear line of difference between explanations and descriptions, just as in historical sciences there are theories which assert that the main epistemic preoccupation of historians should be to capture the unique complexity of occurrence. But Althusser's relation to either of these cannot be very straightforward. This shows that there could be an element of ambiguity in Marxism on this question.

If there had been one contradiction or one structure, it could have caused the event, that is, accounted for it in fullest detail. But since there are many of them, and this is necessarily the case, without reducing the claim of contradictions to determine fully, we can still derive a theory of underdetermined outcomes. The sufficiency of the cause lies in the specific manner in which these combine. Formal explanation is, thus, still left to the 'economic' in Althusser's Marxism, but effective explanation is given over to the 'structure'. 'Structure-in-dominance' is a significant and interesting concept, because it is supposed to provide one of the crucial solutions in Althusser's Marxism. It retains the theoretical injunction of 'determination by the economic in the last instance', but makes this kind of concrete instance historically unavailable. This means that the economic determined in the last instance, not in actual history, but in a particular kind of heuristic and idealising discourse.

Determination in history is made the joint work of multiple contradictions, and the strictly explanatory primacy of the economic is gently taken away. As an orthodox Marxist, Althusser feels obliged to show ritual reverence to the idea of determination in the last instance. But his sense of history, of how events actually occur, does not seem to offer much support to the idea of a deterministic causality. Indeed, he states quite explicitly about the feudal social form, that non-economic levels may, in fact, have dominance, because there is some scriptural support for this notion.[20] In explanation, therefore, the primacy of the economy is avoided,[21] but there is a kind of hollowly linguistic defence of the idea. This leads to the distinction between determination and dominance, and one can see how, in explanatory terms, dominance becomes the effective concept, and discretely pushes out determination. This leads to the curious paradox in the heart of Althusser's Marxism: a sort of division of sovereignty between the two notions. Titular sovereignty still lies with determination, but its function is unmistakably like those of British royalty. It simply stamps with formal approval what the effective concept of dominance decides to do.[22]

Autonomy as Underdetermination

This is attractive from the point of view of historical explanations, no doubt, but a more significant ambiguity seems to result from this. As the two concepts are rooted in two distinct notions of what historical explanation consists in, epistemic propositions of Althusser's Marxism suffer from a fundamental ambiguity. Perhaps one can try to solve this problem by saying that one must, in reading Althusser, exercise an interpretative judgement about which idea is more significant or suggestive, and render his theory coherent by choosing one of them and qualifying the other. Clearly, the verdict in that case would go in favour of explanation as redescription, rather than reduction. Several aspects of Althusser's argument lend credence to this idea—the emphasis on complexity,

[20] Althusser and Balibar, *Reading Capital*, London, 1970, pp. 176–81.
[21] Ibid., Chapter 9 *passim*.
[22] It is significant that some of Althusser's followers have been pushed by his arguments (or perhaps a certain readings of it) into declaring finally that there cannot be any predeterminate primacy that can be ascribed to any single level of the social totality. Hindess and Hirst, *Mode of Production and Social Formation*, London, 1977, p. 5. It is of course difficult to ascertain what these post-Althusserians believe about any serious question, due to the frequency of their autocritiques.

opposition to what he considers to be Hegel's notion of a complexity reducible into simple essence, his unwillingness to accept priorities between contradictions. Dominance has the dominance. But the compromise he arranges becomes suspect in logical terms, because the two notions of explanation are not only different, but in major ways, opposed. Using the language of one to argue for the other leads to recurrent and ineradicable ambiguity.

In Althusser's theory what happens is overdetermination, but what it causes or helps take place relative to each single contradiction is clearly underdetermination. But this is precisely what can be objected to. As this is a plausible model of social explanation, it is hardly surprising that most of the modern departures into political theory begin from Althusser's concepts (Poulantzas, Therborn, Laclau).[23] But conceptually, it is rather a waste to assert first that structures can determine if they exist singly, and then to say that (either normally or exceptionally) such instances never arise in history. From Althusser's point of view, it is a category mistake to expect to find them in history; they can exist only in a specific type of heuristic philosophical discourse. But it is simpler to say that it is in the nature of structures that exist in history to underdetermine their outcomes. This would be a simple alteration of conceptual meaning, which would preserve the explanatory advantages of Althusserian reasoning, but be free from its logical problems, besides doing it more practically and economically. In the social science discourse of Marxism, if not otherwise stated, 'determination'—which is the constraining quality of structures over agency—is equal to underdetermination. It is an exclusion of possibilities, and not rendering one absolutely certain. I shall argue that this also creates some internal space in Marxism for interpretative concepts.[24]

Because of a strong element of objectivism in his thought, a persistent mistrust of all concepts of subjectivity, Althusser does not find the idea of complete determination implausible. But even

---

[23] Nicos Poulantzas, *Political Power and Social Classes*, London, 1973; Goran Therborn, *What Does the Ruling Class Do When It Rules*, London, 1978; Ernesto Laclau, *Politics and Ideology in Marxist Theory*, London, 1978.

[24] I do not mean that concepts from interpretative sociology should be grafted on to Marxist theory, but that Marxists ought to try to generate concepts which would be able to take in interpretative elements of behaviour, instead of trying to bracket them.

on his own terms, since there is a reality to ideology, even though it may only interpolate individuals as subjects,[25] if a single individual turns round to answer, this would disturb the implicit symmetries of his entirely objectivist universe. It is simpler to admit the effectiveness of ideology, the latency of interpretative opportunities within human acts, and to make room for them within our concepts, rather than record their effects, a little disingenuously, by carefully arranging a stalemate between objective things.

In the conceptual reading suggested here, determination is the social process whose precise quality is to underdetermine events. This is not an indeterminacy at the cognitive level, resulting from there being one determination over another, so that one cannot see their lines of force clearly, or a joint causality unascribable to any one. Underdetermination is the quality of what Marxists refer to as historical determination—by classes, structures or situations. This puts underdetermination in the heart of the concept of determination itself. It does not rule out choices, alternative possibilities, but restricts their range with greater or lesser severity. This makes options, or a certain order of indeterminacy, *internal* to the notion of determination, rather than an external condition to be arranged for logically, or attached by adhesive adjectives (like relative not absolute, etc.).

Let us now turn to the point which seems to bind the notions of necessity and determination. The idea of structures implicit in Marxism leaves room for subjectivity; indeed, it considers subjectivity, or agency, to be historically crucial. Problems sometimes arise in this regard from a confusion of tense problems in historical thinking. Obviously, historians and historical actors are placed on different planes, have different ontological relationships, dispositions to occurrences, and quite different orientations in terms of time. Actors live history prospectively; even the most dedicated followers of Dilthey or Collingwood are reduced to mere reconstructions of situations, which work under some limitations. At this level too, there can be hard fallacies to overcome for a reductivist theory of history. If understanding history is through reconstructing situations of actors, some of their dispositions would be unreconstructible. Actors' dispositions towards historical actions

[25] Althusser, *Lenin and Philosophy and Other Essays*, London, 1971.

are determined by the fact that they do not know what will happen. An historian cannot reconstruct this, which by his own conceptual logic, would be a necessary condition of his enterprise. Reliving history, if taken beyond an allegorical phrase, is a misleading notion, bound to collapse, when pushed to extremes into incoherence. Indeed, this is the kind of the ontological bar that constitutes the first and the most fundamental point of the critique of relativist hermeneutic thinkers like Heidegger and Gadamer. Historians can do nothing about their ontological 'privilege' of knowing the future in advance. It is not a privilege they can drop out of. They cannot 'bracket' it in Husserl's sense, for, the need for bracketing itself would set him apart, the entire artillery of Heidegger against the Husserlian 'epoche' would apply against his efforts. The gulf between the positions of actor and observer is unbridgeable. There is a certain residue which would always remain between the events and the knowledge-constructs of events, or as hermeneutic theorists would put it, between knowing and being.[26]

Determination can then be seen as a concept proper to the level at which history is lived, where the tense orientation is prospective; they go with time. Conversely, necessity is a concept proper to the level at which history is studied; it has a tense orientation that runs *against* time. Clearly, the sense in which there is room for agency in living history is quite different from the sense in which there can be an epistemic registration of the room that had once been there for once-living agency in history which is now dead, that is, history as knowledge. To use a different metaphor (which may, in fact, compound our problems), what history as a discursive discipline encounters are traces of agency and subjective decisions having been taken; like fossils of non-compulsory decisions preserved in the strata of time. Room for agency is an idea which can apply realistically only to living history, to history as being. It cannot be applied the same way to the epistemic recovery of being, to history as reconstruction, because the uncertainty contained in the option would have already been spent. It is not the sort of uncertainty that attaches to an unmade choice, but a spent uncertainty of a choice that has been taken. Of course, although the choice has been made, for reasons which are still retrospectively specifiable,

---

[26] The most powerful contemporary argument against this is, of course, Gadamer, *Truth and Method*, London, 1975.

it is still, in principle, different from a situation in which no choice existed.

This is the meaning of determination: it asserts that events that have gone before (this can also come in a different form—of one kind of events exerting pressure on another), create pressures through the continuance of their effects on what is to happen. They restrict possibility and narrow down choice. It cannot be said at any point of historical time that anything can happen, if anything at all has happened before. Evidently, it is a significant part of the historian's enterprise to state what cannot happen, and different theories of history quarrel over which is the best way to know things which cannot take place. Marxists would assert that a detailed consideration of certain types of things, like the level of technology, the stable configuration of social interests, social relations arising out of production (which exerts similar pressure on other spheres of economic life, like circulation and exchange), are particularly and systematically suggestive in understanding excluded choices. Givens of all kinds restrict possibilities of what can happen, or what can be done, to a specific range. This is what is determined. This means that an individual choice, or an individual event is *underdetermined* by the logic of structures which form its context. Determination would never determine in a categorical fashion, what is going to happen. It refers, rather, to what cannot, in principle. This may look at first sight like an evasion. For, to say something about what cannot happen is only a recondite way of saying something about what can. But this accomplishes something which appears to me to be important. What is said about these two respects become asymmetric, logically. Saying something about what cannot happen categorically, is also saying something about what can, but much less definitely. It leaves open a range, a margin of occurrence. What can be extracted from a categorical statement about what cannot happen about what can, is precisely less categorical, and therefore, not open to similar kinds of logical or conceptual objection.

Determination in Marxism is, in this sense, a *negative* concept. To expect it to yield, or to extract from it, a positive outcome is to misconstrue its logical status, to ask it wrong questions, to expect answers it is not equipped to provide. It fixes ranges of possible choice or outcomes. What we denote by determination is not the event, but the space allowed to the event; not what must take place, but the margin in which something must.

When a particular actor chooses, or an historical event takes place, this underdeterminant quality is lost. Of course, each exercised choice within this zone of specifiable indeterminacy would have a further set of reasons or causes. But these reasons cannot be inferred or read off from the initial conditions. These are genuinely underdetermined things. This can also be argued from another angle. A constraining or excluding idea of determination suggests specifying limits. But the idea of limits itself can be seen in two different ways. A more conventional one would say that the range of choice, or its limits, consists of a specifiable set of possibilities or state of affairs, say X or Y or Z; what comes to happen must be one of these. This introduces an indeterminacy of a certain kind. But it seems doubtful if historical possibilities can often be set out and stated in this form. A more suggestive way of talking of limits can be borrowed from linguistics, and its concept of combinatories or a generative structure. An alphabet ensures that only a certain range of things are possible with it; but its way of restricting is different from, and less restrictive than, a straightforward listing of possible outcomes. When Marxists speak of the interests of a class determining its actions or its discourse, the best construction of this idea would be something like this: the class acquires, through its historical experience, its specific alphabet of action or of thought. But what it decides to generate out of this alphabet is underdetermined.

If determination means a list of constraints and delimitation of choice, it can have only one tense mode—the present tense or the very near future. Its use is proper only when we refer to the historical actor, or an observer who is his contemporary, who is living history prospectively, where the actor's tomorrow is also the observer's. If the actor and analyst are related to the event asymmetrically, if the actor's tomorrow is the analyst's yesterday, the notion properly applicable is the second notion of necessity. Its mode is retrospective, it is a tense to which the owl of Minerva is eternally condemned, for it deals with dead choices, with the fossils of agency. It knows the future in advance; its problem is not underdetermined, but wholly determined.[27] Historians usually placed this way, can only try to separate out the space, or levels, in the model in which determination and freedom of choice would have had their play. No doubt, in some cases of spent choice, this

[27] E.H. Carr's exposition of 'determinism' in history is exactly in these terms, though he is not interested in doing it formally. *What is History?*, New York, 1962.

may be difficult to disentangle. Necessity is the concept used to denote the privileged observer's enterprise to understand what happened within the crucially underdetermined part of an historical event. This content of choice can be explained but not forecast. The language of necessity, the only language that Minerva's owl can speak, has no present tense. Determination is in prospective form what turns into necessity in retrospect.

Determination and Structures

Structures are usually considered to narrow down options. By contrast, the idea of a logic of a situation is often used to indicate a peculiar freedom which sometimes arises in history, which loosens up the stuffiness of structures somewhat, a freedom that is not illusory. It is natural to think of situations as intersections of structures or what results when structures meet, or as a result of a stalemate between two pure but contradictory tendencies. But a situation can act on structural logic in both ways.[28] It may narrow down options still more, but the idea generally is that when there are contradictory pulls, this tends to free political agents into a voluntaristic space, to do things much closer to the way they would like. If actors are particularly clever or lucky, they may be able to bring about, acting at the narrow openings that these immense things have between them, even the particular results they intended. Clashes between structures reduce the heteronomy of groups and individuals, if not enhance the autonomous space for political choice. Agents can, as it were, play these heteronomies against each other.

This, of course, is a familiar story in politics. Small states prefer to have two big neighbours instead of one. Western European statesmen, who would agree with the moral preferences of American administrations, would still prefer a bi-polar world to one wholly dominated by the United States. Statesmen work out similar room for manoeuvre by saying that they have to be mindful of a proper trade-off between equally important principles, or claimants of distributive attention, or that they must be just in mediating between equally insistent interests. To be upholding two principles is less constraining than upholding one entirely unambiguous ideal.

---

[28] Althusser observes this point in *For Marx, op. cit.*, p. 106.

There is no reason why this should not apply to abstract things like structures as well. To be placed at the intersection of multiple structures may be less constraining than being swallowed up in one. After all, that is the lesson of Althusser's argument.

But structures are of different kinds, and it is important for the purposes of our argument to distinguish between the precise sense of determination proper to each one of them. For all structures determine, but not in the same way. One obvious distinction to make will be between explicit and abstract ones. In fact, the hazards of deterministic analysis can be traced to the tendency to drop the middle term in analysis, to go straight from an empirical state of facts to abstract things like classes. This is also exhibited in the tendency to think of these two types of propositions, not as things which are legitimate in their proper contexts, but as appearance and essence, in which a statement in terms of the essence would contain all possible true qualities of a statement in terms of appearance. But the distinction must not be seen in those terms.

The structure of imperialism, the structure of cabinet government, the bourgeois class, a political party, a situation—all these things do constrain, and all these would fit into some loose definition of structures. The concept of structure is, indeed, proper to all of them, because the fact that they are the way they are and not otherwise, exerts significant influence on agency. But they constrain in different ways, in different degrees, and these differences are worthy of some attention. I think three distinct implications come out if we analyse these examples. Determination implies somewhat different things when it is related to (i) explicit structures like institutions, (ii) abstract structures like classes, and (iii) situations which are seen as short term compulsions or freedoms. They are significant for political analysis, for politics always happens in the short term.

Explicit and Abstract Structures

The first two types restrict behaviour through complex arrangements of encouragement and sanction. But to speak of rewards and punishments in case of abstract structures, like classes, is naturally somewhat allegorical. This can lead to confusion and misplaced expectation if its qualifications are not specified. In case of explicit structures or institutions, this is unproblematic. A cabinet will dismiss a minister who disobeys rules of collective responsibility, but an individual will not long remain member of the capitalist class if his economic acts are dictated by motives of altruism. In both types of cases, it is common to say, colloquially, that the person has been 'thrown out'. But the second case is clearly different from the first. Evidently, there is a logic at work in the second case too, which supervises the internal coherence of the capitalist class, but it works through a latent structure like the market, which, though abstract, is obviously not ineffectual. Some of the stock arguments against Marxist social theory, that, for instance, it uses metaphysical concepts, are clearly disingenuous. If the concept of class has to be thrown out of the conceptual stock of rigorous social theory, so would the concept of market. That too indicates merely a persistent configuration of effects of explicit acts and institutions. Markets do not exist in the sense in which firms do. Yet, one cannot make sense of a large, and probably the more significant part of the behaviour of firms, without recourse to a conceptual primacy of markets. These are no shadows; they indicate 'logics' which, indeed, compel and explain behaviour of institutions. After all, the distinction between actual and real is still not without its uses in social explanation. In social sciences, it is quite common to have to explain the activity of actual things, only by recourse to things which are real in this indirect way, which would always fail to answer an institutional roll-call.

Curiously, critics of market theory and its reductionist adherents often use similar moves in their thought, particularly in the ascription of political acts to abstract things. At one time, this was considered the fatal flaw of Marxist theory, that it tried to explain and understand the political world in terms of concepts which will fail to pass this most elementary of fitness tests. Governments had a verifiable existence; states were simply metaphysical constructs. As Marxists insisted on the primacy of concepts like the state, which could not be found, in Weldon's elegant condemnation, in the telephone directory, this was supposed to prove the ineradicable metaphysical content in Marxist analyses.[29] Arguments of this sort appear, in retrospect, particularly odd, because they are guilty of precisely the sort of category mistake that Ryle criticised so effectively.[30] The error about calling the concept of the state metaphysical

[29] T.D. Weldon, *Vocabulary of Politics*, Harmondsworth, 1953.
[30] Gilbert Ryle, *The Concept of Mind*, 1949 (1980), pp. 18 ff.

is precisely of the same type as looking for an Oxford University beyond its colleges and other institutions; to mistake the two concepts as competitors or belonging to the same logical class. The state is real, a Marxist can argue, in the same sense in which the Oxford University is real.[31]

Institutional structures are transparent—entities like firms, governments and associations, with names, telephone numbers, explicit rules and clear boundaries. Their definitions are not subject to prior theoretical judgements. We are in no doubt about who are the members of a specific chamber of commerce, what are the rules of membership of a church, and when a person can be expelled from an association. But there are other structures, obviously related to these, but with a more elusive quality about them; a bourgeois class in relation to a chamber of commerce, a religion in relation to a church. Institutions in Marxist political analysis, are not simply embodied versions of classes; they have a more complex relationship. The definition of a bourgeoisie, of the delineation of the ideas which form the core of a religious system, are largely theory dependent affairs. So, the second type of structures depend on, one can almost say they are brought into existence, by, definitional constructs; at least their boundaries certainly are.[32] Rules of institutions are explicit, if not always entirely public. Consequently, the systems of reward and punishment which they work are either well-known or empirically recoverable. At this level, the use of a language of decision is, therefore, appropriate. A person truly decides whether he will become a member of an association; this decision is not previously horizoned by the rules of the organisation; his behaviour of course will be, only if he does join. But it is a necessary quality of determination of abstract structures that it is latent, and can be masked from the person whose behaviour is being determined. At least, seeing that they exist is not a condition for making use of the alphabets they provide.

Although there is often a great difference between what institutions profess and what they actually do, this relation is unmysterious and accessible. But when we use the ordinary verbs of action in

[31] Ibid., pp. 17–18.

[32] This does not imply that classes do not exist if they are not registered in a conceptual definition. Rather, what the concept of class would include, and what it can do in explanation, would depend substantially on how it is defined.

relation to abstract structures, it is done *faute de mieux*, and an ambiguity tends to creep into our language.[33] Ascription of actions to surface structures does not give a complete account of acts in social life; for the world is made up of these other more insidious structures too, and they condition and constrain the actions at the institutional level. And here the distinction between 'surface' and 'deep' structures is of a kind that a deep account does not make a surface account redundant. Just as the concept of firm does not invalidate the use of a concept of market, use of categories like parties or political formations does not close off the logical space for using the notion of class. To argue against this is, paradoxically, a common point between vulgar Marxism and conventional anti-Marxism. Both believe that the conceptual space in political explanation can be occupied by only one set of categories. Thus, the use of explicit concepts close off the use of abstract ones, or vice versa.

[33] This is related to the point made at the beginning of the paper—about some untidiness of expression in Marxist political analyses. This kind of unclarity may be called, after Ryle, 'systematically misleading' expressions. Ryle says:

> There are many expressions in non-philosophical discourse which, though they are perfectly clearly understood by those who use them and those who hear or read them, are nevertheless couched in grammatical or syntactical forms which are in a demonstrable way *improper* to the states of affairs they record (or the alleged states of affairs which they profess to record).

Many political propositions of Marxism would fall under this kind of stricture. However, Ryle's belief that those who read them understand them perfectly, seems to me rather optimistic. Often they lead to confusion, ambiguity or misleading consensus (that is, when two people believe that they agree because they have supported the same proposition, but actually they hold different versions of it). A recent controversy in Indian Marxist historiography comes to mind. Two historians of peasant politics disagreed about the extent of 'autonomy' of peasant political action. Actually, however, the debate remained unclear eventually, because it was not clear whether they differed about terms or about facts of history. It appears that Chatterjee means by dominance a consequence proposition, while Alam means by the same term, a characterisation of origin. Quite often, standard Marxist propositions about politics can be interpreted very differently. For instance, when we say class is dominated, or class X undertakes an act, what we mean (or should mean) is not that the class is the direct actor, but that it is the principal beneficiary. From this point of view, then, to treat these propositions as relating to origins of acts is misleading: they can be suggestive only if they refer to consequences, but sometimes their grammatical form may indicate a reference to origins. It follows from this, however, that the consequences of this sort of 'error' may not be as innocuous as Ryle thought.

Of course, this implies that the sense in which we use the terms 'surface' and 'deep' is not the conventional dichotomy between appearance and reality. Rather, they should be thought of as describing reality at different levels, although the distinction must imply that one considers one group more basic. In explanations of politics there is a kind of reciprocal dependence between them as categories. Both types of descriptions are necessarily incomplete, and the nature of this incompleteness hints at the existence of the counterpart. What categories of the first level can capture, those of the second cannot, and vice-versa. This guards against the common trend towards a sort of class substitutionism in political and cultural analysis in Marxism,[34] in which the class takes over directly from political actors or utterers of discourse. In reductive Marxism, surface and deep concepts are taken in the sense of being high/low, inclusive/exclusive, or appearance/reality. In this view, they are supposed to take in conceptually quite different qualities of the social process, or more precisely, perhaps, qualities which exhibit themselves at different levels of generality.[35]

Abstract structures have their effects only in the longer term, for they constrain indirectly. This is why their logic should be seen as statistical; their effects intensify and wane over long periods. If a

---

[34] The debates about C.B. Macpherson's interpretation of English political thought of the 17th century brought out some of these points quite clearly. Some of the basic objections raised by John Dunn against Macpherson's procedures appear to me to be justified, as also Quentin Skinner's more general objections to reductionist Marxism. Their criticism against Macpherson is right, but against Marxism wrong. For, in much of their criticisms they assume that Marxist interpreters of political thought must ascribe discourses to collective entities like classes, while this seems to be not necessarily true. The work of Lucien Goldmann on Pascal and Racine follows methodological rules and even research procedures that are fairly comparable to their own (except of course a more indirect ascription to class). Clearly, their criticism of prolepsis in interpretation is closely parallel to Althusser's discussions on how to study the philosophy of the young Marx. In my view, their criticisms of Macpherson are well judged, but their view of what Marxist theory allows to an interpreter is too restrictive and wrong. Cf. John Dunn, *The Political Thought of John Locke*, Cambridge, 1968; Quentin Skinner, 'Meaning and Understanding in the History of Ideas', *History and Theory*, 1969; Lucian Goldmann, *The Hidden God*, London, 1964; Althusser, *For Marx, op. cit.*

[35] On the view presented here, Locke does not have the responsibility of thinking the bourgeoisie's thoughts for it. One can retain all the specific peculiarities of Locke's ideas, ranging from ontology to toilet training, and still relate it to the 'discourse' in history of particular classes. In fact, here too it might be a case of what can be plausible as a statement about consequences becoming vulnerable when made about intent.

businessman violates formal laws of company behaviour, his actions will be punished by his government. If he disobeys the subtler but no less insistent laws of the capitalist market, say by excessive altruism, it will restrain him more indirectly. Other things being equal, this will result in his financial ruin and a consequent alteration of his social role. These are laws of large numbers and long periods. When we talk of determination of individual actions by classes, we are using a shorthand, a convenient abbreviation; we are talking not of a single-remove determination, but a double-remove one. In politics, classes do not constrain individuals directly, but through the alphabets of political formations to which these individuals belong. Political formations need not be directly aligned to particular classes or fractions; they still show instances of class politics because they work on an alphabet of decisions whose range is determined by class in a language-like way. In culture, I think Marxists must offer a largely parallel argument, in which determination acts through patterns of discourse, through which thoughts of individuals are coordinated with acts and thoughts of others.

Political formations always exist on the level we have called explicit and they are always the proximate sources of political action. Indeed, actual politics happens on this plane, through relations between agents of this sort. Constraints to which individual agency is subject can be traced to them. Classes and other deep structures do not figure on the political stage as actors; in culture they do not act as actual utterers of discourse. They exist as references to the general alphabet of which discourses are historically formed. It is wrong to refer discourses, or actions, or similar meaning-related things to classes.[36] It is proper, and logically quite

---

[36] This is, stated another way, the central problem about Macpherson's interpretation of English political thought of the 17th century. It is worth noting that his argument about liberal democracy, since it is about an aggregate and not an individual doctrine, has drawn fewer criticisms of inappropriateness. Two types of objections were being made about his procedure. 1. It was doubted whether such direct relations could be established between ideas and behaviour of large groups. 2. It was objected that such general discourses, related to stable interests (that is, assuming that the answer to the first question is positive), could not be attributed to individuals. Individuals create theories with meanings; these may come to have a different kind of historical significance. One way of solving this problem can be Goldmann's suggestion of using the two concepts of meaning and significance, as being proper to individual and collective subjects. Goldmann, *Lukacs and Heidegger*, London, 1974; and *Cultural Creation*, Oxford, 1977.

a different thing, to refer to them as 'creators' of intellectual resources.

Class causes, it may be said, would be condemned to live in a state of suspended animation until they find their way into somebody's reasons. Explanations of revolutions are normally structured in this form. The cost of being fundamental is to have only indirect results. Fundamental structures have always to be 'represented', or mediated (a term not wholly free of ambiguity), and the logic of this representation relation is not one of exact homology between real and perceived interest and between interest and acts. It is through this conceptual space/gap—between class interest and concrete action—that interpretative explanations come to assume great significance in Marxist theory. It is due to this non-homologous relation that the presumptions of reductionism are false. For representation is not a relation of expressiveness, as if representatives of classes are related to them the way spokesmen at news conferences are related to parties. Nor is it that the 'representatives' cannot make up their minds until the class does. The relation between them, on the contrary, goes the other way round. It is basically an area of a critical overlap between individual decisions that is called a class's mind on a particular issue. Classes rarely take decisions in a simple sense, and what is called its mind is something that can only be retrospectively posited. Structures are, then, the names we give to the regularities of relations and effects which the actual behaviour of men and institutions exhibit in history.

Those who analyse politics often find, however, that the complexities of actual situations are not analysable through these two types of determining structures. They still leave an analytical residue. They are cut through by what are called the 'logic of situations'. The precise way in which historical circumstances combine, of course, have an effect on how cleanly the logic of determination can work. But what are called situations, can work in two ways. They can close off options which under normal circumstances, would have been open to actors; or, contrarily, open up choices that normally would not have existed. Thus, if the structural pressures are seen as being statistical, the way situations behave can be conceptualised through something like game theory.[37]

[37] This obviously does not mean that game theory will be able to provide miraculous explanations of political processes, but simply that, within the interstices of long-term and large-scale analyses, there can be room for a purely formal account of

Structural tendencies take long periods to mature or decline, but situational opportunities open and close.

Consequently, it is critical in political activity, not only to be right about what Marxists call the 'political line'—that is, a mapping of these structural tendencies with reference to one's place and preferences within it—but also about timing, that is, not to miss opportunities. A right line means a correct picture of the way structures are tending to move; right timing is to understand circumstantial openings of opportunities, which, if spurned, will soon close off. Compulsions of imperialist control over the rest of the world tend to weaken over time. Classes crystallise or decline in Braudelian long rhythms. Situational logic, critical for both political enquiry and political action, is the realm of opportunities, response and anticipated response. It is the understanding of this that is called statesmanship, and historical materialism does not stop its adherents from distinguishing between statesmen and ordinary politicians with higher rates of mortality. Use of structure-related notions, therefore, does not rule out the use of judgements about opportunities. These cannot assume the conceptual functions of one another. In Gramsci's prison notes in particular, one finds an implied suggestion that to be complete, a Marxist political theory must supplement an analysis of structures by analyses of situations—a suggestion that has been little explored.[38] Reductivism implies, on the contrary, that one can deduce political acts from structural horizons. This is misleading, and utterly impoverishes the conceptual complexity of the political theory of Marxism. From the identification of a mode of production, the stage of growth of a social form, the extent of coalescence of the economic-corporate life of classes, from a reference to what Gramsci calls 'refractory realities', it is possible to infer *not* the actions which *must* follow, but the range in which they are most likely to happen. The language is not one of imperatives. The logic of determination is a logic of probability.

---

how strategies can be worked out. Quite often, the mistrust of Marxists against formal techniques is misplaced. The fault usually lies not with the techniques, but of too large expectations placed on them. There is something very odd about the view that something must be wrong about the techniques rather than the way they are used.

[38] Antonio Gramsci, *Selections from Prison Notebooks*, London, 1971, p. 181.

Structures and Agency

Political analysis within Marxism can take two very different forms. One form, the one that I prefer, would use this probabilistic concept of determination symmetrically, as holding between all levels of social or political reality. And it would naturally follow that if this is the relation between classes and parties, it would admit of a similar relation between individual agents and structures of various kinds. By going for a harder order of determination, out of positivistic delusions, reductionism slides into indefensible generalisations about historical or political causality. The entire point of the foregoing critique of Althusser, however, was to clear some room for reintroduction of some concepts of intentionality within Marxist political theory.

Once more, this is not something new, only not adequately remembered. I have argued before that this was precisely Marx's project, to transcend the sterile dichotomy between positivistic and hermeneutic notions of a social science. This project is clearly announced in the critical *Theses on Feuerbach*, which is the true 'work of the break' in Marx. *The German Ideology*, as Althusser observes, shows the first results of the philosophical reconstitution of his problematic. But it is the *Theses on Feuerbach*, which shows Marx at the experiment. After all, the reason for the preference of underdetermination over overdetermination was that this helped avoid objectivist notions of contradiction (or structures), and made room for interpretative origins of individual acts. It places the concept of interpretation *within* the concept of determination. If determination in history is underdetermination, that is, a combination of constraints which agents in history do not necessarily register (but these are not non-violent things. If actors do not register them, they wreak their vengeance by arranging to ruin the actors' projects), it allows us to reintroduce a concern for agency, and as its precondition, interpretation.

Collective actions are often averages made out of individual actions, but these are what Durkheim called 'social facts'. All qualities of individual actions are not transferable to collective acts; what these lack is precisely the immediacy of meanings that individual projects have. Perhaps, the main distinction between individual actions and what we regard as a collective endeavour is that one cannot attribute simple intentionalities to them. Meanings always attach, to use a Diltheyan phrase, to the 'insides' of actions, and only individual acts can properly be said to have an 'inside'. To go further, one might say that meanings are proper not to acts, but to projects, if acts are taken to denote a stage in the life of the project at which it has already moved out into the world, from the precincts of a purely private intentionality. Meanings, in this sense, can never be unintended. It is useful to deploy Goldmann's distinction between meaning and significance, to indicate the difference between what the author meant to do, and what others took him to have meant, or did with his actions. So, while speaking of class action at the level of institutions or structures, it is misleading to use meaning-related terms. Class actions cannot have meanings, only objectives that can be ascribed to them, after prefacing this by a sufficiently complex argument about structural coincidence of interests. Collective actions are real (because it does not follow from the argument above, that having meanings is the only mode of an action's being real), and they bear significance. The analytic unification that the concept of significance achieves, is external, through somebody else's criteria and act of judgement (usually *ex post*), not the actor's own. Actions carry meanings for their subjects, significance for all others including historians. But significance does not make meanings dissolve; in my view, they simply do not compete as concepts. They occupy two different floors in the explanatory model for social action.[39]

The logic of both kinds of structures are mediated by interpretative acts, through the peculiarly individual faults of individual craftsmanship of meanings by way of which men arrange their relations with the political world. It is in this sense that one must admit an irreducibility of the acts of individual agents, if Marxist analysis of either politics or culture is to be realistic, and not to legislate how the worlds of politics or culture ought to be. Of course, it is men who act, and who must act before classes and other abstractions can act through them. Since these august entities must depend on them, individual actions must assume some priority in the simple sense that these must happen before we can say that through them other more complicated things can. In quite the same way, reasons can claim a priority over causes. The other things simply have no way of happening by themselves, but can

---

[39] Goldmann, *Lukacs and Heidegger*, *op. cit.*, Chapter 4 *passim*.

happen only through these happenings. In politics, men react not to objectively given situations, but to what they consider their situations to be, by means of options which they think are open to them. At both levels, there can be suboptimal decisions. Individuals may have faulty pictures of the way they are placed, or correct pictures of their location but faulty notions of what this entails. They may have a picture of their options that is larger or narrower than what they really are. Practical options are, as a rule, narrower than logical ones, but they are hardly ever so narrow that the analyst (historian) can legitimately bracket interpretative considerations altogether, and can say that whatever way the act came into existence, we shall study only what came of it—its 'after', not its 'before'. It is my general contention that projects are constitutive of acts, they are not things which easily allow such subtracting operations without altering their conceptual values in critical ways. The abbreviation does not really imply that we study a more convenient, or manageable part of what we set out to study. The abbreviation alters it subtly, and gives us something which looks exactly like what we set out to study, but actually is not.

The only way interests can translate themselves into acts is through interpretative understanding, through purposes men posit and meanings men confer on their actions. In this sense, the bifurcation of meanings and interests, and the widespread belief that an explanation in terms of interests can displace one in terms of meanings, appears rather odd. For, it is precisely interests which implicate the sphere of meanings; a pre-interpreted interest is an extraordinarily unhelpful concept. This does not take away from some of the durable distinction between real and perceived interests. People's judgement about their own interests can be shown occasionally to be faulty, but as they remain, nonetheless, real judgements, observers of society have to take account of them and make sense of them. They must be given at least as much explanatory significance as the others, for here, paradoxically, it is the 'correct' judgements which have the status of counter-factuals.[40]

---

[40] Though this manner of speaking is quite common in Marxist analyses of culture, I think it is misleading to say that someone failed to represent the views of a social class. The idea of being a 'faulty', or incomplete representative, actually gives the argument away. It implies, first, that the world view of a class is an existent in a straightforward sense. It does not state that this is necessarily a logical

It is not very suggestive, for instance, to say that Hobbes 'failed' to articulate a bourgeois theory of the state on points X or Y, lacking a prior demonstration of his manifest obligations to have done so. But it does make sense to say that on points X or Y, Hobbes advanced ideas which did not fit into the 'ideal discourse' that can be ascribed (in Lukac's terms, 'imputed') to the bourgeois class, or the real discourse of liberalism which it came to develop historically.

What is thus called an ideal discourse may not square with any actual discourse of an actual bourgeoise. Yet, in a sense, it can be more significant than actual ones, because it can plot the common ground covered by all of them—something close to Foucault's discursive unconscious, or Dilthey's alphabet. By its very nature, this is something that can be seen by the historian, a kind of judgement that can only be made *ex post*. On this argument, Hobbes' theories would be seen as contributing to the conceptual or argumentative alphabet (= resources), through which the bourgeoisie was later to 'think' about the state and allied problems of power, to undermine feudal political discourse, to justify its own claims to legitimate political authority, to try to circumscribe and limit dissidence, by constructing around its social position the astonishingly resilient of ideas. Hobbes, or Locke, or Harrington, did not 'reflect' a mystical thing called the bourgeoisie's views about the state. What they proposed, individually, as reasonable ways of looking at political power, coincide with the parts of the ideal discourse, and helped fashion the rising bourgeoisie's intellectual resources. Instead of the bourgeoisie constituting their discourse, they should be seen as constituting through their theories, the discourse-like thing which we can ascribe to the bourgeoisie.

A possible objection to this argument could be that since social analysis is about behaviour of collectivities—groups, classes, institutions, etc.—and as these are all subject to what Lange called the law of large numbers, individual interpretative nuances must cancel

---

posited idea, something that can be, or needs to be created by the synthesising imagination of the historian. The oddity of the argument lies in the suggestion of something like a prior obligation of a theorist to represent some class which, still more oddly, possesses clear and decisive cultural preferences, such that the theorists can reflect them. On most of these points, Dunn's criticism of Macpherson is suggestive. However, it is not necessarily the case that when a Marxist refers to an author as bourgeois, he is one the Marxist 'greatly dislikes'. Cf. Dunn, *Political Thought of John Locke*, *op. cit.*, p. 205. On the contrary, the ideas they contain are, more often than not, seen as progressive ideas in their age. Consequently, the author is given a kind of approval, it somewhat patronisingly.

each other out statistically. Thus, it could be claimed, it is possible to return to a non-interpretative case. On this view, interpretative aspects of actions would not be denied, but rendered epistemically unimportant. Through the refinements of the notion of overdetermination, Althusser achieves this kind of a 'softening' of structural rigidities. A different and preferable way would turn Althusser's argument round on this point as well: to state that intentionalities give rise to actions, which slip out of the agents' control, and give rise through their unintended consequences over a long term, to what we abstractly term structures. These, grown strange and external, constrain further intentional acts, even of positing intentions. Structures and intentions are then seen as being internally related.

Sartre correctly saw the origin of all human acts in intentionality, but wrongly concluded that the conceptual problem this gave rise to could be solved by inserting into a Marxist theory of the social process, unreconstructed hermeneutic notions taken from Heidegger's philosophy. But here, Althusser's objection that transfer of a concept from one context to another must alter its meaning, would apply. The very act of taking them out of historicist phenomenology must do something to their conceptual values. It is proper to try to generate within Marxism, concepts which could cover the same ground, to cover the phenomenologists' concerns. What this requires is not a theory of intentionality appended to Marxism, but a Marxist theory of intentionality. Of course, this will deal with those things in the world with which the phenomenologist of the hermeneutic theorist deals, but not the way he does. This is not to graft the solutions offered by hermeneutics to the quite other solutions of Marxism, a kind of federalism of philosophies. Historically, both hermeneutics and Marxism grew out of the decline of Hegelianism, their common precondition. Consequently, the two traditions share common concerns, reflected in a crucial overlap between their concepts: superstructure and objective mind; ideology/hegemony and collective representations; underlying structures and alphabets. As concepts, they are not interchangeable, for they presuppose very different assumptions. But they refer, from within different theoretical traditions, to similar areas of social reality.

But, Although a Marxist cannot accept the hermeneutic theorists' solutions, he cannot afford to neglect his problems.

One advantage of the Marxist theory is in its conception of itself as a science, and the room that it provides for internal conceptual experiments—an idea rooted in both the 'emptiness' of some of its concepts, and the corrigibility implicit in the claim to being a science. It has an ability to subsume within itself, critical hypotheses generated within other traditions, without losing its internal coherence. In political analysis, one can use both notions of causes and reasons, or meaning and significance, instead of looking for a dissolution of either of these.

Do revolutions happen through a convergence of reasons, or of causes? It would appear odd to suggest that a historian can do systematically without one of these two notions in his business of explaining actual events in history. The idea of 'class consciousness', particularly of the type that can come only 'from outside', implies that it is of some importance to supply people with reasons to act for, or acquiesce in, a revolutionary initiative. But that does not stop Marxists from believing, entirely without contradiction, that revolutions happen due to the operation of causes; that existence of those causes make men prone to accept the reasons. Causes, again, would stand in the row of second order concepts. The two concepts are not exclusive or contradictory. The notion of reasons captures features of political life, which the notion of cause cannot. Conversely, the idea of cause is not merely a statistical average of the reasons men have, or their simple accumulation.

It is a common experience of those who look for political explanation that both voluntarist and determinist models soon run into difficulty. Their difficulties tend to come from opposite directions. Objectivist models of political explanation, in trying to account for crucial decisions—their forms and timing—have to admit that intentionality is often of critical significance in historical occurrence. No historical law obliged the Bolshevik party to decide to attempt a revolution on the dawn of exactly the seventh of November. Though it was just as true, that this took place within a causal horizon. Agency makes possible the translation of objective possibility into an actual occurrence. Conversely, attempted accounts of history, in purely rational terms, must get involved in problems of the reverse type. For history is, in large part, an unintended story, or intentions gone out of control. Every unintended consequence must, however, have as its logical counterpart an intended occurrence which failed to come off. Historical accounts may justifiably transcend these intents in the larger process of explaining, but they must begin from them.

I wish to suggest that Marx's model of political explanation, properly understood, tries to render this dichotomous discourse of political theory redundant. I think it is crucial for a reconstruction of Marx's theoretical project to see the three dichotomies he tried to transcend. These were the dichotomies between materialist and idealist philosophies; between positivist and hermeneutic notions of science; and between determinism and indeterminism (voluntarism) in explaining politics. These dichotomies are mutually connected.

Among the modern forms of political theory, the Leninist form of Marxism tries, most tenaciously, to avoid a relapse into traditional dichotomies. Part of the reason for this lies in the peculiar structure of this theory, the dual role in which it places its adherents. Marxists try to combine in themselves the roles other theorists usually keep distinct—the roles of observer and actor. Thus, the criterion of praxis holds such a central place in Marxist social epistemics. As historians, Marxists cannot ignore the rather well-known fact that intentions have a way of eluding the control of actors, and becoming, through unintended consequences, remarkably like natural occurrences. As actors in history with strong preferences, they must work against this eventuality, and try to stop history from doing what they know it usually does. They must try to arrange one of those rare occurrences in which intentions, of at least some actors, will bear a reasonably symmetric relation with outcomes; or in which the collective intention of a particular group can adjust effectively to this fugitive quality of events, so that even though they are not mechanically in control, they still have a general grasp over its drift. Eventually, of course, they may be in control in the mildly paradoxical sense that they may have made a revolution, but not the one they wanted. 'Successful' revolutions seem to happen that way, and 'making' them with whatever premediation, must involve a grasp of the contending logics of a variety of structures—of what they disallow, of what they leave open, of how the opportunities in the short term open and close.

This is one way of arranging an adequation between the way events occur and the conceptual structure of Marxist political theory. Events happen through a process which arranges, orders, restricts, narrows, hurries, delays—but never quite excludes choice.

The agony of the choice between determinism and indeterminism is avoided if we simply refuse to make it—by sticking, instead, to a relatively simple conceptual point. Structures can determine agency without destroying it, and agency can exist without laws of history collapsing all around us, if determination is seen as underdetermining outcomes, as an excluding, negative concept. This would save us from sliding into the two counter-intuitive worlds which constantly threaten political analyses—a world which knows no structures, or a world which knows of no choice.

7

Politics—The Dialectics of Science and Revolution in Karl Marx

RANDHIR SINGH

Taking off from the specific and limited, but very rigorously argued, exercise of Sudipta Kaviraj's paper, I shall confine my hurried response to making a few points very briefly on the interrelated issues of Marxism, politics and 'explaining politics'. Nothing original and necessarily general in nature, these points can still bear being restated here for their relevance, albeit a bit rambling, to the theme of this seminar and also to certain 'empty spaces', as it were, in Kaviraj's argument.

Let me state at the very outset that, the finer points of his argument apart, I am in sympathy with Kaviraj's main position, though I would have preferred to have it expressed in a more direct and straightforward manner. However, his is essentially an analytical, or clarificatory exercise, which offers but limited *substantive* help towards sorting out the problem of what he has chosen to describe as 'political explanation in Marxism.' (I am not even sure if this is a happy phrasing of the problem, from a strictly Marxian standpoint.)

Now, in whatever manner one describes or phrases this problem, a discussion in this area needs—among other considerations like the unfinished nature of Marx's theoretical work (especially as it affects politics), the intellectual ethos of his time, what he was arguing with or against, etc.—to take notice of two positions in Marxism, which are also integral to each other. These are Marx's absolute Promethean conception of man ('free, conscious activity is man's species character')[1] and his life-long commitment to revolution (a 'man of science . . . Marx was before all else a

---

[1] Karl Marx, *Economic and Philosophic Manuscripts of 1844*, Moscow, no date.

revolutionist'—Engels).[2] One implication is obvious. Marx's scientific project, the explanatory exercise, I suggest, fully accommodates these positions and thus leaves different areas of human activity, including politics, that are often loosely defined as 'non-economic' or 'non-material', relatively open and unpredetermined, in a manner as to be not entirely amenable to *law-like* generalisations, to *scientific explanation* as it is properly understood.

Marx's scientific project was focused on understanding the society he wanted to overthrow. It is a reconstruction of the way capitalism as a system arises, functions and develops, and prepares the necessary, though not sufficient, objective conditions for the transition to a higher, more rational form of society, a communist society. In this scientific/explanatory enterprise, Marx's method is a model of the practice of materialist dialectics. Thus, the key concepts in his social-scientific theory involve viewing society as a whole, as a *totality* (complex and differentiated, a historically specific structured inter-dependence of parts), which is marked by the predominance, in the long run, of one part within it, the economy ('the mode of production', and more precisely, the *economic structure*), and which is characterised by *contradictions* (principal or structural, and other equally specific secondary ones within and between the various parts), that account for its dynamics, its concrete *over-determined* historical development. Even as he emphasised the special role of the *economy*, 'the direct relationship of the owners of the conditions of production to the direct producers . . . which holds the inner most secret, the hidden foundation of the entire social structure'[3]—without which Marxism would be theoretically indistinguishable from any other 'sociology'—and, more specifically, sought to lay bare 'the economic law of motion' of capitalism. Marx aimed at achieving through 'successive approximations' from different perspectives, a 'mirrored' version of the concrete reality of capitalist social formation as a whole. It is part of the story of Marx's unfinished project that, concerned with all of capitalism, he lived long enough to view it only from the vantage point of capitalist economics (even that incompletely).

A fuller version or understanding would require that it be viewed

[2] Frederick Engels, 'Speech at the Graveside of Karl Marx,' in Franz Mehring, *Karl Marx: The Study of his Life*, London, 1951.
[3] Karl Marx, *Capital*, Vol. III, Chicago, 1909.

from the vantage points of other parts also, of capitalist politics, ethics, culture, etc. Therefore, Marxian explanation of politics requires that, as against the fragmented and surface studies of contemporary political science, the problems of this area be handled in such a way as to illuminate the character of the capitalist system (including its politics) as a whole, in all its structured interconnections and movements—the whole shaping and expressing itself through the parts, and the parts—even as they represent and bear the signature of the whole—constituting, in their interrelatedness, the specific unity that makes it a whole, *the* whole and no other. This goes for the study of any given social formation. For Marxism 'the truth is the whole',[4] as Hegel put it; and in Marxism, as Marx insisted, one seeks to move from 'appearance' to 'the nature of things'.[5] Such is the cardinal methodological thrust behind Marxism's social scientific enterprise, its search for dialectical knowledge as against positivist science.

This Marxist approach or perspective avoids the major *empiricist error* and the minor *holist error* characterising most contemporary writing on politics within the discipline of political science and outside. The former error, found typically on the Right, lies in grasping things only in their appearance and isolation, while the latter error, found typically on the Left, lies in missing out on the richness of the mediations that constitute the whole. Though not written as exercises in social science scholarship, one could draw attention in this connection to what are now rightly recognised as the *political* writings of Karl Marx: *The Class Struggles in France, The Civil War in France*, etc., and above all, *The Eighteenth Brumaire of Louis Bonaparte* which is a model, as it were, of the treatment of politics in Marxism. Here we have, along with a wealth of other insights, Marx's full recognition and masterly exposition, in a Marxian perspective, that is, within the objective conditions structurally constituted by the prevalent mode of production, of the realm of the political, of the class struggle at the level of politics—at a particular juncture in the history of France. Though one must add that just as Marx's proposed work on the state never came to be written, Marx's treatment of politics, as of the realm of the non-economic in general, remained largely *untheorised* by him.

[4] G.W.F. Hegel, *The Phenomenology of Mind*, Preface, London, 1949.
[5] Karl Marx, *Capital, op. cit.*

In this context, the phrase 'relative autonomy of politics', its value against economic and class reductionism apart, could be more misleading than helpful in understanding or explaining politics in a given social formation: it easily tends to give rise to mutually reinforcing empiricist and liberal-reformist errors. On the other hand, 'relative autonomy of the state' is a meaningful concept, denoting as it does the state's *possible* autonomy in a particular historical situation, from any given class or classes, economically dominant or otherwise. However, the state is not autonomous from the socio-economic structure of a class-divided society which it essentially serves. The state remains, always, the organiser of society in the interests of the class (exploitative) structure as a whole.[6]

Marx's scientific and revolutionary projects are not merely interconnected, they grow into each other, and together they put politics at the centre of social practice for our times. At least that is how Marx understood it, and one may legitimately note a divergence between Marxism as Marx himself practised it, and a certain kind of contemporary Marxist scholarship. Given a Marxist understanding of the structured nature of the totality and of the crucial role in it of 'the economy', any fundamental, revolutionary change in a society involves as a necessary, though not sufficient, condition, a changing of its economic structure, of its *real basis*—if I may, contrary to fashion and in a confession of 'orthodoxy' still use that much-maligned concept. Hence the centrality of *politics as revolution* in Marx. ('Revolution is the highest form of class struggle'.)[7] In this sense, the sense in which 'Marx was, before all else, a revolutionist', politics, not economics, has primacy in Marxism. And the obvious corollary is that in the absence of this revolutionary politics changing the structural base of society, the logic of this base shall assert itself, all politics will remain super-structural in its essential character and outcome. This is the basic, a determined and determining choice in politics, within which other, more or less important, choices occur. Such is the dialectics of the economy and politics in the social science of Karl Marx.

[6] See Hal Draper, *Karl Marx's Theory of Revolution*, Vols. I, II, III +, New York, 1977 +. This is possibly the most outstanding work to date on Marx's political theory, including his theory of the state.

[7] Karl Marx, *The Poverty of Philosophy*, London, 1941.

Viewed thus, the political as a whole is the realm of the contingent, of historical conjunctures and changing balance of social forces, a realm of *real* choices and possibilities; and for that very reason devoid of the certainties and predictabilities that politics as 'social science' seeks. Yet, as suggested earlier, these choices and possibilities arise and exist *within* the necessities and constraints of the given objective situation, above all, the economic-structural situation, which sets their context, outer limits and parameters. The economic defines, as it were, the terrain, the 'conditions of existence', the horizon of the non-economic, including the political. Though, it must again be stressed, it does not in a direct, or *reductionist* manner determine it. This determination, insofar as we must use the term, is far more complex and problematic, achieved through any number of mediations, horizontal, vertical and across each other. To put the argument differently, the superstructural instances, these parts or levels of the uneven and differentiated unity that a social formation is, along with the contradictions that characterise them, are not some immediate or epiphenomenal manifestations of the economic-structural base. On the contrary, they have, each one of them, an autonomous, irreducible, and historically specific existence. But this is an existence of dialectical, determined and determining, relationship to each other and the whole. And the dynamics of this existence, the working out of their contradictions, is ultimately and most decisively conditioned by the structural logic of the given mode of production, and the basic contradiction that constitutes it. Thus, whatever happens, every complex historical effect or outcome, is 'overdetermined' in the Althusserian sense. As Marx himself put it: 'The concrete is the product of many determinations.'[8] Furthermore, for Marxism the working out of the structural necessity, the determination by the economic, is not unique. It is essentially a *correspondence* and, therefore, variable. For example, speaking of 'the political form of the sovereignty-dependency relationship', that is, 'the specific form of the state', Marx wrote: '. . . due to innumerable different empirical circumstances, natural conditions, relationships among races (tribes, & c.), outside historical influences, etc., the same economic basis—same in terms of the main

---

[8] Karl Marx, *Grundrisse*, Introduction, Harmondsworth, 1973.

conditions—can show endless variations and gradations in the phenomenon, which can be made out only by analysis of these empirically given circumstances.'[9]

It needs to be emphasised that Marxism is social science not for peers or for policy-makers; it is social science at the service of the people, the exploited and the oppressed. And, insofar as it seeks knowledge of a social formation as a whole, and recognises the decisive importance of its 'economic basis' or structural necessity, it carries with it the imperative, the other necessity, that Marxist political practice be revolutionary. It is not for nothing that Marx insisted: 'The working class is revolutionary or it is nothing'.[10]

It is true that there are problems with the theory and practice of Marxism as social science. But it is also true that most critiques of Marxism in this area are simply nihilistic. Notwithstanding the limitations and inadequacies, even ambiguities, and the unfinished nature of his theoretical work, Marx did open up the continent of social science. And Marxism has provided better knowledge concerning the structure and dynamics of social formations, particularly the capitalist social formation, than anything bourgeois social science has to offer. Equally important is Marxism's explicit assumption about the *growth* of human knowledge. As Engels put it: 'The generations which will put us right are likely to be far more numerous than those whose knowledge we . . . are in a position to correct . . . . The stage of knowledge which we have now reached is as little final as all that have preceded it.'[11]

Pursuit of Marxism as 'science', especially during certain phases of historical development, does tend to produce a loss of revolutionary perspective, its replacement by a complacent concern with 'the historical necessity' at work in the social process. Such, for example, was the Marxism dominant in the Second International; 'irresistible . . . natural necessity' having made socialism 'something *inevitable* (Kautsky),[12] it simply turned its back on the other necessity, which is yet a free choice, namely, a revolutionary struggle for socialism. Lenin's repudiation of this Marxism was in the authentic tradition of Marx himself whose political theory and,

[9] Karl Marx, *Capital*, op. cit.
[10] Karl Marx's letter to Frederick Engels, 18 February 1865.
[11] Frederick Engels, *Anti-Duhring*, Moscow, 1954.
[12] Quoted by Lucio Colletti in 'Bernstein and the Marxism of the Second International', *From Roussau to Lenin*, London, 1972.

still more, political practice throughout his life, never countenanced such deformation of Marxism into an evolutionist, deterministic metaphysics. At other times, a valid, Marxist recognition of the 'historically progressive' character of certain phenomena (men/women, movements, economic developments, etc.) has been deemed excuse enough to eulogise and extend support to them, in a manner as to go soft on the exploiting classes, even to the point of rallying behind them in the name of Marxism. Marx would have none of such political opportunism either. It was on this issue that he, along with Engels, broke publicly with the Lassalleans in Germany and later (1881), apropos Russia, spoke with unconcealed scorn of 'Russian capitalism admirers'.[13] (Apropos India, we may today well speak of 'Indian capitalism admirers', the apologists for 'progressive capitalism', 'independent capitalist development', 'self-reliant economic growth', 'independent economic/national development', etc.) Marx was always allergic to and contemptuous of such doctrinaire or, shall we say, 'scientific' Marxism. If Marx sought to discover the necessity underlying contemporary socio-historical process, it was to establish the objective context or terrain of his political struggle, and to define its revolutionary thrust. And when he recognised the historical progressiveness of certain roles or developments, it was as *fait accompli*, without approval but with all their advantages and drawbacks, so as to make the best possible use of the new starting points or opportunities provided by them for the prosecution of his own political purpose, his uncompromising struggle aimed at overthrowing the system of exploitation and oppression that is capitalism—'progressive' or any other. In this sense, Marx's practice of science was always subject to the logic of his political position, of the choice he had already made in the fight between the people, and those who oppress and exploit them. And he had chosen to stand by the people. A political position for Marx was not a matter of scientific analysis—economic, or social, or historical. It was, always and above all, taking of sides in the on-going class war.

To put the argument in more general terms, Marxism as science, seeks knowledge of the necessity underlying the historical process for enhancing the freedom for *praxis*, for not foreclosing but liberating human practice, for free choices by men, free not in

[13] *Marx-Zasulich Correspondence* in Teodor Shomin, *Late Marx and the Russian Road*, Part II, London, 1984.

some abstract or metaphysical sense, but in the only possible *human* sense, of men choosing and acting with the fullest possible knowledge and consideration of this necessity, the objective situation or circumstances. Such is the dialectics of men and circumstances, of freedom and necessity, of revolution and science in Karl Marx. Moreover, it is of the nature of the structured and changing character of the social process that the relation between freedom and necessity, the ratio between them, varies from one period to another in the development of society. And taking everything into consideration, it seems to me that ours is preeminently an age of freedom, of revolutionary praxis. The alternative is mankind's rapid descent into another age of barbarism.

Within the framework of the reasonably adequate scientific generalisations that Marxism provides about the structure and dynamics of society (and which encompass state and politics also), and within the more limited range of the necessities and the possibilities of revolutionary and non-revolutionary practice of politics respectively, we can, given the requisite data and delicacy of analysis, still make more or less valid, historically specific, explanatory statements about what is generally seen and understood to be *politics*. (Incidentally, 'political scientists' are still having a lot of problems with defining the object of their learned attentions.) But this latter exercise possibly cannot add up to anything that can be legitimately called *science*. I have already suggested as much earlier on. To phrase it a little differently, in politics as elsewhere, men and their choices, all the diverse factors, elements, variables constituting, as it were, the subjective dimension of society, always a most vital part of social reality, are yet not calculable as the objective dimension is. In a famous passage, Marx himself drew attention to the *differing* amenability of the levels of base and *superstructure* in society to scientific treatment. Speaking of the historical transformations set off by the conflict between 'the material productive forces of society' and 'the existing relations of production,' and involving 'the economic foundation' and 'the entire immense superstructure,' Marx wrote: 'In considering such transformations, a distinction should always be made between the material transformation of the economic conditions of production, which can be determined with the precision of natural science, and the legal, political, religious aesthetic or philosophic—in short, ideological forms in which men become conscious of this conflict and fight it out.'¹⁴ Obviously, this fight and its outcome cannot be determined 'with the precision of natural science.' Elsewhere, even as he insists that 'the history of all hitherto existing society is the history of class struggle,' Marx immediately points out that this struggle 'each time ended, either in a revolutionary reconstitution of society at large, or in the common ruin of the contending classes.'¹⁵ There are, thus, no promises of inevitability or guarantees of victory in Karl Marx's politics, only *real* possibilities and *strong* probabilities. Men and women choose and act, but the outcome, the outcome of concrete historical class struggles, is not predetermined, cannot be predicted in advance, least of all with the certainty of natural science. Thus understood, the historical process, in a most meaningful sense, remains open, relatively undetermined. It shall be *ultimately* determined by the activity of men in pursuit of *their* purposes, an activity in which men continually seek to materialise their freedom. And it is quite possible and probable that some time, in the course of this determination, politics itself shall wither away, and with it, the need for explaining politics, scientifically or otherwise.

All this may sound rather dismal to those in the profession who, subject to the 'functional rationality' permeating the discipline, are committed to the search for 'a science of politics'. But do we really want it to be otherwise? I think not. Especially so if *freedom* is indeed 'the essence of man' and if our prime commitment is for man, as indeed was the proud and passionate commitment of Marx, who spoke of 'the categorical imperative to overthrow all conditions in which man is a humiliated, enslaved, despised and rejected being';¹⁶ who laughed at 'the so-called "practical" men with their wisdom', and wrote: 'If one chose to be an ox, one could turn one's back on the sufferings of mankind and look after one's own skin';¹⁷ who, writing to an old friend, expressed his contempt for the philistines who 'consider people like you and me immature fools who all this time have not been cured of their evolutionary

---

¹⁴ Karl Marx, *A Contribution to the Critique of Political Economy*, Preface, Calcutta, no date.

¹⁵ Karl Marx and Frederick Engels, *Manifesto of the Communist Party*, Moscow, 1948.

¹⁶ Karl Marx, A Contribution to the Critique of Hegel's Philosophy of Right, Introduction, in *Early Writings*, London, 1975.

¹⁷ Karl Marx's letter to S. Meyer, 30 April 1867.

fantasies';[18] and who, even as he argued that while 'people make their own history . . . they do not make it just as they please,'[19] and always warned against utopianism and Blanquism in the movement, yet stood up magnificently in defence of the Paris communards for 'storming heavens,'[20] and scorned the socialists who 'keep themselves within the limits of the logically presumable and of the permissible by the police . . . .'[21]

I would like to conclude by pointing out, for whatever it is worth at this stage of the extreme 'specialisation', 'professionalisation' and 'vocationalisation' of the social science disciplines, that it is this commitment that gives its special quality to the scholarship of Karl Marx. Typical of this 'man of science', is his response to the news of the great run his theories were then having in Czarist Russia. On December 14, 1882, Karl Marx, old, sick and dying, wrote thus to his daughter Laura Lafargue: 'Nowhere is my success more delightful to me; it gives me the satisfaction that I *damage* a power which, besides England, is the true bulwark of the old society' (italics added).

Yes, *damage* is the word. How much of even Marxist scholarship can claim this quality for itself today?[22]

---

[18] Karl Marx's letter to J.P. Becker, 26 February 1862.
[19] Karl Marx, *The Eighteenth Brumaire of Louis Bonaparte*, Moscow, 1948.
[20] Karl Marx's letter to L. Kugelmann, 12 April 1871; *The Civil War in France*, Moscow, 1971.
[21] Karl Marx, *Critique of the Gotha Programme*, Moscow, 1947.
[22] It is part of the sociology of Marxism that in recent years, so often, it has come to be reduced to a subject for academic study in the universities with strong fragmentist, scholastic and theoreticist deformations, or, as in the countries of 'actually existing socialism' and even elsewhere, to a legitimising ideology.

8

Weber, Gramsci and Capitalism

ASOK SEN

> **Not summer's bloom** lies ahead of us, but rather a polar night of icy darkness and hardness . . . . Politics is a strong and slow boring of hard boards. It takes both passion and perspective. Certainly all historical experience confirms the truth—that man would not have attained the possible unless time and again he had reached out for the impossible. But to do that a man must be a leader, and not only a leader but a hero as well, in a very sober sense of the word. And even those who are neither leaders nor heroes must arm themselves with that steadfastness of heart which can brave even the crumbling of all hopes. This is necessary right now, or else men will not be able to attain that which is possible today. Only he has the calling for politics who is sure that he shall not crumble when the world from his point of view is too stupid or too base for what he wants to offer. Only he who in the face of all this can say 'In spite of all!' has the calling for politics.
>
> <div align="right">Max Weber, <i>Politics as a Vocation</i>, 1918</div>

> The crisis we are passing through today is perhaps the worst revolutionary crisis . . . . This new tactic is being tried out in the ways and forms to be expected of a class of chatterboxes, sceptics and corrupt dealers. The succession of events . . . with

Acknowledgements: While bearing sole responsibility for the views and analysis presented in this paper, the writer is grateful to Partha Chatterjee and Barun De, his colleagues in the Centre, to Rudrangshu Mukherjee of the Department of History, Calcutta University, and Suren Munshi of the Indian Institute of Management, Calcutta, for their comments and suggestions.

An earlier draft of this paper was published in *Social Scientist*, New Delhi, January 1985.

all their journalistic, oratorical, theatrical and vulgar echoes . . . was like the projection into reality of . . . Monkey-People . . . . Aimless corruption and ruin . . . . The Monkey-People make news, not history . . . . Although these people have damaged the working class and strengthened reaction . . . when the dialectic of the class struggle has been internalised and within every individual consciousness the new man, in his every act, has to fight the 'bourgeois' lying in ambush . . . the evil is not decisive: men of goodwill will still have a boundless field to cultivate again and cause to bear fruit handsomely . . . . If everything lies in ruins, then everything has to be done again.

Antonio Gramsci. Excerpts from
Political Writings,
September 1920-January 1921

Weber on Capitalism

Weber's analysis of the relation between the protestant ethic and the spirit of capitalism is, in some senses, akin to a project of hermeneutics.[1] It is a significant example of the application of the Dilthey-Rickert approach to an understanding of the spirit of industrial capitalism. Dilthey distinguished between the sciences of nature and the sciences of the spirit, the subject of the latter being social reality. For him, positivism offered no adequate insight into the nature of society. The central issue was related to the Kantian question of uniting logic and ethics, the areas which involved a separation in the realm of pure reason. Dilthey emphasised the importance of analysing consciousness as the only means by which one could proceed from merely egoistic experience to an understanding of the unique spirit characterising each specific form of human culture arising in history.

Rickert maintained that there were two methods in science. The natural sciences dealt with materials which are the same everywhere and which could, therefore, be comprehended in universal laws covering all space and time. This is the method of generalised abstraction. The other method is one of individualised abstraction

---

[1] Ephraim Fischoff, 'The History of a Controversy' in Robert W. Green, ed., *Protestantism and Capitalism—The Weber Thesis and Its Critics*, Boston, 1959, pp. 113–14.

which Rickert considered to be appropriate for the historical sciences. It enables us to understand (*Verstehen*, i.e., 'understanding') the relations between phenomena and moral values, the nexuses most pertinent for comprehending the infinite variety of human culture, 'each one of which has to be grasped by a *particular* understanding of its own uniqueness. What is thus grasped is a *life style*, a special form of human living, its modes of thought, its ethical norms, its aesthetic achievements.'[2]

Thus, Rickert's methodological observations and Dilthey's search for the 'unique spirit' are combined in what is mentioned above as the 'Dilthey-Rickert' approach of Weber. My reference to hermeneutics should be subject to several qualifications if we bring in the claims and counter-claims of the empirical method, scientistic knowledge and hermeneutical cognition. More relevant for our present theme is the point that 'Dilthey's main contribution to social scientific thought consists, of course, in his exposition of the method of Verstehen in the "historical Geisteswissenschaften" which occupied Max Weber's methodological reflections and which provided the model for all subsequent approaches concerned with the understanding of "action".'[3]

Weber aims at exploring the factors which motivate and sustain the capitalist system. An exposition was necessary which would bear upon the rich congruency of such diverse aspects of a culture as religion and economics.[4] Neither in *The Protestant Ethic*, nor in his *General Economic History*, did Weber postulate a theory of generalised historical evolution. He was not proving a causal relation between protestantism and capitalism. His main concern lay in an investigation of the influence of certain religious ideas on the emergence of the ethos of an economic system. This should be clear from the following observations in *The Protestant Ethic*:

> We have no intention whatever of maintaining that the spirit of capitalism . . . could only have arisen as the result of certain effects of the Reformation, or even that capitalism as an economic system is a creation of the Reformation. In view of the tremendous confusion of interdependent influences between

[2] John Lewis, *Max Weber and Value-free Sociology*, London, 1975, p. 29.
[3] Josef Bleicher, *Contemporary Hermeneutics—Hermeneutics as Method, Philosophy and Critique*, London, 1980, p. 26.
[4] Ephraim Fischoff, *op. cit.*, p. 113.

the material basis, the forms of social and political organisation, and the ideas current in the time of the Reformation, we can only proceed by investigating whether and at what points certain correlations between forms of religious belief and practical ethics can be worked out.[5]

And again:

Asceticism was in turn influenced in its development and its character by the totality of social conditions, especially economic. The modern man is in general, even with the best will, unable to give religious ideas a significance for culture and national character which they deserve. But it is, of course, not my aim to substitute for a one-sided materialistic an equally one-sided spiritualistic causal interpretation of culture and history.[6]

Weber's point of arrival rests on the recognition that the elements which combine to make a society are too complex and too numerous to yield any neat formula for its causal comprehension. Further, an 'action is "social" insofar as its subjective meaning takes account of the behaviour of others and is thereby oriented in its course.'[7] Identification of human purposes and motives is inseparable from our understanding of social structure and events. Moreover, the potential for change and transformation calls for an understanding of things which have not yet occurred and do not yet exist as actual events. Thus, it becomes impossible to have a scientific system inductively based on the observed frequency of the same causes and the same effects. For Weber, then, purely economic factors were indispensable, but not, by themselves, sufficient for understanding the nature of capitalism. One has to take account of 'subjective factors' for a causally sufficient explanation. The subjective factors are shaped by ideas nurturing special psychic traits. Such ideas act complementarily with habitual social conduct, to produce the personality types with a distinct orientation towards certain determinate 'maxims' or rules. The subjective meaning will

---

[5] Max Weber, *The Protestant Ethic and the Spirit of Capitalism* (Talcott Parsons, ed.), London, 1950, pp. 91–92.
[6] Ibid., p. 183.
[7] Max Weber, *Economy and Society* (Guenther Roth and Claus Wittich eds.), Vol. I, Part I, Berkeley/London, 1978, p. 4.

be called valid 'if the orientation to such maxims includes, no matter what actual extent, the recognition that they are binding on the actor or the corresponding action constitutes a desirable model for him to imitate.'[8]

Considering social sciences as historical, and admitting the crucial importance of subjective influences on historical causality, Weber faced the task of clarifying the most significant specifics of a social system. The 'ideal type' device was used for constructing numerous elements of reality into logical and meaningful categories. It reminds us of Marx's statement: 'In the analysis of economic forms, neither microscopes nor chemical reagents are of use. The force of abstraction must replace both.'[9] The 'ideal type' abstraction consists in what Weber indicated 'by the one-sided accentuation of one or more points of view and by the synthesis of a great many diffuse, discrete, more or less present and occasionally absent concrete individual phenomena, which are arranged according to those one-sidedly emphasised viewpoints into a unified analytical construct.'[10]

There remains the question of the elements constituting such abstraction, such accentuation and one-sidedness. It cannot but be related to an investigator's view of the problematic, to the selection of the essential questions which an historian and a social scientist must always make, 'since they necessarily approach reality from certain points of view which are determined by their value-orientation.'[11] Such pre-suppositions do not, by themselves, ensure conceptual precision. This is where the function of the 'ideal type' comes to have critical significance. It does not imply anything good or noble. Nor does it indicate an extremely novel method of analysis. An 'ideal type' meets the purpose usually served by a hypothesis, or a model, to explain a social system in terms of its central agencies and relations, its intentions and activities. Though not exactly exemplified in reality, an 'ideal type' helps to clarify the action parameters and also the elements of human motivation absorbed in them which govern the significant causal processes of

---

[8] Max Weber, *The Theory of Social and Economic Organisation* (Talcott Parsons, ed.), New York, 1966, p. 124.

[9] Karl Marx, *Capital*, Vol. 1, Preface to the First Edition, 1867.

[10] Julien Freund, *The Sociology of Max Weber*, New York, 1968, p. 60, from E.A. Shils and H.A. Finch, 'Max Weber on the Methodology of Social Sciences'.

[11] Ibid., p. 61.

society. Such is this tool of placing in focus the social phenomenon and its full meaning.

In specifying the various components of capitalism, Weber pointed to the division between property-owning capitalists and property-less workers. He also highlighted the exclusive opportunities the owning class secures for exploiting services on the market, and for control over the means of production, capital funds and marketable commodities. The workers are deprived of all such opportunities. Their wages are kept at the minimum; they can have no other choice, since the system eliminates their occupation of own plots of cultivable land and also the possibility of their craft-work with own tools. To sum up, the essential conditions are:

1. Unrestricted struggle between autonomous economic groups in the market.
2. Money economy.
3. Formally free labour.
4. Unrestricted market freedom.
5. Expropriation of the workers from the means of production.
6. Individual ownership.[12]

In all this, however, Weber sees neither the elements of contradiction leading to economic crises, nor the role of class struggle acting for the supersession of the system. For him, capitalism is based on rational pursuit of wealth and it

> is present wherever the industrial provision for the needs of the group is carried out by the method of enterprise, irrespective of what need is involved. More specifically, rational capitalistic establishment is one with capital accounting, that is, an establishment which determines its income-yielding power by calculation according to the method of modern book-keeping and the striking of a balance.[3]

One commentator rightly points out that 'Weber's pious reverence for the ledger makes it the sacred book of the religion of making

---

[12] Max Weber, *Economy and Society, op. cit.*, Vol. 1, Part 2, pp. 107–09, 161–64; *Theory of Social and Economic Organisation, op. cit.*, pp. 246–50; Max Weber, *General Economic History* (Frank H. Knight, trans.), New York, 1961, pp. 207–09.

[13] *General Economic History, op. cit.*, p. 207.

money. When one first reads the above passage the sudden descent from the sublime to the banal comes with a slight shock—"book-keeping and the striking of a balance".[14] I have noted already how Weber cautioned against overestimating the role of protestantism in the genesis of capitalist society. But his presupposition about the 'ideal type' of capitalist rationality, which Weber also regarded as the value inherent in the subjective choices of the system, placed the highest premium on the idea of Calvinist calling, as 'not a condition in which the individual is born, but a strenuous and exacting enterprise to be chosen by himself, and to be pursued with a sense of religious responsibility.'[15] The emphasis that such 'calling' places on this-worldly asceticism fits with the capitalist pursuit of profit for accumulation.

Thus, the spiritual affinity of a particular world-view with the capitalist economic practice and its achievement-orientation, was central to Weber's arguments about bourgeois rationality. He applied the distinction between 'traditionalism' and the spirit of capitalism, not only to capitalist entrepreneurs and their business-ethic, but also to workers. Traditionalism is characterised by workers who prefer less work to more pay, who seek maximum comfort and minimum exertion, and who lack the ability and willingness to adapt themselves to new methods of work.[16] Weber elaborated a typology of gainful pursuits, to focus on the nature of economic activity thriving on long-range capital investments, application of science-based technology and improvements in productivity. Those were the directions of a rational pursuit of economic gain, distinct from purely speculative profiteering.[17]

But, whether he idealised the aspiring bourgeoisie or revealed the innermost subjective motivations of capitalism, Weber admitted in the concluding pages of *The Protestant Ethic*:

> Since asceticism undertook to remodel the world and to work out its ideals in the world, material goods have gained an increasing and finally an inexorable power over the lives of men

---

[14] John Lewis, *op. cit.*, p. 70.

[15] *The Protestant Ethic*, *op. cit.*, Introduction by R.H. Tawney, p. 2.

[16] Reinhard Bendix, *Max Weber—An Intellectual Portrait*, London, 1969, pp. 51–52.

[17] *Economy and Society*, *op. cit.*, Vol. 1, Part 1, pp. 161–66; *General Economic History*, *op. cit.*, pp. 230–33.

as at no previous period in history. Today the spirit of religious asceticism—whether finally, who knows?—has escaped from the cage. But victorious capitalism, since it rests on mechanical foundations, needs its support no longer. The rosy blush of its laughing heir, the Enlightenment, seems also to be irretrievably fading, and the idea of duty in one's calling prowls about in our lives like the ghost of dead religious beliefs.[18]

Further, *General Economic History* concluded on the following note:

> The religious root of modern economic humanity is dead; today the concept of the calling is a *caput mortuum* in the world . . . . Economic ethics arose against the background of the ascetic ideal; now it has been stripped of its religious import. It was possible for the working class to accept its lot as long as the promise of eternal happiness could be held out to it. When this consolation fell away it was inevitable that those strains and stresses should appear in economic activity which since then have grown so rapidly.[19]

Such statements notwithstanding, the historical prospects for transcending capitalism had no place in Weber's theory. His tone remained rather pathetic, 'trying to understand the meaning of all existences, individual or collective, endured or chosen, without concealing either the weight of social necessities pressing on us or the ineluctable obligation to make decisions which can never be scientifically demonstrated.'[20]

The issues become more complicated, as Weber proceeds to explain the structure of legitimate capitalist domination in terms of rationality. Among his three 'ideal types' of power, rational domination abides by belief in legal ordinances and the legality of those who administer power. Weber considered such legal authority the essential element of the modern rational state. Apart from bureaucracy, parliamentary administration and all sorts of collegial authority would be covered by this type. The idea of rational

---

[18] *The Protestant Ethic*, op. cit., pp. 181–82.
[19] *General Economic History*, op. cit., p. 270.
[20] Raymond Aron, *Main Currents in Sociological Thought*, Vol. 2, Harmondsworth 1968, p. 259.

action in relation to a goal is inextricably connected with the concept of rational domination. The other two types, traditional and charismatic, are associated with sentiment and emotion respectively. Weber did not, however, rule out the possibility of the mixing of types in particular kind of real authority.[21]

As observed by Weber, bureaucracy promotes expertise, connects job security with regular and consistent performance of duties which are clearly defined, builds a coherent system of authority and subordination, and ensures the right of the superior to regulate the work of his subordinates.[22] Given the Weberian propositions about capitalist rationality, such a system unceasingly strives for creating conditions which would allow a maximum of productivity and a maximum degree of efficiency. Correlatively, the further advance of capitalism was inevitably tied up with the rise of ever more efficient bureaucracies, and an even greater degree of formal rational organisation at all levels of social interaction.[23]

No doubt, the political conditions of Germany in the post-Bismarckian era influenced Weber's formulations regarding the role of bureaucracy in the expansion of industrial capitalism. The unification of Germany under the leadership of Prussia was attained at a premium on the latter's semi-feudal autocracy resting upon Junker landlordism, the civil service bureaucracy and the officer corps. In 1848, Marx characterised the bourgeoisie of his own fatherland as being 'without initiative, without faith in itself'.[24] About half a century later in 1895, Weber felt:

> *The threatening thing* in our situation . . . is that the bourgeois classes, as the bearers of the power-interests of the nation, seem to wilt away, while there are no signs that the workers are beginning to show the maturity to replace them. The danger does not lie with the masses. It is not a question of the *economic* position of the ruled, but rather the *political* qualification of the

---

[21] H.H. Gerth and C. Wright Mills, *From Max Weber: Essays in Sociology*, New York, 1958, Ch. VIII; Wolfgang J. Mommsen, *The Age of Bureaucracy—Perspectives on the Political Sociology of Max Weber*, Oxford, 1974, Ch. III.
[22] Gerth and Mills, *op. cit.*, p. 196.
[23] Ibid., pp. 232–44; Mommsen, *op. cit.*, p. 57.
[24] Karl Marx, 'The Bourgeoisie and the Counter Revolution', in *The Revolutions of 1848*, Harmondsworth, 1973, p. 194.

ruling and *ascending* classes which is the ultimate issue in the social-political problem.[25]

Perhaps this explains why Weber needed an 'ideal type' bureaucracy to fulfil, what he considered, the rational conditions of capitalist development.

One can note a deep tension in Weber's writings, as his theoretical system ends up, in what was characterised by him, as a 'cage of bondage' for men who were supposed to act freely and rationally in keeping with the Weberian 'ideal types'. A process of rationalisation working in society was built into Weber's system, point by point, as the essential condition of capitalism. The capitalist dynamics, its internal contradictions and conflicts, led to consequences which, apart from the questions of exploitation and misery of the multitude, could not even be reconciled with the rationale for pursuing more and more profits. As noted already, Weber himself observed that 'the idea of duty in one's calling prowls about in our lives like the ghost of dead religious beliefs.'

For Weber, again, bureaucratic domination results from the requirements of the division of labour, of technological and professional expertise, which are indispensable for the implementation of rational technology in production. This is the point Weber uses to argue that socialist transformation would not do away with bureaucratisation. Bureaucratic domination corresponds to an inescapable techno-economic law, in Weber's scheme of things. Only this can ensure a full implementation of all the elements listed under Weber's type of pure legal rule; they are now 'administered by an almighty bureaucracy in accordance with a closely knit network of laws and regulations of a purely formalistic nature, which would leave little or no space for individually oriented creative action.'[26] To obviate extreme oppression and routine stagnation under such systems, Weber, of course, admitted the possibility of their fusion with some charismatic elements, namely, his concept of plebiscitarian democracy.

---

[25] Anthony Giddens, *Politics and Sociology in the Thought of Max Weber*, London, 1972, p. 17. The excerpt is cited in translation from 'Gesamelte politische Schriften', the standard collected edition of Weber's political writings.

[26] Mommsen, *op. cit.*, p. 82.

Weber's own portrayal of such a state of things was dark enough:

> No one knows who will live in this cage in the future, or whether at the end of this tremendous development entirely new prophets will arise, or there will be a great rebirth of old ideas and ideals, or, if neither, mechanised petrification, embellished with a sort of convulsive self-importance. For the last stage of this cultural development it might well be truly said: 'Specialists without spirit, sensualists without heart; this nullity imagines that it has attained a level of civilisation never before achieved.'[27]

Weber refrained, however, from 'judgements of value and faith' and could not perceive the 'spirit' of any civilisation beyond capitalism. To the extent Weber started from the conviction that social actions expressed a deeper reality of subjective intentions and ethic, he was trying to adopt an emanative approach in his understanding of the capitalist system. This was evident in his concern for the 'spirit', and also in the construction of his 'ideal types' of rational behaviour. The rest of Weber's system takes recourse to analytic logic (empiricism, rationalism, positivism), and offers causal explanations of human actions without adding anything to their external aspect.[28]

Moreover, Weber used reason to close and enclose the world in a rigid system of capitalism working for its profits. And science was supposed to ensure that the world would be tidied up in order that reason could prevail in the 'ethical' pursuit of private profits. This world had its classes, strata, institutions of domination and modes of expropriation. But all this is subsumed under rational calculation, which shapes into a kind of economic determinism to transform 'what previously was only a "means" (rational pursuit of gain in a specialised vocation) into the "end" of human activity.'[29] There is, indeed, an element of paradox in this journey from the calling of this-worldly service to God, to an inexorable economic determinism expressed as follows:

---

[27] *The Protestant Ethic, op. cit.,* p. 182.
[28] Lucien Goldmann, *The Human Sciences and Philosophy,* London, 1970, p. 125.
[29] Anthony Giddens, *Capitalism and Modern Social Theory—An Analysis of Writings of Marx, Durkheim and Max Weber,* Cambridge, 1971, p. 241.

> This masterless slavery in which capitalism enmeshes the worker or the debtor is only debatable ethically as an institution. In principle, the personal conduct of those who participate, on either side of the rulers or of the ruled, is not morally debatable, as such conduct is essentially prescribed by objective situations. If they do not conform, they are threatened by economic bankruptcy which would, in every respect, be useless.[30]

Capitalism can work, but not without its satanic wheels.

While Weber's 'ideal types' are all immersed in protestant ethic and bourgeois consciousness, his method of analysis rules out the theory that contradictions within capitalism generate the forces to resolve such contradictions. All his concern for religious ethic notwithstanding, Weber bases himself on the premise of human individuals as self-contained atoms, and finds no clues to collective consciousness as something more than an arithmetical sum of autonomous and independent unities. His 'ideal types' are not understood in terms of a dialectical interaction within the totality of relations, the whole and its parts. And so, Weber's categories did not enable him to identify the potential for superseding capitalism, even though he once declared that 'the fact that the maximum of formal rationality in capital accounting is possible only where the workers are subjected to domination by entrepreneurs, is a further specific element of substantive irrationality in the modern economic order.'[31]

From Weber to Gramsci

We have pointed to the paradox and pessimism of Max Weber's analysis. The strength of his position lies, no doubt, in not abstracting the socio-economic experience of capitalism from its basic value-system. He knew capitalism as he found it, and also in terms

[30] Gerth and Mills, *op. cit.*, p. 58. Also *Economy and Society, op. cit.*, Vol. 2, p. 1186, where the translation reads as follows:

> From an ethical viewpoint, this 'masterless slavery' to which capitalism subjects the worker or the mortgagee is questionable only as an institution. However, in principle, the behaviour of any individual cannot be so questioned, since it is prescribed in all relevant aspects by objective situations. The penalty for non-compliance is extinction, and this would not be helpful in any way.

[31] *Economy and Society, op. cit.*, Vol. 1, Part 1, p. 138.

of the absolute presuppositions inherent in the bourgeois ethic. Weber made it clear that the overthrow of capitalism would require a change in the very ethos of human social action which made sense to individuals in terms of their belief in an 'oughtness'. He stressed the correspondence between a set of moral principles and a particular social and historical context. In his appraisal of the Marxian theory, however, Weber took a position assailing economic determinism and the so-called prediction of 'increased pauperisation', criticisms which would not apply to Marx's system, except in its vulgarised and mechanistic versions.

For Marx, the way to founding a new mode of production depends on its validity as an entire social alternative. The faculty of a class to become really revolutionary and eventually the ruling power, in society and state, has to emerge and achieve hegemony in this process of validation. The building of such hegemony comprises all the dimensions of human social living, not only the instruments of enriching a particular class, but also the whole complex of advancing social production, ideas and ethos, whereby the gains of a particular class can acquire the leverage of historical progress.

This concept of progress does not hang on a purely metaphysical belief. It is based on the comprehension of history as a significant movement which is subject, in its cunning passages, to aborted opportunities, reversals, or even denials, but also provides the criterion by which production forces and production relations could be reorganised in terms of a perspective envisaging the end of all exploitation of man by man and the human social preference for life, health and sustenance rather than death, disease and alienation. All this is man's making and unmaking, and relates human consciousness to the course of history. While progress is possible and necessary in history, it cannot be realised without conscious human action.

Another part of Weber's diagnosis has more lasting relevance for our understanding of social transformation through the present century. As noted already, Weber argued that socialism would provide no solution for the problem of bureaucratic domination. While most of Weber's observations had a necessary connection with his logic of the consistent working out of the bourgeois ethic, increasing bureaucratisation was caused by the needs of developed industrialism which, in Weber's view, would become stronger under socialism. Indeed, Weber's perspective for the future, which he set forth in reaction to bureaucratic absolutism in imperial Germany, amounts to what has been called an 'early formulation of George Orwell's 1984':

> It is horrible to think that the world could one day be filled with nothing but those little cogs, little men clinging to little jobs and striving towards bigger ones—a state of affairs which is to be seen once more, as in the Egyptian records, playing an ever-increasing part in the spirit of our present administrative system, and especially of its offspring, the students. This passion for bureaucracy is enough to drive one to despair. It is as if in politics . . . we were deliberately to become men who need 'order' and nothing but order, who become nervous and cowardly if for one moment this order wavers, and helpless if they are torn away from their total incorporation in it. That the world should know no man but these: it is in such an evolution that we are already caught up, and the great question is therefore not how we can promote and hasten it, but what can we oppose to this machinery in order to keep a portion of mankind free from this parcelling out of the soul, from this supreme mastery of the bureaucratic way of life.[32]

And Weber's premonition is confirmed in what responsible and committed sociology of our day considers to be a major problem: 'I do not know the answer to the question of political irresponsibility in our time or to the cultural and political question of the Cheerful Robot. But is it not clear that no answers will be found unless these problems are at least confronted?'[33]

Weber's observations cannot belie the Marxist understanding of capitalist contradictions and their revolutionary supersession in history. This is not to ignore the changes which result from new technological revolutions, the increase in the weightage of skilled personnel among the working class, and the expansion of the service sector. No less important are the points of coalescence

---

[32] Reinhard Bendix, *op. cit.*, p. 464. The excerpt is quoted from J.P. Mayer, *Max Weber and German Politics*, London, 1943, pp. 127–28. These remarks were made in the course of a debate at the convention of the *Verein fur Sozialpolitik*, in 1909. Bendix makes the comparison with George Orwell.

[33] C. Wright Mills, *The Sociological Imagination*, 1970, p. 195.

between bourgeois state power and the world of oligopolies in the stage of state monopoly capital. There is also the permanent arms economy which uses up, rather, which squanders, an enormous amount of resources that capitalism cannot direct towards the production of 'instruments of life'.[34] Such are the ways and means of late capitalism to concede a part of the trade union demands and to make up for the extremes of unemployment with a growing tertiary sector and chronic inflation.[35]

But post-Keynesianism and the so-called 'supply-side' masks notwithstanding, capitalism shows little evidence of becoming free from recurrent recessions and the persistence of considerable unemployment, even at the peak of each cyclical boom. In its international dimension, the experience is even more sinister when one takes account of the endless squabbles over common or exclusive markets, and of the economics and politics of neo-colonial rampage in the poor countries of the world. Thus, even in conditions of maximum 'prosperity' under late capitalism, the capitalist contradiction between private property and social production still proves insoluble within the structural limits of that system.[36]

The issues are more complex when we take up the question of the proletariat becoming a 'class for itself', of its clarity of awareness and conscious commitment to change the world. For the Marx of *The Communist Manifesto*, the inexorable contradictions and conscious revolutionary action by the exploited would come together, since he had reasons to assert that capitalism did lack even the competence 'to assure an existence to its slave within his slavery.' But capitalism today engineers an economy of armaments and waste, to give to its workers 'the place of the slave within his slavery,' a process aiming to reduce the working people to the atrophy of Marcuse's 'one-dimensional man'. This has a critical bearing on the pattern and orientation of the working masses, including, among them, the new middle class variant of professional workers and white-collar employees.

Such are the historical circumstances that must have influenced

---

[34] Shigeto Tsuru, 'Has Capitalism Changed?' in Shigeto Tsuru, ed., *Has Capitalism Changed*, Tokyo, 1961, p. 37.

[35] Ernest Mandel, *Late Capitalism* (Joris Do Bres, trans.), London, 1980, Chs. 12, 13, 17.

[36] Ibid.

the state of things, which Perry Anderson interprets in his survey of developments in 'Western Marxism' since 1920:

> No matter how otherwise heteroclite, they share one fundamental emblem: a common and latent pessimism. All the major departures or developments of substance within this tradition are distinguished from the classical heritage of historical materialism by the darkness of their implications or conclusions . . . . The confidence and optimism of the founders of historical materialism, and of their successors, progressively disappeared. Virtually every one of the significant new themes in the intellectual muster of this epoch reveals the same diminution of hope and loss of certainty.[37]

No less pertinent are Perry Anderson's observations regarding the historical context:

> Born from the failure of proletarian revolutions in the advanced zones of European capitalism after the First World War, it developed within an ever increasing scission between socialist theory and working-class practice. The gulf between the two, originally opened up by the imperialist isolation of the Soviet State, was institutionally widened and fixed by the bureaucratisation of the USSR and of the Comintern under Stalin.[38]

We should then consider the emphasis that Antonio Gramsci placed on the struggle for class hegemony, for cultural and moral predominance prior to the capture of state power by the working class. For the theme of this paper, some of Gramsci's ideas become all the more relevant because of the apparent similarity between his emphasis on the superstructure and what is often understood as the primacy of religious and cultural factors in Weber's interpretation of history. This has to bear upon the different interpretations of the base-superstructure of relationship.

Further, with reference to the problems of retarded working class consciousness and Perry Anderson's picture of pessimism, we must remember Gramsci's own experience of the failure of the

[37] Perry Anderson, *Considerations on Western Marxism*, London, 1979, pp. 88–89.
[38] Ibid., p. 92.

proletarian revolution in the countries of advanced capitalism, the emergence of the Fascist state, the 'New Deal' type reforms of capitalism from above, following the world slump of 1929, and the aggravation of contradictions in the course of socialist construction in the Soviet Union. No elaborate discussion of Gramsci's thought is intended in this paper. Let us simply focus upon the central issues of building socialist counter-hegemony under conditions of late capitalism and also in the more underdeveloped stages of contemporary history. In view of the nature of the problem I have already stated, such tasks not only mean the posing of a real historical antithesis to Weber's premonition, but are also indispensable for a reversal of the mood of pessimism which concerns many Marxists like Perry Anderson, and, which again is implied in the analysis of a thinker who is not anti-Marxist by calling or commitment: 'Bureaucratic terror and the cult of personality are just another expression of the relation between the constituent dialectic and the constituted dialectic, that is to say, of the necessity that a common action as such (through the multiple differentiation of tasks) should practically reflect upon itself in the untranscendable form of an individual unit.'[39]

For Gramsci, hegemonic power is not only coercion, but also 'directing' by the token of consent obtained from the governed. Civil society defines the sphere where such a 'directing' role is achieved. It encompasses significant ethico-cultural dimensions which are not amenable to adequate understanding in terms of the economic factor alone. This is not to ignore the criterion of advancing production forces, since 'this consent is "historically" caused by the prestige (and consequent confidence) which the dominant group enjoys because of its position and function in the world of production.'[40]

The political struggle of the proletariat and its party has to aim, therefore, at an alternative hegemony. The question of social hegemony had its vital place, both in earlier Marxian writings and in Lenin's statement of the total task, in *What Is To Be Done?* The latter embraced its own specifics of tactics, strategy and organisation in the historical context of Czarist Russia, typifying state

[39] Jean-Paul Sartre, *Critique of Dialectical Reason* (Alan Sheridan-Smith, trans.), London, 1982, p. 662.
[40] Quintin Hoare and Geoffrey Nowell Smith, eds., trans., *Selections from the Prison Notebooks of Antonio Gramsci*, London, 1971, p. 12.

omnipotence and immature civil society. The importance of ethico-political and cultural factors was writ large over the entire evolution of Gramsci's politics and philosophy of praxis. For example, while focusing upon worker's productivism in the Turin factory councils, Gramsci was never simply advocating improved industrial management per se. He strove to initiate the factory councils for critical ethico-political mediations of proletarian values, and a new cultural totality in the making.

It should be clear to communist orthodoxy that Gramsci was moving with historical reality by not placing the entire emphasis on the contradiction between production forces and production relations, or, in other words, on capitalist production relations being outpaced by the advance of production forces. In his comments on 'Americanism and Fordism', Gramsci clarified the directions of advanced capitalism to newer manoeuvres of assimilating wage-workers to 'scientific' management and advancing productivity.[41] Such tendencies have assumed a multiplicity of forms in the development of capitalism since the Second World War. Consequently, the development of productive forces is combined with an enormous growth of differential practices within the working class. These are the processes which fragment and parcellise the proletariat under the sway of advancing technology. Moreover, an expanding volume of 'institutionalised waste'—exemplified by the growth of the tertiary sector securing cultural domination of capital and its commodity fetishism—is realised with the support of huge profits from technological advance.[42]

All this coincides with increasing state intervention in the social sphere. State monopoly capitalism leads to extensive politicisation of social conflicts. By its work in the economy, the state transforms politics and influences the class structure and its dialectic. Gramsci characterises as 'passive revolution', these tendencies and their contribution to forming a mass consensus in favour of capitalism. It amounts to a restructuring of capitalism through state initiative to consolidate bourgeois domination by means of new forms of mass integration.[43] Against this complex of capitalist domination,

---

[41] Ibid., pp. 277–318.

[42] Shigeto Tsuru, ed., *op. cit.*, Ernest Mandel, *op. cit.*; Harry Braverman, *Labour and Monopoly Capital*, New York and London, 1974.

[43] Hoare and Smith, *op. cit.*, pp. 277–318. Also, Anne Showstack Sassoon, *Gramsci's Politics*, London, 1980, pp. 204–17.

Gramsci's concept of hegemony, his 'war of position'[44] to evolve a 'historical bloc',[45] and his emphasis on ethico-cultural mediation in civil society, sets the political task of the communist struggle in its totality.

While Gramsci's 'philosophy of praxis' is obviously more relevant to the historical context of advanced capitalism, it is noteworthy that:

> . . . . so far from being marginal, the concept of passive revolution as a critical corollary of the Marxian problematic of transition possibly allows for a new, global interpretation of the involvement of politics in the overthrow of a mode of production. If we take the study of politics of transition to consist in a critical analysis of the dialectic between historical bloc and institutional forms, then passive revolution emerges as 'a general principle of political art and science.'[46]

Gramsci contraposed the struggle for social hegemony against state expansion and the passive revolutions of capital.

Coming to our proximate national experience, an analogy is visible in conditions of relative underdevelopment, when bourgeois domination endeavours to continue its rule through an amalgam of expanding state sector, bureaucratic power, and populist mobilisation.[47] This may be combined again with the political slogan of justice for the poor, while in reality, extreme inequalities

---

[44] 'War of position' refers to struggle in the area of civil society, as distinguished from 'war of movement/manoeuvre', which indicates conflict over the state machine in the narrow sense. They are conceived as parts of one dialectical process. Vide Hoare and Smith, *op. cit.*, pp. 229–39.

[45] Ibid., pp. 360, 366, 377. Also, Antonio Gramsci, 'Some Aspects of the Southern Question' in Antonio Gramsci, *Selections from Political Writings (1921–26)* (Quintin Hoare, ed., trans.), London, 1978, pp. 441–62. A historical bloc describes the way in which different social forces relate to each other. What is particularly emphasised is the nexus of structure and superstructure which articulates the ability of a progressive class to form an alternative historical bloc. Also, Anne Showstack Sassoon, *op. cit.*, pp. 191–92.

[46] Christine Buci-Glucksmann, 'State, Transition and Passive Revolution', in Chantal Muffe, ed., *Gramsci and Marxist Theory*, London, 1979, p. 210.

[47] Asok Sen, 'Bureaucracy and Social Hegemony', in *Essays in Honour of Prof. S.C. Sarkar*, New Delhi, 1976, pp. 667–85. Also, Asok Sen, 'Marx, Weber and India Today', in *Economic and Political Weekly*, Bombay, Annual Number, February 1972, pp. 307–16.

characterise an economy infested with corruption, black money, and slow and uneven growth. Above all, there exist the conditions of duality, in which about 20 per cent or a little more of the population are increasingly assimilated into the realm of capitalism, the rest being abandoned to a peripheral wilderness. Amidst such historical circumstances, socialist and national motivations can fuse only at a level where anti-imperialism also resolves to struggle against internal capitalist expansion. On the contrary, as those conditions of duality take shape, the politicians, the officials, the experts and even the working people and their agencies, are integrated in the segment of capitalist assimilation. There is only a passive participation in the continuous extension and growing legitimacy of the institutional processes of the capitalist state order. They all move in the vicious circle of private or corporative egoism and bureaucracy, and act through their ignorance, their greed, their 'formal reason' and ethic of self-seeking divorced from the premises and ends of an alternative hegemony.

Indeed, in such historical circumstances, the formula of capitalist advance of production forces provides no adequate criterion for identifying a progressive historical phenomenon. The point is inherent in Gramsci's idea of 'transformism' as one variant of the passive revolution of capital. It is characterised by ways of domination, in which the capital relation does not lay the base of a sufficiently clarified civil society, nor does it eliminate the numerous labour forms which remain subject to pre-capitalist constraints and exploitation. Even then, the strength of bourgeois political power may succeed in combining some elements of hegemony with its apparatus of coercion. There lies the essence of Gramsci's idea of molecular changes through bourgeois initiative. The dialectical process of historical change is blocked by the ability of the capitalist order to absorb even the so-called representatives of its antithesis.

Under such conditions, again, Marxism is required to take up the task of combining, with its political goals, the social and ethico-cultural initiative which Gramsci considered to be of vital importance. Thus, the characteristic contradictions may call for the same level of praxis in countries of advanced and backward capitalism, even though their socio-economic conditions are so widely different. While admitting the need for different programmes, such variations will justify the same concern for the task of alternative social hegemony

Coming back to Weber's despair about the hiatus between formal reason and substantial rationality, we can now link it to the general problem of social hegemony and power in the stages of historical transition. It should then be possible to recognise Gramsci's 'passive revolution', 'as a potential tendency intrinsic to every transitional process.'[48] As regards the transition from feudalism to capitalism, the ongoing debate through the recent decades makes it clear that Marx's 'two ways' are associated with the variants of absolute monarchies, their different mercantilist policies, and the role of a nascent bourgeoisie in building its own social hegemony.[49] We have noted earlier the interaction between the specific context of German history and Weber's identification of bureaucracy as the institution of rational domination, for the advance of industry and technology. A reference can also be made to Gramsci's reflections on the experience of a 'passive revolution' in the history of capitalist transition in Italy.[50]

The three couples in Marx's theory, namely, production forces/production relations, base/superstructure and society/state, still serve as vital elements in our understanding of historical processes. Gramsci's use of categories like 'social hegemony', 'historical bloc', 'passive revolution', 'war of position' and/or 'manoeuvre', clarify, with several examples, the interaction of those vital elements in specific conjunctures ot history. And, what is perhaps of more importance for avoiding a positivist predilection of Marxist orthodoxy, Gramsci's analysis reveals how, in the logic of dialectics, the reality of interaction and praxis prevails over causal primacy and determinate reduction.

Thus, the metaphor apart, the relation of the base to the superstructure must not be considered as that of two different planes, where the former determines the latter. In his letters and notes on the historical role of ideologies, Engels clarified that a historical factor can react upon its own conditions. In his famous historical writings, Marx never reduced the multiplex reality of revolution and counter-revolution to a scheme of economic determinism. His reflections on civil society encompassed the totality of economic and non-economic factors in their continuous reciprocity. For Marx, 'History, to be intelligible, must show the economic and

---

[48] Christine Buci-Glucksman, *op. cit.*, p. 208.
[49] Asok Sen, 'The Transition from Feudalism to Capitalism', *Economic and Political Weekly*, Bombay, July 28, 1984, PE54–55.
[50] Hoare and Smith, *op. cit.*, pp. 105–20.

social origin of events in their oecumenical validity.'[51] Gramsci's concept of social hegemony is rooted in the same necessity for validation.

The emphasis on reciprocity does not ignore the crucial role of the mode of production in Marxian analysis. No such default creeps in when we duly recognise that the base/superstructure couple clarifying our understanding of the mode of production is complementary to the state/civil society relation in our total comprehension of historical processes. There obtains the dialectic of the parts, and also of the parts and the whole, in the totality of a decentred structure. This should take us to the crucial problem of mediation in Marxian theory, which points not only to the genesis of a new stage within the 'womb' of the old order, but also to the role of a rising class and its consciousness in such a making of history. We can then answer the question of a dichotomy between 'scientific' and 'critical' Marxism, raised in one incisive sociological analysis of our time.[52]

Indeed, the orthodox understanding of the base/superstructure relationship may have been influenced by some peculiarities of the emergence of capitalism in history. The origin of the bourgeoisie within the feudal mode of production instantly objectifies some alternative forms of production and circulation. It can even suggest a priority of the economic base in the general course of historical transition. Lenin pointed out the other experience associated with the transition from capitalism to socialism:

> One of the fundamental differences between bourgeois revolution and the Socialist revolution is that for the bourgeois revolution, which arises out of feudalism, the new economic organisations are gradually created in the womb of the old order, gradually changing all the aspects of feudal society . . . the difference between Socialist revolution and bourgeois revolution lies precisely in the fact that the latter finds ready forms of capitalist relationships; while the Soviet power—the

---

[51] H.P. Adams, *Karl Marx, in his Earlier Writings*, London, 1965, p. 153.
[52] Alvin W. Gouldner, 'The Two Marxisms', in *For Sociology*, 1975, pp. 425–62. Alvin W. Gouldner also points to a tension-filled conjunction of science and politics, of theory and practice in Marxism, since it is a philosophy of praxis and also the political economy of the laws of capitalism.

proletarian power—does not inherit such ready-made relationships, if we leave out of account the most developed forms of capitalism, which, strictly speaking, extended to but a small top layer of industry and hardly touched agriculture.[53]

In fact, even the most highly developed capitalist concentration is quite different from a system of socialist relations, while the advance of capitalist production, both in terms of forces and relations, was often significant within the feudal order. Analysing the role of class consciousness in history, Luckas also noted that 'Capitalism already developed within feudalism, thus bringing about its dissolution.'[54] Also, 'The rival systems of production will not co-exist as already perfected systems (as was seen in the beginning of capitalism within the feudal order). But their rivalry is expressed as the insoluble contradiction within the capitalist system itself: namely as crisis.'[55] Gramsci realised how the dominant bourgeoisie aimed at absorbing this crisis in a passive revolution. His counter-strategy placed emphasis on the 'war of position' for achieving alternative social hegemony. It followed that ethico-political mediation would have a premium in that strategy. There is, therefore, little reason to hold that Gramsci works out an inversion of the base/superstructure relationship. True to the Marxian tradition, he, in fact, implied no one-way reduction of the superstructure to the base or, vice versa, of the base to the superstructure.

On a more elaborate analysis, it is possible to discover some ambiguities and antinomies[56] in Gramsci's *Prison Notebooks*, written under obtrusive conditions and extraordinary circumstances. The central point of his arguments remains extremely valuable, insofar as it immensely enriches the content and perspectives of Marxist praxis, by locating the element of consent in the material structure and cultural components of class rule and exploitation.

---

[53] V.I. Lenin, 'Report on War and Peace to the Seventh Congress of the R.C.P.(B), 1918', in *Selected Works*, Vol. II, Moscow, 1947, pp. 293–94. Also quoted in Alvin W. Gouldner, *op. cit.*, p. 140.

[54] Georg Luckas, *History and Class Consciousness*, London, 1971, p. 283.

[55] Ibid., p. 243.

[56] Perry Anderson, 'The Antinomies of Antonio Gramsci', *New Left Review*, London, No. 100, November 1976-January 1977, pp. 5–78.

The more complex question to answer, is, how such mediation will take place. No less complicated is the real task of avoiding reformism and adventurism in giving effect to the strategies of the 'war of position' and the 'war of manoeuvre'. Gramsci himself would even evoke an 'optimism of the will' against the 'pessimism of the intellect', and he did conceive of the task of counter-hegemony long before 'passive revolution' emerged as a general phenomenon of contemporary capitalism.

We cannot ignore the unknowns and the uncertainties of real history. While there is evidence to indicate that 'Eurocommunism' in Italy promises the new to be born,[57] one cannot wish away the practical and ideological factors accounting for the differences between 'Gramscians of the left' and 'Gramscians of the right'.[58] The very fact of passive revolution can lead to a duality between two types of endeavour—one to achieve hegemonic structural reforms based on mass support, and the other to secure significant strength within the existing parliamentary system.

Again, at a different world pole, the Maoist empathy for 'revolution from below', and for the critical role of the peasant communes, appears to have produced results not quite consistent with its goals. One need not be blind to the achievements of socialism through this century in order to give Sartre's diagnosis its due—the danger of scarcity being schematised as the universal crystallisation of bureaucracy, after every socialist revolution in the backward countries.[59] Capitalism provides a far worse alternative for such countries. We can perceive Gramsci's aim as one of preventing 'the proletariat of Western Europe and the United States from being kept quiet by bread and circuses, passively

[57] Carl Marzani, *The Promise of Eurocommunism*, Westport, Connecticut, 1980.
[58] Walter L. Adamson, *Hegemony and Revolution—A Study of Gramsci's Political and Cultural Theory*, Berkeley/London, 1980, p. 231. Also, Massino Salvadori, 'Gramsci and the PCI: Two Conceptions of Hegemony', in Chantal Muffe, ed., *op. cit.*, pp. 236–58; and Biagio de Giovanni, 'Lenin and Gramsci: State Politics and Party', in Muffe, ed., *op. cit.*, pp. 259–88. The two essays present the different positions of the PCI and the PSI in the post-1976 debate in Italy. Salvadori holds that the current strategy of the PCI distorts the theories of both Lenin and Gramsci. It amounts to making Gramsci a 'hinge' between revolutionary seizure of state power and current reformism. Giovanni's counter-argument stresses the differences between the Leninist and Gramscian concepts of hegemony and points to the new situation in Europe after the 1930s. It led to the exhaustion, as argued by Giovanni, of the hypothesis tied to the dichotomous opposition of party and state.
[59] Perry Anderson, *Western Marxism*, *op. cit.*, pp. 85–89.

waiting for decadence and destruction.'[60] Things are not improved when, in our own circumstances, we can have circuses even without bread for the multitude.

This has been a long journey from Weber's 'pessimism of the intellect' to Gramsci's 'optimism of the will'. Even then, the point of arrival may require more clarification in the light of what is conventionally known of politics, as the art of the possible. Let us not miss the dangerous portents faced by mankind today by its passage to a technological stage, where even the threat of nuclear destruction can be a tool of wild imperialist strategy. In all probability, we may have completely exhausted the political process which, in Weber's view, 'is a complete parallel to the development of the capitalist enterprise',[61] and where 'the internal premiums consist of the satisfying of hatred and the craving of revenge.'[62] For Weber, again, such reflexes of class struggle were associated with the immutable bourgeois ethic and its external premiums of incentives and returns.

Gramsci proposed to reach beyond the very limits of the bourgeois rules of the game, in his calling for ethico-political mediation. The real issues of such praxis take us once again to what Marx observed about the distinct goal of his materialism: 'The standpoint of the old materialism is civil society; the standpoint of the new is *human* society or socialised humanity.'[63] It is something more than mere philosophical affinity that links Gramsci's ethico-political mediation with Marx's social humanity. In Weber's vocabulary, the identity is one of a new ethic, of a new *Weltanschauung*. True to that identity, Gramsci's challenge of alternative social hegemony acquires immense significance when capitalism manages to live on an involution of expanding production forces, which can thereby advance and also perpetuate the exploitative production relations. Such manoeuvres do not remain confined to the advanced capitalist countries only.

There are the questions of mediations, of its form and content encompassing what Marx and Lenin considered the task of

---

[60] Bo Gustaffson, 'Friedrich Engels and the Historical Role of Ideologies', *Science and Society*, Summer, 1966, p. 274.
[61] Max Weber, 'Politics as a Vocation', in Gerth and Mills, *op. cit.*, p. 82.
[62] Ibid., p. 125.
[63] Karl Marx, 'Thesis on Feuerbach', in *Selected Works*, Vol. 1, Moscow, 1941, p. 354.

'educating the educators'. Gramsci could not live to work out the practical directives of a new programme for his 'modern prince'. It is necessary to appreciate that Gramsci's emphasis on the superstructure is not in opposition to Marxism, but a development of the tradition committed to changing the world. No less significant is the historical tendency toward passive revolutions in many conjunctures of transition, from both developed and underdeveloped capitalism. But no ready answers automatically follow the many critical questions of mediations, or the principles and style of organisation suitable for Gramscian politics. This, surely, is the terrain on which Gramsci is to be deployed most usefully;[64] the ground on which his philosophy of praxis can be conducted for the elimination of capitalism. Capitalism evolves new ways of domination by bringing the masses into politics. In this process, capitalism functions today as an 'artful perverter of joy and keen exploiter of strength' by binding man to be an animal 'that has learned to survive "in a fashion", to multiply without food for the multitudes, to grow up healthily without reaching personal maturity, to live well but without purpose, to invent ingeniously without aim, and to kill grandiosely without need.'[65] Here lies the crucial import of Gramsci's resolution to sufficiently fulfil the socialist function of mediating historical advance towards a human renewal. He strove to achieve mass initiative for unceasing ethico-political action, which would create a consciousness with the will and an ability to transcend capitalism, that Weberian cage of 'cowardly' 'little men'.

---

[64] Keith Nield and John Seed, 'Waiting for Gramsci', *Social History*, Vol. 6, No. 2, May 1981, p. 221.

[65] Erik H. Erikson, *Insight and Responsibility*, New York, 1964, p. 227. Erikson comments on man's 'socio-genetic evolution' which has reached 'a crisis in the full sense of the word.' Equally pertinent for our conclusion, is what Erikson adds: 'At the point, however, when one is about to end an argument with a global injunction of what we must do, it is well to remember Blake's admonition that the common good becomes the topic of "the scoundrel, the hypocrite, and the flatterer", and that he who would do some good must do so in "minute particulars"' (ibid., pp. 227–28). Erikson's point had a place in Gramsci's mediation of 'collective will' which 'requires an extremely minute, molecular process of exhaustive analysis in every detail' (Hoare and Smith, *op. cit.*, p. 194).

9

Relevance of Max Weber for the Understanding of Indian Reality

YOGENDRA SINGH

Max Weber is amongst the few Western sociologists who has, directly or indirectly, generated much social science thinking about India for over several decades. Indologists, historians, political scientists, theologians, sociologists and intellectuals in general, have debated Weber's contributions and their implication for the understanding of Indian social and cultural reality. Both in political science and sociology, Weber forms an essential reading in the curricula of most universities. Despite this wide acceptability, access to the writings of Weber has two important general features among Indian students and scholars. First, it is almost entirely through English translations, as very few among Indian sociologists and social scientists read Weber in German. Secondly, there is widespread ambivalence among Indian scholars about Weber's writings of Indian society and religion. His postulates about religious ethic and cultural values and their implication to modernisation of the Indian society in the economic, scientific and technological fields, have not evoked favourable response from most Indian social scientists. More important, these postulates have proved to be unsustainable in the light of empirical facts, and processes of economic development and social changes in India during the past decades.

The Paradox of Max Weber

This seeming paradox of Max Weber in India, his wide reading and acceptability as a social science thinker on the one hand, and on the other, deep skepticism about the utility of most of his substantive propositions about Indian culture and society, poses important problems of approach in evaluating the relevance of his contributions for the understanding of Indian social reality. Much responsibility for this paradox also results from inadequate access of Indian scholars to Weber's writings. The translations of Weber into English which are available to Indian readers are faulty, as Detlef Kantowsky has documented. The translated material is often published disjointedly, without reference to the context or without proper periodisation. Kantowsky writes:

> Everybody will agree that it is almost impossible to translate Weber's German style of thinking into English: there simply is no equivalent. In their 'Preface' to the *Essays in Sociology* Gerth and Mills have made that clear enough. No matter how careful a translation is rendered, the specialist will still find points to disagree on. But when I say that in comparison with the original the Gerth-Martindale edition of Hinduism and Buddhism is unreliable, misleading and sometimes quite simply wrong, it is not inaccuracies in minute details that I have in mind. According to Johannes Winckelmann there was 'a cry of horror' ('Aufschrei des Entsetzens') from Max Weber specialists when *The Religion of India* appeared in 1958.[1]

There are also complexities in abstracting clear, substantive propositions about India from the writings of Max Weber. This holds true in respect of Weber's famous propositions about the relationship between religious ethic and economic development, his statements on the 'rationality' of the capitalist model of the Western industrial society, and his final position with regard to the pre-eminence of the Western cultural model over that of the East. Kantowsky, quoting from a correspondence of Winckelmann, a Weber specialist, writes that '... Weber would never have thought of the idea to teach the East or to persuade its people to take over the Euro-American form of civilisation and rational domination of world (letter dt. 25.9.80).'[2]

Indeed, it is widely known how Weber expressed his own disenchantment about the techno-industrial civilisation capitalism triggers, as a 'nullity' in his *The Protestant Ethic and the Spirit of*

---

[1] D. Kantowski, 'Max Weber on India and Indian Interpretation of Weber', *Contributions to Indian Sociology* (NS), Vol. 16, No. 2, 1982, pp. 150–51.
[2] Ibid.

Capitalism. This is affirmed by his writing as early as 1905 following his visit to the U.S. He wrote:

> When asceticism was carried out of monastic cells into everyday life, and began to dominate worldly morality, it did its part in building the tremendous cosmos of the modern economic order. This order is now bound to the technical and economic conditions of machine production which today determines the lives of all the individuals who are born into this mechanism, not only those directly concerned with economic acquisition, with irresistible force. Perhaps it will so determine them until the last ton of fossilised fuel is burnt. In Baxter's view the care for external goods should lie on the shoulders of the 'saint like a light cloak, which can be thrown aside at any moment.' But fate decreed that the cloak should become an iron cage.[3]

This, by implication, shows us Weber's negative value judgement on the Western industrial social order. As a positive construction, according to Kantowski, Weber would probably have preferred a social order closely resembling Tolstoy's conception. He finds some affinity between Weber's notion of moral order of society, and that of Tolstoy and Gandhi. 'In his last months Weber probably came very close to this world view of a rural Hindu', writes Kantowsky. Marianne Weber's biography of Weber relates to an episode from his life which supports this thesis. She writes:

> Weber sat on the bench by the stove . . . His kind eyes reflected his complete readiness to empathise with the young people. What agitated them was the belief that by means of communist oases (rural settlements and the like) the natural cells of a new, higher world order could be created—the peaceful overcoming of capitalism, or at least liberation from it for those who seriously *wanted* to be free from it. And by living off the soil together they hoped to remain free from specialisation in working for a living, for in this way they saw a soul destroying compulsion . . . .[4]

Complexities in evaluating Weber's relevance to understanding Indian social reality also arise from the breadth and depth of his

---

[3] Ibid., pp. 167–68.
[4] Marianne Weber, *Max Weber: A Biography* (Harry Zohn, trans., ed.), New York, 1975, pp. 674–75, quoted in Kantowski, *op. cit.*, p. 171.

social science paradigm. He belongs to the classical mould of scholarship, and as Peter Worseley says about Karl Marx, it is also difficult in the case of Max Weber, to bracket his contributions to any one single paradigmatic frame. The range of interpretations of Weber's paradigm of social science varies from the extremes of the nomological[5] to existential, phenomenological[6] forms of theorising. Weber has, rather explicitly, criticised in his *The Methodology of Social Science*,[7] the tendency among social scientists to formulate formal nomic generalisations, or to imitatively attempt to impose such 'scientific' models for the explanation of social reality. The objectivity in social sciences, unlike those in the natural sciences, is, according to him, value-mediated. Hence interpretive understanding is essential. Yet, Carl Hempel and a few others find in his conceptual schemes an inner logical consistency whose rigour approximates formal requirements of theory building in sociology. Luckmann, Berger and Schutz carry the interpretive focus of Weber's sociological method to existential-phenomenological directions of theorising. The element of typification in his ideal-types is seen to offer a dialectical linkage between the realms of the subjective and objective, value and motive, symbols and objects, and individual and society. One could also notice in Weber's formulation of ideal-types, an emphasis towards comparison and evolutionary construction of the historical movement of societies differing in space and time. This is quite evident from his comparative analysis of religious systems of the West and the East. It is also evident from his treatment of the passage of societies from feudalism to capitalism, through a series of structural transformations as contained in his lectures on *General Economic History*,[8] *Economy and Society*[9] and his *Essays in Sociology*.[10]

There is, thus, not one paradigm of sociology in Weber's

[5] Carl Hempel, *Aspects of Scientific Explanation and Other Essays in the Philosophy of Science*, New York, 1965.

[6] A. Shutz, *On Phenomenology and Social Relations*, Chicago, 1979; Luckmann and Berger, *The Social Construction of Reality*, New York, 1966.

[7] *The Methodology of Social Sciences* (Edward Shils and H.A. Finch, trans., eds.), New York, 1949.

[8] *General Economic History*, New York, 1950.

[9] *Economy and Society: An Outline of Interpretive Sociology* (G. Roth and C. Wittich, eds.), Berkeley, 1978.

[10] *From Max Weber: Essays in Sociology* (Gerth and Mills, trans.), London, 1952.

contributions taken in totality; rather, a set of paradigms contest for a position of pre-eminence. This multiplicity, or even polarity of paradigms, raises questions as to whether there is any central integrative principle in Weber's shifting positions on the paradigms of social science through which his theoretical and methodological position could be clearly postulated. Two types of solutions to this question could be offered: one, to look at Weber's theoretic position from the perspective of 'levels' and not of 'continuum'. The notion of levels lends the treatment amenable to pluralism of paradigms for analysis of different sets of social reality, which the notion of continuum does not offer. The second solution is to single out one from the varying sets of paradigms of Weber, as the most basic and central to his contributions, and proceed to analyse social reality from that frame of reference. Both types of attempts have been made by social scientists, in respect of the uses of Weber's sociological theory and methodology.

Supporting the significance of the notion of 'levels' in Weber's theory, Walter M. Sprondel writes:

> .... it seems expedient to differentiate between different theoretical levels of his historical and comparative sociology. A great deal of confusion could be avoided, if the respective level of analysis, to which a given proposition belongs, were clarified. Such a clarification is not always an easy task, because Max Weber very often refers to them all in one paragraph. For this differentiation of levels I would follow a proposal made by Guenther Roth in an essay which was published in the *British Journal of Sociology* in 1976.[11]

In this article, Guenther Roth suggests that one could treat Max Weber's contributions to theory at three levels. The first is the level of the 'historical individual', or a social reality constituting a unique configuration. His theory of ideal types belongs to this level of analysis. The second level is that of the 'developmental or secular theories' which deal with processes of evolution of systematised social forms, such as bureaucratisation, movements

---

[11] Walter M. Sprondel, 'Max Weber's Study on the Protestant Ethic in Context: Another Weberian View on South Asia', paper presented at the Seminar on Max Weber's Study of Hinduism and Buddhism—A New Evaluation, 1–3 March 1984, New Delhi.

towards rationalisation or routinisation of charisma, etc. The third level is that of the 'situational analysis' where Weber undertook historical analysis of specific social phenomena, such as 'the struggle of military nobility and merchants in medieval Venice, politics in Tzarist Russia in 1905; the internal structure of the German university system', etc.[12]

The context of each level of analysis is in response to a specific question to which Weber addresses himself. Sprondel writes:

> In this illuminating essay Guenther Roth made clear that Max Weber stood at a crucial juncture in modern historical sciences and 'began to ask questions that are indicative of a reflective stance in a situation of reorientation'. Unlike many predecessors as well as contemporaries, Weber maintained, that history could no longer be analysed with reference to laws of history—Weber called them 'phantoms' or 'ghosts'. His main questions were: 'Who are we that we came so far?' 'How did we get there?' 'Where are we likely to go?' 'And where should we go from here?' It was Weber's conviction that answer to these questions could best be given within the perspective of universal history. Thus he outlined his historical sociology which came to stand between historiography on the one side and the explanation of history by referring to iron laws, on the other.[13]

To the questions posited above, Weber deals with issues of 'historical individual', in response to the first question; developmental process and its theory as a reply to the second question; and the political social interest groups and their internal processes as a solution to the third question, respectively. The last question: 'Where should we go from here?', however, could not be answered according to Weber within the framework of science, as it involved value-judgement. The normative choice of such a path should be founded upon rationality, but such rationality could be derived, not empirically or historically, but only from within the cultural and normative framework of a society.

The second solution: as to which of the paradigms in Max

---

[12] Walter M. Sprondel, 'Max Weber's Study on the Protestant Ethic in Context', *op. cit.*, p. 7; G. Roth, 'History and Sociology in the Works of Max Weber', *British Journal of Sociology*, Vol. 27, 1976, pp. 306–18.

[13] Walter M. Sprondel, ibid., p. 6.

Weber's contributions is the most over-arching and subsuming, there could be different answers. Yet, the central issue with which Weber has been concerned, in and through most of his writings, relates to the historical and interpretive nature of social sciences. This is closely related to his formulation of the notion of causality, objectivity, and historicity in social sciences. This also ties well with his attack on the positivism of the time, and his emphasis on the place of values in social sciences. The notion of rationality is an integral element in this formulation of a methodology for social sciences in general. It is true Weber arrives at these problems through his analysis of the specific historical reality of the European civilisation. Yet, in all such analysis his concern is not merely substantive, but pre-eminently theoretical or methodological. Weber does not attempt mere narrative history, although several good examples of it could be found in his writings. His main concern in studying historical societal realities was comparison, generalisation and causal explanation of an interpretive kind, for establishing a universal history of mankind.

His notion of the ideal types, historical individuals, and process of rationalisation in societies, make no sense except in a concrete cultural historical context. This context, according to Weber, distinguishes a social science study from the natural science pursuit of explanatory models, where the treatment of the notion of objectivity is unmediated by values and devoid of historical moorings. The objectivity of social sciences lies in establishing their facticity through a series of historical experiments, using comparison as the basic tool of analysis. This comparison is attempted through a set of logically consistent concepts, or conceptual schemes (ideal types, historical individuals), as cognitive constructs derived from the historical cultural contexts concerned. This kind of analysis offers the meeting point in Weber's methodology, between the substantive and the theoretical. It also constitutes the zone of convergence between social science and natural science methodologies. Weber does not renounce the use of rational categories. The concepts he uses are rational as they are of a cognitive nature and defined logically. But these concepts are not mere abstractions from a random set of empirical observations, devoid of meaning content of the specific observations. Nor are they pure hypothetico-deductive categories, derived from a set of *a prioristic* postulates about the nature of social reality. The concepts in Weber's sociology are rational categories, but their rationality is culturally embedded. Without it, concepts would cease to be representative of reality. Weber, thus, rejects both formal theories of *a prioristic* idealistic types, as well as the positivistic theories modelled after inductive empiricism of the natural sciences. This flexibility in his notion of theory renders his method for studying specific historical societies and their processes, more meaningful and more comparative. In any evaluation of the relevance of Weber's contributions to social sciences of India, this aspect of his contributions, together with the notion of levels in his sociology, will have to be kept in mind.

Question of Relevance

So far we have attempted to bring out the complexities in the *appraisal* of Weber's social science contribution in general, from the standpoint of his substantive and theoretical positions. Indeed, this task is difficult, considering the competing sets of both substantive and paradigmatic positions held by Max Weber in his monumental contribution to social sciences. A similar complexity exists about determining his relevance for the understanding of Indian social reality. Partly, it is inherent in what we have called 'paradoxes' in Weber's social science contributions. The significant issue here, is, what degree of centrality did the Indian phenomenon occupy in Weber's scheme of analysis? To what extent do his substantive statements on India merit, or have met with, affirmation? What advantages do his theoretical and methodological insights into the social sciences offer to the Indian sociologists in their own analysis of the Indian social reality?

Most debate in India about the relevance of Max Weber, emanates from his *Religion of India: The Sociology of Hinduism and Buddhism*,[14] *The Protestant Ethic and the Spirit of Capitalism*,[15] *Economy and Society* and several essays interspersed in his *Essays in Sociology*. The propositions contained in these volumes have been debated in India with respect to the relationships between the processes of economic development and Indian ethico-religious

---

[14] *Religion of India: The Sociology of Hinduism and Buddhism* (H.H. Gerth and Don Martindale, trans., eds.), London, 1958.
[15] *The Protestant Ethic and the Spirit of Capitalism*, London, 1965.

values; the place of rationality and its nature in the Indian social and cultural systems, and in the context of the question of objectivity, or adequacy of proof, used in Weber's substantive statements about the Indian religion and culture. Some questions of methodological adequacy and relevance about Weber's sociology in general, have also been raised. Any evaluation of Weber's relevance to the understanding of Indian social reality would have to deal with these and related sets of questions that have arisen among social scientists in India and abroad.

A section of Weber specialists strongly holds the view that India occupied a position of auxiliary interest in Max Weber's historical sociology. The crucial theme in his intellectual concern was western rationalism and its historical sociological explanation. His interest in other cultures or civilisations was only a means to test his European propositions, rather than studying these other civilisations *per se*. At the most, his concern was to seek out possible comparisons to establish areas of divergence, or convergence, in terms of his propositions about the processes of rationalisation in cultural values. Walter M. Sprondel makes this point rather sharply, saying:

> The question arises: How much relevance can be attributed to such an approach (of Weber), if the focus of interest is shifted to other cultures or—in Weber's own term—world-religions. In considering this, again, it must be unequivocally clear that Max Weber was a child of his time and culture, notwithstanding his interest in, as well as his sensitivity to, fundamentally different ways of thought and action. Therefore, in Weber's view Occidental Rationalism is *our*, i.e. our European point of view, from which *we* look at a particular section of world history. This rationalism is claimed by *us* of being of 'universal significance and value', if and only so far we are interested in its continuity . . . . How much sense does it make to contemporary Indian social scientists to turn their attention to this apparently hopeless Eurocentricity? . . .
>
> I believe that Max Weber's advise to Indian sociologists would have been: You have to follow the tortuous paths of your own history upto the present if you are interested in what happens to India today. I would like to remind of the constitutive questions

which Weber asked when he attempted to understand the European situation: Who are we that we had come so far? How did we get there? Where are we likely to go?[16]

That Weber's central concern in terms of both substantive and theoretical issues was anchored in European reality is evident from the process of evolution of his ideas. Sprondel identifies three main stages in Weber's intellectual progress. His basic ideas were formed by his study of *The City*[17] from where he discovered the tools necessary to observe the process of rationalisation in lifestyles. It generated the ideal-types of political, social and cultural structures of a medieval city in the process of transition. It identified the process of disintegration in the feudal environment with replacement of the landed aristocracy by mercantile patriciate and artisans, the emergence of new principles of legal legitimacy of autonomous association of citizens, freed from feudal burden, and the implication of all this to the possibility of the emergence of sect as a structural type, which assumed basic significance in the period of early reformation. The emergence of autonomous association of citizens broke down the ritually sanctioned kinship ties and replaced it by the notion of a new universalistic moral community. This type of social process did not exist or emerge, according to Weber, in the Oriental cities. This was a typically European phenomenon. Max Weber further built upon his theory of social and economic implications of religious ethic in his essay on 'The Economic Ethic of World Religion',[18] and the evolutionary religious typology of rationality and rationalisation in *Sociology of Religion.*[19] The culmination of the thesis on rationalisation can be seen, according to Sprondel, in his lecture on 'Science as Vocation', where the most decisive structural principle of modern society, based on the values of rationalism, is propounded.[20] Throughout these stages of Weber's intellectual odyssey, the emphasis on European experience remains at the centre of his cognitive concern.

[16] Walter M. Sprondel, 'Max Weber's Study on the Protestant Ethic in Context: Another Weberian View on South Asia', *op. cit.*, pp. 15–16.

[17] Max Weber, *The City*, Glencoe, Ill., 1958.

[18] 'The Economic Ethic of World Religion,' in Essays by Max Weber, quoted in Walter M. Sprondel, *op. cit.*

[19] *The Sociology of Religion*, London, 1966.

[20] Walter M. Sprondel, 'Max Weber's Study on the Protestant Ethic in Context', *op. cit.*

A second response to the question of the relevance of Weber to the understanding of the Indian reality, is that his method of 'interpretive understanding' should inform the formulation of relevant questions about the analysis of social phenomena in India. Given this broad methodological parameter, the substantive issues about India could be analysed in terms of its specific symbolic and cultural content, which is difficult to universalise. On the relevance of Weber to Indian sociology, Detlef Kantowski writes:

> How to construct an Indian theoretical point of view? May I as an outsider offer a few concluding thoughts? The first task should be to reformulate Weber's questions according to the penetrating insight of the native speakers of Indian languages, who alone can concern themselves 'with the interpretive understanding of social action and thereby with a causal explanation of its course and consequences'. Having lived for the short span of altogether not more than some three years in Indian surroundings, I have come to the personal conclusion that my 'explanations' of Indian behaviour will always remain defunct since I can never dream of grasping 'the subjective meaning' of it. I think, therefore, that the definition of sociology and social action in the true Weberian sense of the above quotation, would be a good basis for a genuine theoretical standpoint.[21]

The above statement of Kantowski, about the difficulty of a person alien to a culture in grasping the 'subjective meaning' of its symbols, raises many difficult problems of method, to which sociologists both from within the same culture and those alien to it might be concerned. Yet, his suggestion about utilising Weber's basic epistemological framework, in terms of questions relevant for the principles, or codes, of a specific social or cultural system, merits appreciation. It means that the relevance of Weber to Indian sociologists lies in his theoretical contribution to what is called 'interpretive understanding' of reality, and the logico-philosophical rules it offers for formulating the concepts for the observation of social reality. Once we accept the theoretical position and its methodology, its operationalisation could be

[21] D. Kantowski, 'Max Weber's Contribution to Indian Sociology,' draft paper presented at the Seminar on Max Weber's Study of Hinduism and Buddhism—A New Evaluation, 1–3 March 1984.

undertaken in the culturally and socially unique setting of each society.

Once we formulate Weber's relevance to Indian sociology in theoretical or methodological terms, there are many variations in which it could be postulated. There is a basic distinction which Weber always emphasised. It is between a purely intuitive-subjective understanding of social reality, which he rejected, and a subjective understanding of social reality that is at the same time causal and explanatory, which he proposed. Weber did not view social science as a product of mere subjective interpretations, but as an objective and comparable set of observations of social universe that could lend themselves to interpretive causal explanation. He, however, rejected, as Talcott Parsons rightly pointed out, the 'radical positivistic' theory of social explanation. Social objects, according to him, are not objective in the same sense as natural objects are, but their objectivity is culturally mediated and is to be comprehended meaningfully. For this, an understanding of history and tradition is essential. It is this emphasis on historicity and symbolism, in respect of viewing social reality, that distinguished Weber from the positivists of the nineteenth and early twentieth century. It bears enduring significance for social scientists in all societies.

There is yet another aspect that offers a basis for examining the relevance of Weber's sociological theory and methodology. It belongs to the field of social change and social development. There is a point of view, that the primary concern of Weber was not with the theory of social change. His interest was in establishing a cultural basis for the organisation of Western industrial capitalism and its social structure. The conceptual typologies he used for the analysis of social systems were for understanding their inner social organisation and for their comparison, rather than for establishing a theory of social change. On the contrary, the main concern in the developing societies, particularly in India, is directed to social change and development. This is reflected in the themes that most Indian sociologists select for their studies, and the aspirations of Indian people and public men.

Possibly, Weber's contributions in the Indian context are apt to be evaluated more as a sociologist of change than an analyst of social or cultural structure, or as a social science philosopher. There are many levels of analysis in Weber's treatment of cultural and social systems, however, that link his contributions directly to a theory of change. Weber's main focus is on rationalisation as a process in cultural systems. Associated with this process is the mechanism of legitimation in the types of social orders. Weber formulates his famous trilogy of social order—traditional, charismatic and legal, each reflecting principles of rationalisation of the legitimate authority in the social and cultural systems.

In his lectures on *General Economic History* in contra-distinction to his *Theory of Social and Economic Organisation*[22] or even *Economy and Society*, Weber is refreshingly historical in his treatment of the transition in the European social order, from feudal-agrarianism to capitalism. He identifies social and cultural forces of transformation in the culmination of European capitalist social structure. These come quite close to those of Karl Marx, but for his very different and distinctive analytical methodology. These works of Max Weber, taken in their totality, offer both comparative-historical and theoretical insights into how his sociology could offer not only methods, but also conceptual schemes, that could be further operationalised to analyse specific processes of change in the historical context of non-European societies. Innovation and improvisation would, of course, be necessary in the uses of Weberian categories.

Some of the leading concepts from Weber's sociology that can be adapted to the study of the Indian process of change, are: prophecy and charisma, and its routinisation, the process of rationalisation in structural forms, the emergence of rationality, both formal and substantive, and the relationship between major cultural themes, value systems and their role in the emergence of modern social institutions and organisations, in the fields of economic, political and intellectual activities. In examining these relationships, the distinctive contribution of Weber's sociology would rest in the manner his approach to 'interpretive' causal explanation is kept in mind. It would appear that in most studies claiming affinity with Weber's methodology, not much attention has been paid to the interpretive aspect in the treatment of social relationships. The issue of causality, too, has not been taken up 'interpretively' in examining substantive propositions. A balanced appreciation of Weber's relevance to India would depend upon the extent to which

---

[22] *The Theory of Social and Economic Organisation* (Talcott Parsons, ed.), Glencoe, Ill., 1964.

both the substantive and the theoretico-methodological elements of his sociology are together kept in view.

The Indian Experience

The references to India in Weber's monumental writings are widely interspersed. The more significant treatment of the Indian reality, especially the Indian ethical and institutional systems to which much closer attention has been paid by scholars, can be found in his *Religion of India: The Sociology of Hinduism and Buddhism, Essays in Sociology, Economy and Society* and *General Economic History*. In other works on religious systems, and also in his numerous comparative essays, Indian institutions and practices are mentioned to support his arguments. In these writings, the institutions that come under scrutiny by Weber have quite a vast range of scope: the agrarian structure and village community, caste and guild, literati and intelligentsia, occupational groups, typology of legal systems and its relationship with ethical systems, and above all, the religious ethic of Hinduism and Buddhism and its institutional consequences for the Indian society in contra-distinction to that of the West. In most of these analyses, treatment of ethical systems is also linked with the analysis of role types and forms of social structure. This makes Weber's study of religion essentially sociological. The response of scholars to Weber's writings on India is, however, focused on mainly his proposition on the Hindu and Buddhist religions, and its implication for the development of rational, economic, social, political and cultural institutions. Since, in Weber's sociology, the primacy is that of the value system, such as rationality and rationalisation as a dialectic of religious ethic, much attention in Indian sociology has gone into the evaluation of this proposition.

We have already discussed how risky it is to accord primacy to Weber's statements about Hinduism and Buddhism, as a basis of his general attitude to the relationships between religious ethic and economic development. The difficulties arise, not only from faulty translations which are often the sources of evidence, but more than that, from a-contextuality of the statements that are the subjects of evaluation. Despite this, much debate on Weber's propositions, that have come under critical review in India, relate to the general relationship between culture and economic development and modernisation. Is Hinduism and its other-worldly ascetic ethic a hindrance to the growth of modern rational institutions of economic development? Are caste, traditional joint-family, and membership of religious sects in India, constraints in the adoption of rational attitudes to science, technology and economy? Has the modern type of economic entrepreneurial activity suffered in India because of the hold of the traditional religious ethic of Hinduism and Buddhism? These are some broad propositions that have been examined during the past decades by students of Indian society.

In the early 1960s, a symposium on the theme of 'Cultural Values in the Economic Development of India' was organised, in which M.N. Srinivas, D.G. Karve and Milton Singer, among others, participated. There was an overwhelming convergence in the viewpoint of participants, that traditional cultural values of Hinduism did not impede the process of economic development in India. It was erroneous to compare the cultural and religious traditions of the two distinctive civilisations—of India and Europe—at two different scales of time and devoid of historical contexts. Hinduism, it was postulated, placed equal emphasis on pursuit of material goals, as well as on the spiritual path of *dharma*.[23] S.C. Dube, writing in 1965, concluded that it was, firstly, difficult to define clearly the essential or uniform principles of Hinduism as such. Hinduism comprises complex sets of sects and belief systems, often mutually exclusive, and even if one could define Hinduism culturally, it was not antithetical to economic development or rational principles of organisation. Empirical observations in India's process of development do not support the thesis of religious factors being impediments to economic development.[24] Milton Singer, on the basis of his study, 'Industrial Leadership, the Hindu Ethic, and the Spirit of Socialism', critically examines many postulates of Weber on Hinduism, its notion of predestination, and its impact on industrial and economic enterprises. He writes:

> The problematic aspect of Weber's assumptions emerges when the ideal types are confused with empirical realities. In an ideal

---

[23] Cf. Myron Weiner, ed., *Introduction to the Civilisation of Developing India*, 1961.

[24] See S.C. Dube, 'Cultural Problems in the Economic Development of India,' in R.N. Bellah, ed., *Religion and Progress in Modern Asia*, pp. 43–55, New York, 1965.

typical 'traditional' order governed by an 'iron law' of ritual, there may well be ideal typical Hindus living in magical dread of change and innovation and seeking to escape from the wheels of rebirth and redeath through other-worldly ascetic austerities or orgiastic mystical rites. At this level of imaginative construction, perhaps the only way to change the 'traditional' order is to construct an ideal typical 'modern' order in which ideal typical secular Indians, completely liberated from traditional institutions and beliefs, can proceed to modernise their economy and society.

What has all this to do with empirical realities? 'Traditional' Indian society has been a changing society, and the Hindus who have been agents of these changes have not been prevented by caste, ritual, or religious beliefs from making innovations. Even Weber pays tributes to their flexibility and resourcefulness . . . there are several striking parallels between Calvinistic and Hindu eschatology and it is not clear why the psychological effects of the one belief system should be so diametrically opposed to those of the other. Through their emphasis on personal destiny and fate, both systems should arouse 'salvation anxiety' in believers. In both, a vocational ethic enjoins industriousness and dedication to one's 'calling' as a moral duty. Competence and success in one's calling are also linked in both to a transcendent goal of spiritual salvation. In Hinduism, the link has been described in the lofty philosophical doctrine of the *Bhagavadgita*, which assures to householders, women, and Sudras a path of salvation in the performance of their daily work, provided their performance is not motivated by a desire for the selfish enjoyment of the fruits thereof. Tilak, Gandhi and other modern Hindu leaders applied this analogue of the 'Protestant Ethic' to justify programmes of political and economic activism.[25]

Singer's study of industrial leadership supports his argument empirically. Many of the basic traditional Indian institutions such as caste, joint family, religious affiliation and traditional occupations, in Madras, do not seem to hinder the growth of industrial entrepreneurship. On the contrary, these traditional institutions

---

[25] Milton Singer, 'Industrial Leadership, the Hindu Ethic and the Spirit of Socialism,' in Milton Singer, ed., *When a Great Tradition Modernizes*, pp. 279–80, New York, 1972.

Relevance of Max Weber for the Understanding of Indian Reality / 227

and their accompanying value systems work out an adaptive relationship towards a viable growth of modern roles and institutional innovations. This has been established at the all-India level, in my work on the *Modernization of Indian Tradition*.[26] Much difficulty in analysing Weber's propositions on religion and economic development, apart from other difficulties which we have pointed out earlier, arise from the ambiguity of levels at which his thesis is examined. One set of levels, as Singer rightly indicates, could be textual, contextual and ideal-typical. The major limitation in Weber's analysis of Hinduism, or other Indian institutions, rests at the textual and contextual levels. It is indeed difficult to come by a uniformly acceptable textual view of what are the central values of Hinduism. Even if a textually common set of values could be agreed upon, at the contextual level, both the transcendental and the pragmatic principles have co-existed in the Hindu ethic. Weber recognises the role of the magic and magico-religious nature of ethic in the religious systems. This also obtains for Hinduism. But because of the limitations of the access to the contextual reality of religion and culture in traditional India, there are bound to be shortcomings in Weber's treatment of Hinduism and its ethic. The operation of the pragmatic principle in Hinduism dealing with a variety of ecological, cultural, economic and other utilitarian aspects of life, escaped Weber's attention because of the limitations of the data through which he had to work. Moreover, his main concern possibly, was not to study the Hindu ethic *per se*, but to highlight those aspects of its system which served to sharpen the contrast with Western Calvinistic tradition.

To the students of the modernisation process in India, it is no longer academically feasible to posit the negative role of religious ethic in economic development. Whether it is industry, agriculture, adoption of modern technology, education, modern communication, new managerial skills or access to modern organisations, people in India as a whole, with the Hindus in the forefront, have adopted rational methods and operations.[27] The pessimism voiced in this regard by scholars such as Gunnar Myrdal and William Kapp, has proved to have been ill-founded. These scholars did not adequately realise the elements of flexibility and pragmatism in

---

[26] Yogendra Singh, *Modernization of Indian Tradition*, New Delhi, 1973.
[27] Ibid.

the structure of the Hindu ethic. Such elements of Hinduism have come into evidence as empirical studies on the adoption of modern institutions of development in India have multiplied, adding fresh insight into the pragmatic aspects of the Hindu ethic.

The weakness in establishing the linkages between the textual and the contextual elements of Hinduism and Buddhism in India in Weber's writings, led him to formulate ideal types about the nature of rationality, and the process of rationalisation in the Hindu society, which were bound to have limited significance. An ideal-type must mirror the 'historical individual' of a society in an objective and comprehensive manner. The limitation in Weber's generalisation about the Hindu ethic, its other-worldliness, asceticism and mysticism, the role types of caste, guild etc., suffer from paucity of a comprehensive view on the 'historical individual' of Hinduism and its related doctrines. It may well be argued that some Hindu sects and schools of thought not only recognised, but gave a place of pre-eminence, to this-worldly pursuits. Indeed, if we compare the *Dharma Shastra* with the *Artha Shastra* of Kautilya, the contra-distinction of the two different ideologies of Hinduism become striking. If one took into account the Buddhist and Jain ethical systems of interpreting the meaning of reality, the multiplicity of ethic would be further enlarged. The need is to draw from the Hindu religion on the one hand, and the behavioural manifestation of its ethic in the day-to-day life of people, on the other, and then use it as a comprehensive basis for constructing a 'historical individual' of Hinduism, to derive sets of ideal-types for Indian studies. This has not yet been attempted.

Max Weber and the Understanding of Indian Social Reality

We could now come back to the question we posed earlier. What is the relevance, today, of Max Weber's sociology to the understanding of Indian social reality? We could analyse this question at two levels: substantive and theoretical (methodological). At the substantive level, Max Weber's statements and generalisation about social institutions and ethical systems in India are subject to various limitations. Even if one could agree that Max Weber has been misunderstood in India because of a lack of access to him in German, there are numerous propositions that Weber formulates about the relationship between the ethic of Hinduism and the nature of social institutions and structures in India, which are questionable and faulty. We have indicated some of them in this essay. These limitations in Weber's empirical propositions on India have been confirmed as concrete studies of Indian culture, value system, ethic and their implication to modernisation processes have gained momentum, and have grown in size. These studies of the process of social, economic, political and cultural transformation in India, have brought out the complexity and flexibility of traditional institutions and values in response to social change. The 'historical individual' of the Indian society that emerges from these observations is considerably different from what Weber formulated on the basis of data available to him at his own time.

As Sprondel suggests, there is always a possibility of reformulating Weber's propositions about the relationship between, what he called, 'existential knowledge' and 'normative knowledge' on the one hand, and between the contextual level and the ideal-typical level of the construction of social reality on the other. This would shift the question of Weber's relevance from his statements on substantive processes and interpretation about the Indian society, to those of the methods of formulating the questions or propositions themselves—propositions that could be examined with the help of ideal type concepts for interpretive understanding of reality.

Weber's theoretical formulation of sociology, and his method of interpretive causal explanation, are the crucial elements of his contribution that have enduring relevance. It has many qualities that harmonise with, and set into perspective, several contemporary trends in sociological theory. The disenchantment from nomological explanations, growing emphasis on reflexivity in social observations, increasing significance of language forms and symbols in interpretation of culture and society, emphasis on historicity and identity in understanding social formations, and the universal tendency in social sciences to recognise the limitations of the positivistic approach in social sciences, reconfirm the relevance of Max Weber in today's theory and practice of social science. As the recognition of symbolic and emic perspectives for the study of social and cultural realities increases, the significance of 'interpretation' in the formulation and use of concepts also increases. In fact, many widely accepted categories of Indian sociology, such as 'caste', 'class', 'community' or 'ethnicity', etc., which have been widely used in social sciences, have undergone increasingly new formulations of meanings, or even operationalisation, as the focus in studies has become more concrete, historical and symbolic. The uses of indigenous terms and symbols add new perspectives to the meanings these categories have in people's life. Thus, the demand for reflexivity in concept formation, emphasis on interpretive understanding, semiology, structuralism, and phenomenology, have opened up new possibilities in giving Weber's methodology new operational relevance for Indian sociology.

Weber's relevance to Indian social science lies in his metatheory and methodology. His substantive propositions and conceptual schemes about Indian religious and cultural systems could only provide the curious ground for formulating new questions about the nature of Indian social reality. Weber over-emphasised the significance of cultural aspects, to the neglect of structural principles of society. Indeed, he always attempted to interpret the structural principles of society through the principles of symbolic forms, values and processes of symbolic transformations called 'rationalisation'. Here, Weber unconsciously introduces the role of ideologies in the formation of social institutions, such as capitalism, bureaucracy and other modern social organisations. Thus, rationality and rationalisation, which emerge from within the transformative process of the religious ethic, also set into motion the process of *disenchantment*, which grows as an organic and critical element in the social organisation of modern society. This insight of Weber is one of his more enduring contributions to an understanding of the process of modernisation, with universal relevance to social sciences. It sharpens our awareness about the dialectic of social transformation in the emergence of modern industrial society and nation state. At this stage, Weber's otherwise culturological approach to the study of social reality begins to come to grips with issues of social structure, power and ideology. Apart from his methodology, it is this element in Weber's sociology that adds new relevance to his contribution for the study of Indian social reality.

10

State Power and Capitalist Democracy

RALPH MILIBAND

I

The purpose of this essay is to extend an argument which I presented in an article in *New Left Review* in the Spring of 1983, concerning the relationship between the state and dominant economic interests in advanced capitalist societies. In the article in question, I suggested that the traditional Marxist view on the subject was that the policies and actions of the state were mainly (or even wholly) impelled by forces external to it: either by a ruling or dominant class, so designated because of its ownership and control of the main means of economic activity, or by the impersonal constraints generated by the capitalist mode of production, which are taken to compel the state, whatever may be the dispositions of those who are in charge of it, to serve the requirements of capital. Nor, obviously, are the personal forms of constraint incompatible with the impersonal ones; on the contrary, the two complement each other. This view of the dynamic of state action, I also suggested, greatly understated the degree of autonomy which the state in these societies enjoyed. I also said that the notion of the 'relative autonomy of the state', which was intended to qualify the state's subordination to external capitalist forces, still left it far too strictly subordinated to them.[1]

The state is, of course, an ensemble of institutions: the executive

---

[1] 'State Power and Class Interests', *New Left Review*, No. 138, March-April, 1983.

Author's Note: Earlier versions of this essay were presented in 1983 to seminars at York University, Toronto, and the New School for Social Research, New York, and to a Marx Centenary Colloquium at the Vrije Universiteit, Brussels. I derived much benefit from the discussion which followed the presentations, and I am grateful to the participants.

power, by which I mean presidents, prime ministers and their cabinet colleagues and other immediate advisers; the top layers of the administration, in departments of state, and also beyond ministerial departments, for instance in central banking institutions or public enterprises; military and police chiefs; the judiciary; the legislative branch; and various forms and levels of local and regional government. However, it is the first of these—the executive power—which is of the greatest immediate relevance here, since it is presidents, prime ministers, and their colleagues and advisers who are ultimately responsible for making policy decisions and initiating actions which stem from these decisions. In this sense, the autonomy of the state refers primarily to the autonomy of the executive power of government. And it is with the executive power of the state that I shall be mainly concerned here.

The problem, which the notion of 'relative autonomy' points to but does not resolve, is to combine a view of the state in advanced capitalist societies which takes due account of the forces and constraints to which the state is clearly subjected; and yet, to make due allowance also for the crucial role which the state plays in these societies, and which it plays, in regard to vital issues, quite autonomously.[2]

The answer to the problem which I proposed in my article was the notion of a *partnership* between the state on the one hand, and dominant capitalist forces on the other. And I suggested that this partnership should be viewed as involving 'two different, separate forces, linked to each other by many threads, yet having each its own separate sphere of concern'.[3] The terms of that partnership, I also noted, 'are not fixed but constantly shifting, and affected by many different circumstances, and notably by the state of class struggle. It is not at any rate a partnership in which the state may be taken necessarily to be the junior partner'.[4]

The burden of the present essay is that this last formulation is much too weak; and that, insofar as there exists a 'partnership'

[2] My repeated references to 'advanced capitalist societies' are intended to stress the fact that it is only these societies, and their capitalist-democratic regimes, that I deal with here. The relationship of the state to capitalist and other social forces in 'less developed' capitalist countries presents a different set of problems, and requires separate treatment. So, of course, does the relationship of the state to society in Soviet-type regimes.

[3] 'State Power and Class Interests', *op. cit.*, p. 65.

[4] Ibid., p. 65.

between the state and dominant capitalist forces, the state should be seen, in advanced capitalist countries, as by far the more senior of the partners, and, more often than not, able to use its power without any reference to forces external to it.

II

The notion, which has been a central part of Marxist political sociology, that the capitalist state is primarily, and even exclusively, moved by capitalist forces, and that the defence of these forces is virtually its only purpose, and certainly its most important one, may be attributed to a deep-seated 'economistic' bias in Marxist thought, which was particularly marked in the period of the Second International. The bias undoubtedly owed much to the extraordinary development of capitalism in that period—the period of the Second Industrial Revolution—and to the emergence of what were then industrial, financial and commercial giants. In the light of this capitalist development, it is not very surprising that governments and states should have been thought to be mere pawns in the hands of captains of industry, financial tycoons and 'robber barons'.

This 'economistic' perspective persisted well into the twentieth century, and was given as appearance of plausibility by the further development of capitalism. In fact, it received even more pronounced emphasis with the notion of 'state monopoly capitalism', which has long been the official Soviet view of the state in advanced capitalist societies, and which has also been adopted by western Communist parties. In this perspective, the capitalist state and monopoly capital are not only inextricably intertwined, which is a reasonable enough view, but form an ensemble in which the state is hardly more than the pliant tool of monopoly capital.

This seems to me to be a profound misreading of the true relationship of the state to capitalist forces in advanced capitalist countries in the present epoch. For it fails to take account of the degree to which the state itself has grown, from the relatively ramshackle and non-interventionist state of the nineteenth century, into the highly organised and pervasively interventionist one of the twentieth. Nor is the point simply that the power and scope of the state have grown tremendously in the twentieth century, but also, that the state plays its role with a very high degree of independence from *all* social forces in society, often amounting to absolute independence.

Moreover, the 'economistic' perspective also fails to take into account the extent to which capitalist democracy, including as it does, political competition and overt pressure from below, has itself helped to shift the balance of power towards the state. The state imperatively *needs* more elbow room if it is to effectively contain pressure from below. And power holders who depend on electoral legitimation, *want* more elbow room in order to enhance their chances of holding on to office.

Marx and Engels made full allowance for the independence of the state under capitalism, but viewed it mainly as the result of what Engels called 'exceptional circumstances', notably, when no class was able to assert its domination. And they saw it as assuming, then, more or less pronounced authoritarian and 'Bonapartist' forms.[5] In the twentieth century, however, it is by no means only under properly authoritarian forms that the state achieves a high degree of emancipation from external pressures: it is also in the 'normal' circumstances of capitalist democracy that it assumes, in relation to a vast array of policy decisions, some of them of vital importance, the kind of independence which Marx and Engels attributed to the authoritarian state.

I will presently say more about this pervasive and independent role of the state in the present epoch, but must note here that, in thus stressing its independence, I do not in the least seek to belittle the influence and power which capital exercises in society, and vis-a-vis the state. Capitalist forces have vast means at their disposal, whereby they can hope to shape public opinion and affect the fortunes of candidates and parties in elections. Nowhere is this more true than in the United States, where business deploys

---

[5] For example, Marx: 'The Empire . . . was the only form of government possible at a time when the bourgeoisie had already lost, and the working class had not yet acquired, the faculty of ruling the nation'. K. Marx, 'The Civil War in France', in *Political Writings*, Vol. 3, *The First International and After*, Harmondsworth, 1974, p. 208; and Engels: 'By way of exception, however, periods occur in which the warring classes balance each other so nearly that the state power, as ostensible mediator, acquires for the moment a certain degree of independence of both'. F. Engels, *The Origin of the Family, Private Property and the State*, in K. Marx and F. Engels, *Selected Works*, Moscow, 1949, 11, p. 290. For a useful exposition of the place of autonomy in Marx and Engels' work, see H. Draper, *Karl Marx's Theory of Revolution*, Vol. I, *State and Bureaucracy*, New York, 1977, Ch. XIff.

immense resources for what is, in effect, ideological and political indoctrination and pressure, and where few candidates in elections can hope to get very far without strong business support. Business is by far the most powerful pressure group in all capitalist countries, compared to which all other 'interests', notably labour, must be reckoned to be weak. Moreover, capital controls strategic means of industrial, financial and commercial activity, and no government can, as a result, ignore the power which this confers upon the controllers, and the degree to which that power can be used to embarrass a government and make its life more difficult.

All the same, the weight which capital has on public affairs, however great, does not amount to mastery over the government or the state. A difference has to be made between influence and power which are brought to bear on the political process on the one hand, and on the state on the other. Obviously, there is a link: the influence and power which are wielded by business in the political process impinge upon the state itself, and are, in any case, directly deployed in regard to the state itself. Nevertheless, there is a difference: a candidate to the presidency of the United States, for instance, depends upon business support a lot more than does someone who *is* President of the United States, and a President of the United States has, himself, vast resources of power which a candidate to the presidency does not have. More generally, the executive power of the state speaks with an authority—or at least can do so—that no 'interest' in society can begin to match. Governments armed with the legitimacy conferred upon them by electoral procedures deemed 'democratic' (whether they are or not), and claiming to speak in the name of the majority (whether they do or not), cannot reasonably be thought to be helpless in the face of capitalist opposition.

There are, of course, occasions when any government is forced to act in ways which it finds very disagreeable, and capital is one of the forces which may compel it to make highly unwelcome decisions. But it is not usually the case that the executive power in advanced capitalist countries has no option but to adopt a course to which it is strongly opposed, on matters of fundamental importance. The possible alternatives open to governments vary from country to country, and according to particular circumstances; but governments do, almost always, have some choice of alternatives.

This means that, if the state acts in ways which are congruent with the interests and purposes of capital, it is not because it is driven by dire compulsion to do so, but *because it wants to do so*. There are strong reasons for this. One of them is precisely the influence and power of capital. It is much easier to go along with strong capitalist interests, and to conciliate them, than to oppose them, most of all on matters of great importance. Another reason is that, in any case, most of the people who have traditionally occupied positions of power in government and other parts of the state, have viewed the interests of capital as being broadly congruent with what they conceived to be the 'national interest'. They might oppose the policies and actions of this or that firm, and find that its behaviour represented the 'unacceptable face of capitalism'. But the face of capitalism has generally been perfectly acceptable to power holders in these societies, and the point is scarcely less valid for social democratic governments than for conservative ones. These ideological dispositions provide a firm basis for the 'partnership' I have referred to.

However, it is governments which ultimately decide what policies and actions the interests of capital and the 'national interest' require. There are, let it be said again, important and even vital policy choices to be made. And, while governments do take into very careful account the opinions expressed by the representatives of capital (who may not, in any case, speak with one voice), and must include in their calculations the actions which capital may undertake or threaten to undertake, it is they who will, from a range of alternatives, choose what policy to adopt—and the range is wider than the traditional Marxist perspective has generally allowed for.

On this view, it seems more useful to take the state as being concerned with *the defence of the given social order* rather than simply with the defence of capital. Of course, the given social order constitutes a particular structure of exploitation and domination, a particular order of property and production relations of privilege and power, and capital is at its very centre. The defence of the social order is, therefore, also, and even pre-eminently, the defence of capital. Nevertheless, the notion of the state as the defender of the social order makes possible a more accurate perception of the state's place in capitalist society than is afforded by the narrow 'economistic' view of the state as the defender of capital. For the larger view, while not for a moment losing sight of the fact that the social order which the state defends *is* an order of exploitation and domination, also indicates that the state's purposes and concerns far transcend the immediate—or even the longer term—interests of capital, and encompass whatever those in charge of state power deem to be necessary for the defence and stability of the social order. It also indicates that the people in charge of the state do not necessarily want to use the state in order to help capital, but want to help capital because they believe this to be required in order to strengthen the state—a purpose which may stem from many different ideological, political, religious, moral and other concerns.

The notion of the state as the defender of the given social order—and as its more or less independent defender—is perhaps best supported by way of a review, however brief, of the main areas in which it is involved.

To begin with, the state intervenes in crucially important ways in the economic life of capitalist society. However much conservative governments may proclaim their attachment to 'free enterprise' and the unfettered operation of the market, they are, nevertheless, irremediably involved in the national and international economy. Much of what the state does in this area is done in close consultation with capitalist interests. But even here, where these interests are most closely involved, the decisions which the state takes in regard to economic life are taken by presidents, prime ministers and their immediate colleagues and advisers as *they* ultimately think fit.

Furthermore, there is a great deal which the state does by way of the regulation of business, which business has traditionally found irksome, but which has been imposed upon it, precisely because the state, as the defender of the social order, could not allow business to disregard altogether the social costs of its pursuit of profit. These regulatory activities of the state may be carried out halfheartedly and ineffectively; but they *are* performed, notwithstanding the opposition they encounter on the part of the interests concerned.

The same considerations apply even more strongly to a second area in which the state intervenes, namely, the social provisions subsumed under the rubric 'welfare state'. Here too, governments, whether reluctantly or not, cannot avoid shouldering major responsibilities for the provision of a wide range of social services. The question in this realm is not 'whether' but 'how much?', or, perhaps more accurately, 'how little?'. Much, if not most that has been achieved in terms of welfare rights and social protection, may be attributed to direct or indirect pressure from below. It is safe to assume that a mass of legislation which regulates the labour process, and most of the social provisions which make up the 'welfare state', would not have come into being without pressure from below, and the fears of the consequences in terms of social instability and conflict that might be produced by the refusal of regulation and reform. But it is the state, usually in the face of strong opposition from capitalist interests, which turned expectations and demands into measures with the force of law.

It may well be said—in fact, it needs to be stressed—that the measures of regulation and reform which were achieved, were never of such a nature as to pose a major challenge to capitalist interests; that these interests were always in a position to put a brake upon the scope and impact of the reforms which they were unable to prevent altogether; and that the state was usually the willing partner or accomplice in these limiting endeavours. This is, undoubtedly, very important in the assessment of the meaning and significance of reform in a capitalist society. Nor is it to be ignored that reform has helped to contain conflict and to legitimate capitalist democracy. But none of this can be taken to suggest that, because the reforms that were introduced did not actually destroy the existing structure of power, they were, therefore, of no consequence, mere matters of detail in the ways in which exploitation and domination are organised and conducted. Such a view is unwarranted. The reforms in question did not destroy capitalism, and were never intended to do so. But their introduction, and their cumulative effect, did make a considerable difference in the ways in which exploitation and domination were experienced in these societies, and in the capacity of the subordinate classes to resist the conditions of their subordination, or to challenge subordination itself. This is precisely why reforms have always been opposed, and often opposed fiercely, by all conservative forces in capitalist society. It is also why the state itself has always been halfhearted in its regulating and reforming endeavours. But it did, nevertheless, play an indispensable role in the implementation of the measures in question; and it could not have played that role if it had not had a very considerable degree of independence from dominant economic forces, and thus, been able to act as the guardian of the true interests of these forces—a task made absolutely essential by the 'structural' and all but insurmountable shortsightedness of dominant classes.

Thirdly, the state is ever more thoroughly involved in the 'engineering of consent', the manipulation of opinion, the business of propaganda and indoctrination. The struggle for the 'hearts and minds' of the subordinate populations of capitalist societies was once a task largely undertaken by dominant classes in control of what Marx called the 'mental means of production' as well as the material ones. But that struggle is now also waged, with great intensity, by the state itself, so to speak on its own account, and with all the formidable resources it has for the dissemination of propaganda, mis-information and plain lies.

Fourthly, the state is ever more deeply and comprehensively engaged in the surveillance and 'technological control' of its population, in the business of repression, in which it plays a unique role, and in the discouragement of dissent and the harassment of dissenters. Some of the things it does in this area are of direct and specific help to capitalist employers—for example, the harassment and repression of strikers—but most of its policing and repressive activities, are intended to serve the larger purpose of defending the social order against all those who are taken to be its internal enemies. Here too, what the state does is done quite independently of any pressure external to it, out of a dynamic generated in the state itself. Moreover, the amount and forms of repression which the state uses, which are a matter of very considerable importance, with very large implications for the whole of society, are also decided inside the state, not outside it.

Finally, for present purposes, there is the whole area of external affairs, to which may be linked defence, and in which the state alone, or rather the executive power of the state, exercises an exclusive prerogative of ultimate decision-making. Of course, the state is greatly constrained in its external dealings by a wide variety of internal and external limitations. But when all these have been duly taken into account, it is still the case that there is much that the state can choose to do, or not to do, quite independently of capitalist or any other forces in society. Its area of choice is greater or smaller, depending on the country's power and resources: it is obviously much greater for the United States than for any other advanced capitalist country. But it is not negligible for any of them. Thus, to take one recent example among many, it was possible for a British Government, quite autonomously, and without any reference to anyone outside the state itself, to embark on the Falklands enterprise. In so doing, it could, no doubt, count on a large measure of support in the House of Commons (as it turned out, all but unanimous support), and in the country at large. But that support was obtained *after* the decision to act had been taken. An earlier example is that of the Suez expedition in 1956. That enterprise floundered because of internal and external (decisively American) opposition. However, the significant point here is not the failure of the expedition, but the fact that it was initiated by the British Government without reference to anybody outside the state. The extreme example of such decisions and actions—fortunately still only potential—would be the decision of the President of the United States to start a nuclear war which would devastate a large part of the planet. Such a decision would be taken by the President, without reference to anybody outside a small circle of advisers.[6] There could be no more dramatic example of the meaning of the autonomy of the state.

It would not be difficult to lengthen this enumeration of 'the areas of activity' in which the state is engaged as the defender of the social order. But what has been said about it may suffice to recall how pervasive its involvement is, and how much is done by the state 'on its own', for whatever purposes those who are in charge of it deem desirable. This independence of the capitalist-democratic state is one of its most notable and important features, and it is a feature which is becoming more marked with every decade that passes. If the control of the state by society is taken to be an essential part of a democratic regime, it is fair to say that the regimes of advanced capitalism are anything but democratic. True, the state in these regimes does not have the degree of freedom from control which is enjoyed by the authoritarian state. Legislative constraints, judicial review, electoral and popular pressures, the influence of the press and of a multitude of diverse pressure

[6] However, the adoption of 'launch on warning' systems, which entail the initiation of nuclear war by automatic computer responses to given warning signals, would constitute an even further stage in the autonomy of the state, insofar as the decision to destroy a large part of the planet and its inhabitants would be taken independently of any human agency—by grace of machines invested with all the power of the state.

groups, associations, interests and lobbies, all serve, to some degree, to place obstacles on the capacity of the state to act as it wills. But there is an evermore pronounced tendency for the executive power in these regimes to seek emancipation from all such constraints, and to curb all power except its own. This is particularly true in the area of 'law and order', defence and external policy. Much of the relationship between the state and society in these regimes, thus, turns into a permanent struggle of the former for freedom from the latter.

The main reason for the inflation of state power within the constitutional shell of capitalist democracy, is not, *pace* Max Weber, the irresistible march of bureaucracy; or the hunger for evermore power from people who already have a lot of it (though this is not to be discounted); or the ever greater sophistication of the technology of social control. All such explanations miss the essence of the matter, namely, that the social order which the state is seeking to defend *requires* its intervention evermore imperatively, if the the prevailing patterns of exploitation and domination which are constitutive of that social order are to be preserved, given conditions of permanent economic, social, political, cultural and moral crisis. The state has always played an essential part in the defence of the social order: its intervention is now more essential than ever. But it is the more effectively undertaken, the freer the state is from the constraints which a capitalist-democratic regime imposes upon it.

There is one factor which has enormously accelerated the tendency towards the 'autonomisation' of state power in these regimes: this is the permanent anti-revolutionary purpose, conveniently legitimated by the bogey of the threat of Soviet aggression, which has been at the core of the defence and external policies of advanced capitalism. These policies aggravate the difficulties which these regimes confront, and which, themselves, make for the 'autonomisation' of executive power. They also require a strenuous and sustained mobilisation of the population and the greatest possible marginalisation of dissent from the left; and they involve the extension of police powers in the name of 'national security'. Only the state can perform the tasks required by dedication to anti-revolutionary purposes.[7] This entails not only the inflation of

---

[7] I use the term 'anti-revolutionary' rather than 'counter-revolutionary', because the latter term denotes the intention to destroy existing regimes. This is certainly

state power, but its emancipation, in crucial areas of policy, from constraints which are proclaimed to be dangerously detrimental to the 'national interest'.

III

Given the power which belongs to the governments of capitalist-democratic regimes, and the degree of freedom which they have in wielding it, the obvious question which arises is, how far this power could be used to subvert rather than support the given social order. If governments can act without reference to capitalist forces, how far is it possible for these governments to go on acting against them? How feasible is it for the government of an advanced capitalist country to act in ways which must entail the dissolution of the state's partnership with capitalist forces, and to forge a new partnership with the hitherto subordinate class, or classes, for the purpose of transforming the social order in socialist directions? What, in other words, are the limits of radical change in capitalist-democratic regimes?[8]

There is a remarkable dearth of historical experience with regard to such questions. Of course, there is a vast amount of evidence in the twentieth century of counter-revolutionary movements directed against reforming governments (and also against governments that were not particularly reform-oriented). But this evidence, though relevant, concerns countries and situations in which capitalist democracy was poorly implanted, as, for instance, in Italy,

---

part of 'western' policy wherever possible. But, insofar as the intention is more commonly to prevent revolutionary movements from coming to power, and generally to contain the left, 'anti-revolutionary', except in the case of policies and actions directed against revolutionary regimes, seems the more.

[8] This would involve many different measures in the economic, social and administrative fields, all of which would be intended, in one way or another, to serve the purpose of moving closer to a radically more democratic, egalitarian and cooperative social order. Nor could governments and movements determined to pursue such policies continue with the defence and external policies which have been pursued by the governments of advanced capitalist countries, whatever their specific political coloration, since the end of the Second World War. The notion of 'socialist directions' and 'radical change' is now inextricably linked with profound changes in defence and external policies, based upon the withdrawal, at a minimum, from the anti-revolutionary and counter-revolutionary coalition, in which all such governments have been involved in that period.

Germany, Spain and Eastern Europe in the inter-war years. There is also Chile, which was a capitalist democracy, with a strong tradition of constitutionalism; and what happened there between 1970 and 1973, and particularly in 1973, is directly relevant to the question, and needs to be carefully remembered and pondered. But any such experience has its own specificities, and can never, therefore, be taken to be finally conclusive for what would happen in other settings.

Historical experience is scanty, despite the long history of reform and reforming governments in the capitalist-democratic regimes of advanced capitalism. Since 1945, a succession of such governments, of social democratic character and inspiration, have come to office in one or the other advanced capitalist country. Social democratic governments were a rare occurrence in the inter-war years, save in Scandinavia: they became a common experience in the post-war decades. But while these governments generally came to office with very large programmes of social renewal, they very carefully confined themselves in office to measures of reform, which, though often substantial, were clearly and even explicitly not designed to bring about a wholesale transformation of the structure of power, property and privilege in the society in question. These governments did want reform, but they also wanted to defend the social order, and, indeed, wanted reform not least because this seemed to them to be the best guarantee of social stability. As a result, the opposition of conservative forces to these reforming governments might be determined and often fierce; but it was also kept within fairly narrow bounds. There was no need for these forces to seriously consider actions which would strain to a really dangerous point, the 'normal' workings of the political and constitutional system.

Furthermore, these reforming governments always had a critical point of contact and accord with the conservative forces which were opposed to them—with regard to defence and foreign policy. Social democratic governments naturally differed from their conservative opponents about specific items of policy in these fields. But they were wholeheartedly agreed on the absolute necessity for their countries to be part of the NATO alliance, under the leadership of the United States. And social democratic governments had no difficulty at all in aligning themselves with the United States in the waging of the anti-revolutionary crusade, to which I referred earlier, even though they might object to this or that move by the American government. Consensus in this area greatly, even decisively, eased the relationship of reforming governments and conservative oppositions.

In short, there has been no occasion in the history of well-implanted capitalist democracies (save for Chile), when the executive power of the state has been used, to push to their farthest possible limits, the opportunities for radical change which the possession of office afforded them—and even Chile is doubtful in this respect, given the relative modesty of the programme of reforms which Salvador Allende was seeking to implement. All social democratic governments have retreated, or given up power, long before they reached these outer limits: there was always more that they could have done, had they chosen to do so. The main reason for their choosing not to do so was not the strength of the opposition which they encountered, but rather, that further advances would have required them to adopt policies and measures likely to aggravate conflict, an option from which their whole cast of thought led them to recoil.

For their part, many Marxists, out of a proper concern to combat 'reformist' illusions, have tended to argue that, even if a government intent upon radical changes was allowed to take office, it would very soon find obstacles on its path, which it could not hope to negotiate within the constitutional and political framework of capitalist democracy.

Two different points may be made about this view. The first is that it would, undoubtedly, be foolish and reckless to underestimate the opposition, which a government intent on the transformation of the structure of property and power must encounter. This opposition would arise from within the state itself, as well as in society. It would include a vast array of forces, of which capitalist interests would be one, and some of which would proclaim their 'non-political' nature. And opposition from within the state and the country would certainly receive strong encouragement and support from abroad.[9]

The question, however, is not whether a government determined upon radical courses must expect strong conservative opposition: that may be taken for granted. The real question is how *effective*

[9] For some further discussion of the topic, see my *Marxism and Politics*, Oxford, 1977, Chapter VI, 'Reform and Revolution'.

this opposition would be. An answer to it must depend on the specific circumstances in which the struggle occurs. But—and this is the second point—the stress on the strength of the opposition, however necessary and reasonable it may be, runs the risk of blurring and even occluding the fact that a duly elected government in a capitalist-democratic regime *also* has a great deal of strength at its disposal, provided it is backed by a legislative majority (which Allende did not have), and that it enjoys a large measure of solid, organised and reasonably united support in the country.

These may seem to be rather onerous conditions in the political climate of the present period, when the left in advanced capitalist countries has suffered much demoralisation and many defeats. Nor, in any case, is it to be denied that they *are* onerous conditions, insofar as they demand not only electoral support, but the 'internalisation' by large segments of the population of that new 'common sense', of which Gramsci spoke. On a longer term view, however, and in the light of the shortcomings and derelictions of advanced capitalism, these conditions, apart from being inescapable, are not unrealistic. But there is one further condition whose fulfilment is essential if the government is to have any chance of coping effectively with the problems and obstacles it would confront, namely, that it should itself be determined to proceed with the implementation of its programme, and that it should accept the 'radicalisation' which that implementation must inevitably entail. This *is* a large condition: its realisation largely depends on the nature of the movement from which the government is issued, on its political maturity, its coherence, its combination of principle and flexibility. The question, in other words, is not one of 'good leaders', but of the quality of the movement they lead, and of the manner in which leaders and movements relate to each other.

The paradox, however, is that the power which is at the disposal of a government determined on radical change, and adequately supported in the country, cannot, from a socialist point of view, be a matter of unalloyed satisfaction. On the one hand, this power is indispensable, not only to achieve and safeguard the desired transformations in the social order, but also to fulfil the many administrative and arbitrating functions which must fall upon the state in a 'post-capitalist' society. On the other hand, the power of the state must (or should) evoke intense suspicion in socialist eyes— very much, it may be added, in the tradition of Marx himself, if not in that of many of his disciples. One of the main items in the indictment which socialists direct at capitalism today, is that it must rely evermore heavily upon an inflated statism, which assumes more and more authoritarian forms. The socialist purpose is not to substitute one statism for another, but to create the conditions in which the state is assigned its necessary, but subordinate sphere, by a social order securely in command of it. How to bring this about comes very high on the list of problems, which it is the task of socialism to solve.

11

The State and Development of Capitalism: The Third World Perspective

REHMAN SOBHAN

The central argument of this paper is that the State has become the principal agent for the development of capitalism in post-colonial societies of the Third World. The extent to which the State plays a dominant role in the process of capitalist development depends upon the constellation of class forces in the post-independence period. The extent to which the emergent capitalist classes can acquire autonomy from the State depends upon the capability of the class to reproduce itself through its capacity to generate surplus. Within this analytical perspective, the question of the autonomy of the State from the dominant class forces within the society becomes of less significance as a theoretical construct and a policy variable. The operative issue is whether the apparatus of State power is directed towards building an indigenous capitalist class, or, in effect, to pre-empt its emergence by using the instruments of state power and institutions as a direct instrument of class struggle.

Capitalism in the Third World

The historical process of colonial conquest and domination of the Third World was a powerful factor in inhibiting the growth of capitalism within these societies. The penetration, control and eventual establishment of hegemony over the economies of the Third World by a metropolitan bourgeoisie was instrumental in frustrating the development of an indigenous capitalist class. The initial penetration of Third World markets by the manufacturing produce of the developing capitalist economies of Europe, gave way to the struggle to establish political hegemony by particular colonial powers. The virtues of free trade and the supremacy of free competition in the market place were not to be extended to the Third World. Here, the dominant colonial power used its superior military power to create a captive market for the manufactured exports and capital of its metropolitan bourgeoisie. This was realised through the exclusion of competing colonial powers from the market place, and the suppression of the indigenous producing classes. The hegemony of the metropolitan bourgeoisie over the economy of the colony was thus established, not by the interplay of market forces, but by coercion and the introduction of non-market factors in the direction of the colonial economy and the conduct of economic policy. The indigenous trading and artisan classes, where such existed, were liquidated by non-market restrictions on their access to the metropolitan market, and by constraints on their continued access to the domestic market. Such constraints even included the use of physical force to suppress a more competitive artisan class.

The process of surplus extraction from the colonial economy further contributed to the immiseration of the indigenous population, and imposed constraints on the development of the home market. The only role which was open to the indigenous elites of the colonial society was the role of intermediaries for the metropolitan bourgeoisie with the indigenous producers, whether as a revenue collecting *rentier* landlord, or tribal chief, or as a middleman between the metropolitan trading houses and the petty commodity producers. Beyond this, a class of service holders took root in the lower echelons of the colonial administration to provide various services to the expatriate bourgeoisie.

The phase of using the colony as a market was accompanied by the process of penetration of metropolitan capital to exploit the natural resources of the colony to feed the manufacturing sector and consumption needs of the metropolitan market. Investments in the development of the infrastructure of the colonial economy were guaranteed by the colonial government to ensure satisfactory rates of return for the metropolitan investors. There was no scope for calling international tenders to build the railway system of colonial India.

The Post-Independence Scene

The incidence of domination and control over the economies of the Third World varied widely, depending on the size of the economy and the development of indigenous classes as a consequence of the colonial system. In a few of the larger Third World countries, an embryo trading bourgeoisie could create some space for itself in competition with, and eventual contradiction to, the metropolitan bourgeoisie. This led to the creation of some domestic industry financed from the surpluses accumulated by the indigenous trading bourgeoisie. Where direct colonial rule was withdrawn, as in Latin America, some of the bigger economies could even take protective measures to foster industry. However, here, as in India, it took two wars and a global recession to provide some basis for indigenous industrial development.

In most of the Third World, however, there was no such scope for the development of an indigenous mercantile bourgeoisie or for any form of domestic industry to take root. At the time of independence, these economies were completely dominated by metropolitan capital which controlled their principal exports and supplied their imports.

Thus, in the post-colonial phase, three broad stages of development were manifest in the newly emergent nation states of the Third World. In a very few States, such as India, an indigenous trading bourgeoisie, and/or owing capital in industry had developed along with a class of government officials, professionals associated with trade, the judicial system, education and public services. This class constituted the emergent ruling class of the post-colonial society. Their values were bourgeois and they aspired to build a bourgeois State where capitalism could take root as the dominant mode of production.

In attempting to build a bourgeois capitalist State, this aspirant class had to contend with an indigenous landed elite which not only controlled the land and monopolised the surplus generated by the rural economy, but exercised power and influence in rural society. This power had been used to good effect by the colonial power, who used this class as their agent in exercising political control over rural society, and as an instrument of surplus extraction. This class of rural elites became the natural partners, rather than potential competitors, of the aspirant urban bourgeoisie. In many newly independent societies, part of the surplus was directed into trade and small/medium industry.

As a class, the rural elites looked to the State to preserve their hegemony over the rural society, by channelling public resources to elements within this class in the form of development funds, rural credit, subsidised agricultural inputs and scope for marketing the produce of public enterprise. As a consequence, the economic and social power of segments of the rural elite was considerably enhanced through the enhanced presence of State power and public resources in the rural areas. Conflicts with the urban elites over the pricing of agricultural products, and claims on public development funds, were more apparent than real. Elements of the rural elite not only crossed class lines in their role as trader and aspirant industrialist, but thrived on the scarcity economy in the rural areas. This class was willing to live with a relatively small share of public resources going to the rural areas, as long as elements of this class could mediate the flow of these resources to the rural areas.

This reasonably coherent world view of the aspirant bourgeoisie, both urban and rural, was, however, exposed to some challenge by the exigencies of a plural political system. The post-independence government could not exercise the spectre of the masses who had participated in, and given substance to, the independence struggle. Nor could they overlook the fact that as long as the forms of parliamentary government were retained, the constituents and the class of vote brokers would need to be propitiated by a combination of populist rhetoric, and through limited access to public resources. Within such societies, the compulsions of the political process and the scarcity of public resources, in relation to the growing number of claimants amongst the urban and rural elites, created contradictions within the polity which constrained the unchallenged hegemony of the aspirant bourgeoisie over the post-colonial State.

Power of the State

However, those factions of the bourgeoisie, which sought to embark on the path of capitalist industrialisation, had to come to terms with the fact that it was the State which could create the necessary infrastructure for their growth as a class. It was thus the government which became the principal instrument to mobilise capital on a sufficient scale to build up the necessary infrastructure needed to sustain a quantum change in the fortunes of a capitalist class. It was the State which became the principal instrument to mobilise domestic resources, foreign aid and loans, and to provide the necessary guarantees to foreign capital, to retain their investments and/or make new investments in the domestic economy.

The latter aspect of the post-colonial State, as guarantor of the security and profitability of foreign capital, was an important factor in those societies where the confidence of the metropolitan bourgeoisie had been shaken by the withdrawal of the formal trappings of colonial rule. It was, again, the State which became the mediator between the aspirant foreign investor and the emergent bourgeoisie. It deployed the resources of State power to secure a stake for the aspirant domestic capitalists within the domestic market, at the expense of metropolitan capital. The use of State fiat, to compel foreign business operating in the domestic economy to take on locals as partners, and in cases, even as majority partners, contributed to enhancing the resource base, access to foreign management skills, technology and social power of the domestic bourgeoisie. It also contributed to the process of linking capitalism within the Third World with the world capitalist system.

Within this construct, the debate over the relative role of the public and private sector becomes essentially academic. The public sector emerges as an essential element in the development of the capitalist mode of production in the post-colonial State. It provides an essential resource base to provide infrastructural services, such as modern public utilities and communications, and it provides the trained manpower to run the capitalist sector. It also provides massive access to credit from public development finance institutions, and mediates access to foreign resources. Above all, it serves as the largest and most dynamic market for the produce of the capitalist sector, and as a major source of private accumulation through capital acquired through the role of intermediary to the State system, whether as commission agent, contractor or distributor of public goods. A significant part of these transactions between the public and private sector are undertaken at sub-market prices, so that the built-in scarcity premium provided by the marketing of public goods and services constitutes a massive unrequired transfer of public resources to a selected segment of the bourgeoisie.

Thus, debates over the efficiency, or lack of it, of the public sector is again rendered academic. The public sector was not intended, and perhaps in a bourgeois system cannot expect to be 'efficient' in the way of maximising profits in relation to equity. The public sector is, however, an important source of surplus which can be appropriated by various categories of beneficiaries of State patronage. This class may include both foreign and domestic suppliers of goods and services, a privileged class of public sector employees, private sector consumers of public sector products as also the public revenue budget. The balance of class forces which contend for the surplus to be generated by particular public enterprises will determine how the surplus is distributed, and whether and how much of it is retained within the enterprise to provide the basis for expanded reproduction within the public sector.

Aspirations of the Capitalist Classes

Within this system, a stage will come when some factions of the national bourgeoisie will feel constrained by the administrative hegemony of the State. This may arise where the State occupies space which the now more established capitalist class feels it is equipped to occupy. Therein lies the contention over the concept of the 'reserved' sector. Where the domestic capitalist class is now generating enough investible surplus to create the basis for its expanded reproduction, it can aspire to some autonomy from the State. However, there are, as yet, few examples of a national bourgeoisie which has created an autonomous resource base for itself, where they would not expect public institutions to provide them with subsidised capital and to share the risks of a new investment. They would continue to depend on the State to provide subsidised public services, to control the working class and maintain sufficient coercive power to contain any challenge to the bourgeois system.

In the case of the more developed capitalist bourgeoisie in the newly industrialised States, the State is expected to play an active role in mediating this class's growing transactions with the world capitalist system. This would range from lining up to finance both private lending, and the growth of the public sector markets through the medium of this aid-financed development plan, to providing guarantees for private borrowing in the international capital market, and collaboration with foreign investors. The use of State power to secure a share for the dominant factions of the capitalist class in world markets, to unfettered access to technology, to realise a relocation of industry away from the metropolitan centre to the periphery, has come to constitute what is termed, the realisation of a New International Economic Order. These recent compulsions to promote the international fortunes of a domestic bourgeoisie serve to reinforce the symbiotic relationship between the State and the domestic capitalist classes in the more industrialised Third World countries.

This category of States is, however, representative of only a small fraction of the Third World. In most parts of the Third World there was no nascent bourgeoisie to speak of at the time of independence. In many such States, independence turned out to be notional, and the economy continued to be dominated by the metropolitan bourgeoisie, who retained control over foreign trade, remained the sole source of capital and technology for the erstwhile colonial economy, and continued to control access to foreign markets for the traditional commodity exports of these economies.

In some of these countries, however, the hegemony of the metropolitan bourgeoisie was challenged by the process of mass mobilisation, which became a necessary instrument of the liberation struggle. A number of these movements culminated in a process of armed struggle, where colonial rule was terminated within a process of violence and massive social upheaval. In most such cases, there was a consequential and abrupt withdrawal of the metropolitan bourgeoisie, and, in many cases, a drastic abridgement in the power of their local factors. As cases in point, one can think of Vietnam, Algeria, the Portuguese dependencies in Africa, and Bangladesh in relation to Pakistani domination. As a variation to this process, there was the victory of various mass struggles against neocolonial domination and their local surrogates, as in the case of China, Cuba and more recently, Iran. In all such cases, an immediate social vacuum was created by the withdrawal of the metropolitan bourgeoisie, and/or the sudden collapse in the power of their local agents.

In such situations, one witnesses a dramatic extension in the role of the State to fill the vacuum created by the withdrawal of the metropolitan bourgeoisie, in order to keep the economic system from running down and creating serious dislocation in the supply of goods and services. Such societies may, however, evolve in various directions. In some societies the States may commit themselves to the path of class struggle, where they consciously seek to pre-empt the emergence of a capitalist class, and aspire to build a society drawing its sustenance from the support of the masses.

Crisis of External Dependence

However, in other societies this process of State intervention is itself only an interregnum. State power itself experiences a process of atrophy as a result of unresolved contradictions within the polity between factions of the State-patronised bourgeoisie, over the appropriation of the surplus from public enterprises. The failure to generate surpluses from public enterprises makes it difficult for the process of expanded reproduction to take root. This may, in turn, contribute to the growth in external dependence. This dependence may manifest itself through official financial transfers, largely from advanced capitalist countries (AIC), or multilateral institutions controlled by them, or through a process of mounting private debt to the AIC-dominated international banking system.

The process of degeneration in the national economy creates political instability, and provides the precondition for intervention by external forces and their local intermediaries, acting usually through the armed forces, but with the backing of the AIC aid donors and the international financial agencies. The post-coup phase of military, or military-backed rule, usually goes through a process of 'liberalisation', suppression of the working class, the privatisation of the economy, and, above all, the re-opening of the economy to penetration by foreign capital.

The 'open' economy, so beloved of the World Bank and International Monetary Fund (IMF), is, of course, not just the logical consequence of the incapacity of State-dominated systems to create an autonomous basis for expanded reproduction. Few post-colonial societies even went through the phase where foreign capital could be uprooted so that in these cases the economy always remained 'open'. However, in most such neo-colonial societies, various forms of the military or autocratic role remain as essential safeguards for

The State and Development of Capitalism: Third World Perspective / 255

the 'open' economy. Here, the State serves as guarantor of foreign capital, coerces labour to work at sub-market wages, and equips itself to contain mass mobilisation against foreign hegemony. This deployment of State power covers dissent from those factions of the domestic bourgeoisie who are not dependent on linkages with foreign capital for their development, and see their own aspirations as a class frustrated by the external domination of the economy. However, here again, there would be many Third World countries which even today, have yet to witness the emergence of such a class.

The development of capitalism in these 'open' societies is, by its nature, highly dependent on the role of the State. The continuing external domination of these societies, or the fact that there was a period of State domination of the economy where the nascent bourgeoisie witnessed a serious erosion of their power base, means that such classes retain little autonomous strength. They remain deficient in entrepreneurial experience, command over modern technology, management skills and, above all, in the capacity to generate surpluses. Their sole exposure to the world of business is as a trader or intermediary. In both activities, they hope to prosper as instruments of foreign capital, or as a client of State patronage. Where the bourgeoisie remains in a State of underdevelopment, the only way in which a capitalist class can aspire to develop, remains through massive State patronage. The State may choose to invest its power and use patronage to reduce the domination of foreign capital on the economy. Or, the State may act at the behest of its foreign patrons, who feel that military power is an unstable basis for preserving an open economy, and the policy must be anchored to clearly articulated domestic forces with a stake in such a policy.

The process of State-sponsored capitalist development, therefore, begins with the state initially deploying its patronage to provide a basis for capital accumulation. The most extreme demonstration of this process is being witnessed in the oil-exporting States of the Middle East. Here, the vast influx of oil revenues which was expended on imports, development projects and arms procurements, led to sizeable fortunes being accumulated in a very short period by members of the ruling families and classes who were close to them. Those same classes, which made their fortunes as agents of foreign suppliers of goods and services, are, in the next phase, seeking partnership with the same suppliers to create a capital base in the domestic economy. But the very creation of the base is contingent on massive State financial patronage, subsidy and protection.

This phenomenon witnessed in the oil rich States is, however, evident in most 'open' societies where the State becomes the initial source of wealth for a narrow faction of the bourgeoisie. In the second phase, the State becomes the source of development finance for factions of this class. This, in many cases, becomes, not a source of domestic capitalist industrialisation, but another source of export of capital, and/or the expansion in the trading activities of the domestic bourgeoisie. For this class to maximise returns on capital does not necessarily mean well-conceived investment projects, choice of equipment and efficient plant management, but the exploitation of the scarcity value of the public capital resources to which they have been given privileged access. As a result, we witness slow, and in some cases non-implementation of private investment projects, low levels of capacity utilisation and very poor repayment of loans to development finance institutions (DFI). This leads to a degeneration in the viability of DFIs, the inability of expanded reproduction to take root and provide the basis for a domestic capitalist class to reproduce itself. Thus, capitalist industrialisation comes to be sustained by new injections of capital to DFIs provided by foreign donors.

Since the essential feature of this system is a highly selective process of channelling public financial resources to a narrow segment of the bourgeoisie, the policy generates its own social tensions. The incapacity of the system to generate its own internal dynamism means that the State must continue to commit itself to this highly skewed pattern of public resource distribution. The resultant tensions tend to destabilise the polity and make it prone to mass unrest. In the absence of a radical political leadership committed and organised to transform the system, frequent changes of regime outside the constitutional process become a recurring feature of the society.

Autonomy of the State

As it stands, the paper does not provide a basis for contributing to the debate on the autonomy of the State, which was raised by

Marx in his path-breaking works on the *Civil War in France* and *The Eighteenth Brumaire of Louis Napolean*, and which has been carried on by Miliband, Poulantazas and Hamza Alavi among others. Whether, in effect, the State acts in autonomy of the dominant classes, and whether a state bureaucracy, for various reasons, chooses to challenge the dominant class acting ostensibly in the name of other classes, seems to be of considerable academic interest but of limited relevance to the course of political action and policy-making. Within the above framework of analysis, the character of the State is manifested in the direction of state policy, the external patronage it attracts, the mode of distribution of public resources and the beneficiaries of state patronage.

The autonomy of the State presumes a consolidation in authority of the State, and a coherence in its ability to act autonomously of contending social forces within it. Presumably, Louis Napolean as the all-powerful monarch of France could act decisively and above the conflicts within the French polity. Contemporary history of Third World countries does not record many instances where the State can act either decisively or coherently above the fray. The State is an aggregate of contending social forces. Its policies tend to reflect the contradictions within the polity. The State can, thus, hardly be autonomous of the social forces which sustain it.

In particular Third World societies, however, the state machinery moves more decisively to act in the service of a particular class. This compels it to suppress other contending class, and to thereby put into suspension the institutions of the plural state which accommodated these contradictions. Military regimes acting in the service of an aspirant capitalist class, as in Brazil or South Korea, or constitutional autocracies as in the case of Taiwan or Philippines, are examples of the move to subsume contradictions within society, by arbitrary action in support of a particular class. In such situations, the State may indeed be autonomous, in the sense that it is not dominated by the bourgeoisie whom it serves. Such regimes may be run by a more socially heterogeneous officer corps and bureaucracy. However, to the extent that the State continues to act in the service of a capitalist class, its autonomy has no functional significance for the conceptualisation of the nature of the State.

Such situations are more likely to arise where the capitalist class itself is not fully developed, but is, indeed, dependent on State power for its development and consolidation. It is only when it has reached a more mature stage that the capitalist class can be inducted into its rightful place in the hierarchy of State power, which it may share with the feudal elite and/or the army and state bureaucracy. Till such a time as a capitalist class has emerged from its embryo, the State, acting through the medium of the officer corps and senior bureaucracy, will serve as the patrons and the proxy of capitalist interests. In the process, fractions of the officer corps and bureaucracy may make themselves the beneficiaries of their own patronage, as they use State power to promote their friends, relations, and even themselves, as aspirant capitalists. Thus, the autonomous State may not be subservient to a class but remains committed to the creation of a capitalist class and to the establishment of the hegemony of this class.

Conclusions

The argument in this paper, to interpret the role of the State in the development of capitalism in the Third World, has been developed in a somewhat simplified form to provoke debate. It needs to be further refined and validated by more comprehensive analysis of the historical experience of particular Third World countries in varying stages of development and class formation. The thesis, that the State has been critical to the development and sustenance of a capitalist class in Third World countries, remains at the centre of the argument in this paper.

In a small number of Third World countries, an indigenous capitalist class may have developed some autonomy from the State and developed a capacity to reproduce itself. Though even here, the State plays a critical role in promoting the further growth of this class by mediating the linkages of this class with the world capitalist system.

However, in most Third World countries, the State is the progenitor of capitalist development, and the class survives by courtesy of State patronage. Thus, the nature of the State remains critical to the fortunes of the embryo capitalist class. A withdrawal of State patronage through a change in the balance of class forces within the State would see the withering away of what passes for a capitalist class in particular Third World countries.

About the Contributors

Amiya Kumar Bagchi is Professor of Economics, Centre for Studies in Social Science, Calcutta, and Member, State Planning Board, Government of West Bengal. He has also held the distinguished posts of Visiting (Professorial) Fellow, University of Bristol, U.K.; and Professor of Economics, Presidency College, Calcutta. The Institute of Social and Economic Change, Bangalore, awarded him the V.K.R.V. Rao prize in Economics for 1980. Professor Bagchi is the author of *Private Investment in India 1900–1939*; *The Political Economy of Underdevelopment*; and *Change and Choice in Indian Industry* (co-edited).

Krishna Bharadwaj is Professor of Economics at the Centre for Economic Studies and Planning. Amongst the distinguished positions that Prof. Bharadwaj has held are: Dean, School of Social Sciences, Jawaharlal Nehru University, New Delhi; Visiting Fellow, Clare Hall and Trinity College, Cambridge; Visiting Professor, Stanford University, USA; and Visiting Senior Simon Fellow, Manchester, UK. In 1979 she was awarded the V.K.R.V. Rao Eminent Social Scientist National Award. Professor Bharadwaj's major publications include *Themes in Value and Distribution: Classical Theory Reappraised; Production Conditions in Indian Agriculture; On Some Issues of Method in Analysis of Social Change; Classical Political Economy and Rise to Dominance of Supply and Demand Theories*.

P.R. Brahmananda is ICSSR National Fellow. Prior to this he was Professor of Monetary Economics, and Director, Department of Economics, University of Bombay. Professor Brahmananda's major publications include *Productivity in the Indian Economy; Growthless Inflation and Stockless Money; Explorations in New Classical Political Economy; Studies in Economics of Welfare Maximization*; and *The Development Process of the Indian Economy* (co-edited).

Sukhamoy Chakravarty is Professor of Economics at the Delhi School of Economics, University of Delhi; Chairman of the Indian Council of Social Science Research, New Delhi; and Chairman, Economic Advisory Council to the Prime Minister. Amongst the distinguished positions that Professor Chakravarty has held during his career are Visiting Fellow, Sidney Sussex College, University of Cambridge, U.K.; Visiting Professor, Johns Hopkins University, USA; and Member, Planning Commission, Government of India. Besides articles in reputed Indian and foreign journals, Professor Chakravarty's publications include *Capital and Development Planning; Development Planning: The Indian Experience; Contributions to Indian Economic Analysis—A Survey* (co-author) and *The Relationship between Food Aid and Non-Food Aid* (co-author). Prof. **Chakravarty was the 1978 recipient of the V.K.R.V. Rao Eminent Social Scientist Award.**

Sudipta Kaviraj is Associate Professor, Centre for Political Studies, Jawaharlal Nehru University, New Delhi, and Fellow, Nehru Memorial Museum Library, New Delhi. Prior to this he was Agatha Harrison Fellow, St. Antony's College, Oxford. Besides numerous articles in reputed journals and edited volumes, Professor Kaviraj is the co-author of *The State of Political Theory*.

Ralph Miliband is Professor of Sociology at Brandeis University, Massachusetts, USA. His major publications include *Marxism and Politics; The State in Capitalist Society; Parliamentary Socialism*; and he has been the co-editor of *The Socialist Register* since 1964.

Mihir Rakshit is with the Centre for Economic Studies, Presidency College, Calcutta. Besides articles on macroeconomics and problems of LDCs, Professor Rakshit has written *The Labour Surplus Economy: A New-Keynesian Approach* and *Studies in the Macro Economics of Developing Countries*.

Asok Sen is Professor of Economics at the Centre for Studies in Social Sciences, Calcutta. Prior to this he was with the Indian Statistical Institute, Calcutta. Prof. Sen has contributed numerous articles to reputed journals and edited volumes, and is the author of *Iswar Chandra Vidyasagar and his Elusive Milestones; Three Studies on the Agrarian Structure in Bengal 1850–1947* (co-author); and *Problems of the West Bengal Economy and Planning* (co-edited).

Randhir Singh was formerly Professor of Political Theory, University of Delhi. He is currently National Fellow, Indian Council of Social

Science Research. An outstanding teacher and committed activist, Prof. Singh is the author of *Reason, Revolution and Political Theory*.

Yogendra Singh is Professor of Sociology at the Centre for the Study of Social Systems, Jawaharlal Nehru University, New Delhi. Professor Singh's contributions to contemporary Indian sociology have been acknowledged both in India and abroad. His major publications include *Indian Sociology: Social Conditioning and Emerging Concerns; Essays in Modernization; Social Stratification and Social Change; Modernization of Indian Tradition; Towards a Sociology of Non-violence and Peace; Social Aspects of Scientific and Technological Revolution* (co-author); and *Sociology of Culture for India* (co-edited).

Rehman Sobhan is Chairman, Bangladesh Institute of Development Studies, Dhaka. Renowned for his significant contributions in the area of development problems in the Third World, Professor Sobhan is the author of numerous articles and books in this field. The latter include *Basic Democracy, Works Programme and Rural Development in East Pakistan; Public Enterprise in an Intermediate Regime—A Study of the Political Economy of Bangladesh*; and *Crisis of External Dependence: Political Economy of Foreign Aid to Bangladesh* (co-author).

List of Seminar Participants

Professor S. Chakravarty
Delhi School of Economics
University of Delhi
Delhi 110007

Dr. Mihir K. Rakshit
Centre for Economic Studies
Department of Economics
Presidency College
Calcutta 700073

Professor Krishna Bharadwaj
Centre for Economic Studies and Planning
School of Social Sciences
Jawaharlal Nehru University
New Delhi 110067

Dr. Sudipta Kaviraj
Centre for Political Systems
School of Social Sciences
Jawaharlal Nehru University
New Delhi 110067

Professor P.R. Brahmananda
Department of Economics
University of Bombay
Vidyanagri, Kalina
Bombay 400098

Professor Yogendra Singh
Centre for Social Systems
School of Social Sciences
Jawaharlal Nehru University
New Delhi 110067

Professor A.R. Desai
Department of Economics
University of Bombay
Vidyanagri, Kalina
Bombay, 400098

Dr. Utsa Patnaik
Centre for Economic Studies and Planning
School of Social Sciences
Jawaharlal Nehru University
New Delhi 110067

Dr. Sheila Bhalla
Centre for Economic Studies and Planning
School of Social Sciences
Jawaharlal Nehru University
New Delhi 110067

Dr. Sudipto Mundle
Economic Advisor
Ministry of Finance
North Block
New Delhi 110001

Dr. Prabhat Patnaik
Centre for Economic Studies and Planning
School of Social Sciences
Jawaharlal Nehru University
New Delhi 110067

Dr. N.K. Chandra
Professor of Economics
Indian Institute of Management
Joka, Diamond Harbour Road
Calcutta 700027

Dr. Surendra J. Patel
Director
Technology Division

UNCTAD, Palais des Nations
CH-1211, Geneva 10 (Switzerland)

Dr. N.S. Sidharthan
Institute of Economic Growth
University of Delhi
Delhi 110007

Dr. R.P. Sengupta
Centre for Economic Studies and
Planning
School of Social Sciences
Jawaharlal Nehru University
New Delhi 110067

Dr. Profulla Sanghvi
61 Lodi Estate
New Delhi 110003

Prof. Yogendra Alagh
Member
Planning Commission
Yojana Bhavan
Sansad Marg
New Delhi 110001

Dr. K. Subbarao
Institute of Economic Growth
University of Delhi
Delhi 110007

Professor Rehman Sobhan
Chairman
Bangladesh Institute of Development Studies
Adamjee Court, Motijheel Commercial Area
Dhaka 2 (Bangladesh)

Professor Ralph Miliband
Department of Sociology
Brandeis University
Waltham
Massachusetts 02254 (U.S.A.)

Dr. Arvind Vyas
Centre for Economic Studies and
Planning
School of Social Sciences
Jawaharlal Nehru University
New Delhi 110067

Professor B.B. Chaudhari
Department of History
Calcutta University
Calcutta

Professor Asok Sen
Professor of Economics
Centre for Studies in Social
Sciences
10 Lake Terrace
Calcutta 700029

Professor Amiya Kumar Bagchi
Director
Centre for Studies in Social
Sciences
10 Lake Terrace
Calcutta 700029

Professor Ashok Guha
School of International Studies
Jawaharlal Nehru University
New Delhi 110067

Dr. Anjan Mukherjee
Centre for Economic Studies and
Planning
School of Social Sciences
Jawaharlal Nehru University
New Delhi 110067

Professor Randhir Singh
52, Hemkunt Colony
New Delhi 110048

Dr. Amal Sanyal
Centre for Economic Studies and
Planning

School of Social Sciences
Jawaharlal Nehru University
New Delhi 110067

Professor Surendra Munshi
Indian Institute of Management
Joka, Diamond Harbour Road
Calcutta 700027

Dr. Dipankar Gupta
Centre for Social Systems
School of Social Sciences
Jawaharlal Nehru University
New Delhi 110067

Dr. C.P. Chandrasekhar
Centre for Economic Studies and Planning
School of Social Sciences
Jawaharlal Nehru University
New Delhi 110067

Dr. A.K. Mathur
Centre for Regional Studies and Development
Jawaharlal Nehru University
New Delhi 110067

Dr. Pradhan H. Prasad
A.N. Sinha Institute of Social Studies
Patna 800001

Professor C.T. Kurien
Director
Madras Institute of Development Studies
Gandhinagar, Adyar
Madras 600020

Professor L.K. Deshpande
Department of Economics
University of Bombay
Vidyanagri, Kalina
Bombay 400098

Dr. D.D. Narula
Institute of Development Studies
B124A Mangal Marg
Bapu Nagar
Jaipur 302015

Professor K.A. Naqvi
Delhi School of Economics
University of Delhi
Delhi 110007

Mr. Mohit Sen
110 Amrit Apartments
Kaladia Lane
Samajiguda
Hyderabad 500482

Prof. T.S. Papola
Senior Consultant
Planning Commission
Yojna Bhavan
Parliament Street
New Delhi 110001

Professor R. Radhakrishna
Director
Centre for Economic and Social Studies
Nizamia Observation Campus
Begumpet
Hyderabad 500016

Professor K.R. Ranadive
A/15, Shefalee Makar and Sahanivas Cadell Road
Mahim
Bombay 400016

Professor Tapas Mazumdar
Zakir Hussain Centre
Jawaharlal Nehru University
New Delhi 110067

Professor P.C. Joshi
Institute of Economic Growth

University of Delhi
Delhi 110007

Professor R.S. Sharma
Department of History
University of Delhi
Delhi 110007

Dr. Arun K. Ghosh
Vice Chairman
West Bengal State Planning Board
6, Camac Street
Calcutta

Professor B.C. Parekh
211 Victoria Avenue
Hull HU5 3EF
UK

Professor Rasheeduddin Khan
Centre for Political Systems
Jawaharlal Nehru University
New Delhi 110067

Professor C.P. Bhambri
Centre for Political Systems
Jawaharlal Nehru University
New Delhi 110067

Professor Harbans Mukhia
Centre for Historical Studies
Jawaharlal Nehru University
New Delhi 110067

Professor Satish Chandra
Centre for Historical Studies
Jawaharlal Nehru University
New Delhi 110067

Professor Moonis Raza
Vice-Chancellor

University of Delhi
Delhi 110007

Professor K.L. Krishna
Delhi School of Economics
University of Delhi
Delhi 110007

Dr. Arjun Sengupta
Prime Minister's Secretariat
New Delhi 110001

Dr. S.K. Goyal
Indian Institute of Public Administration
Indraprastha Estate
New Delhi 110002

Dr. Amaresh Bagchi
Director
National Institute of Public Finance and Policy
18/2, Satsang Vihar Marg
Special Institutional Area
New Delhi 110067

Dr. Susheela Kaushik
Department of Political Science
University of Delhi
Delhi 110007

Professor Manoranjan Mohanty
Department of Political Science
University of Delhi
Delhi 110007

Dr. Nirmal Singh
Centre for the Study of the Social Systems
Jawaharlal Nehru University
New Delhi 110067

Index

Abramovitz, M., 95
Adams, H.P., 206
Adamson, W.L., 208
Alam, 162
Althusser, L., 132, 142, 143, 145–54, 158, 159, 163, 165, 171
Alvi, H., 257
Anderson, Perry, 200–01
Arrow, K.J., 25, 114

Bagchi, A., 10, 13
Bailey, S., 67
Baranowski, T., 105
Baumol, W.J., 50
Baxter, 213
Bendix, R., 191
Benjamin, D., 118
Bentham, J., 32
Bentinck, W.C., 118
Berger, 214
Bhagwati, J., 114
Bharadwaj, K., 114
Bharadwaj, R., 98, 102
Blaug, M., 93
Bleicher, J., 187
Bodin, Louis, 32
Bohm-Bawerk, E.A.V., 59, 61, 74–75, 89, 97–98, 105–07, 114–16
Brahmananda, P.R., 10, 12–13
Braudel, F., 122
Buci-Glucksmann, C., 203
Bukharin, N., 136

capital theory debate, 60–61, 70–71; a critique of orthodox theory of interest rate, 70–71; a structural critique of neo-classical theory of value and distribution, 60–61
capitalism, development of, in post-colonial societies, 18, 247–58; failure of market mechanism in, 10–11, 20, 23, 29, 31–33, 36–40; laissez-faire capitalism, 27; liberal capitalism, 20; maladies of, 39, 43, 52, 53; structural basis of instability characterising, 10–11, 25, 33–34, 43, 73; western capitalism, changing face of, 198–200
Carr, E.H., 157
Carver, T., 132
Cassell, G., 114–15
Chakravarty, S., 10–11, 19, 114
Chamberlin, E.H., 114
Chatterjee, 162
Chicago school, 120
Clark, J.B., 102
Clower, R.W., 69
Cohen, G.A., 132
Colletti, Lucio, 180
Collingwood, R.G., 154
Comte, A., 33
Condorcet, 33
Cournot, A., 85, 105, 114–16

Dasgupta, A.K., 25
de Finetti, 25
Dillard, D., 30
Dilthey, W., 154
Dilthey–Rickert approach, 186–87
divide in theories, 56, 58
Dobb, M., 30, 58
dominant technique, 62–63, 81
Draper, H., 178
Dube, S.C., 225
Dunlop, T.T., 29
Dunn, J., 163, 170
Durkheim, E., 167

effective demand, applied in analysis of accumulation, 72; short- and long-run, 71–72; theory of, 20–42; within surplus theory, 60

Elster, J., 132
Engels, F., 133, 135, 139, 180–81, 234
Erikson, E.H., 210

Fellner, W., 88
filled and empty concepts, 14, 140–42
Fischoff, E., 186, 187
Fisher, I., 56
Forrester, N.B., 96
Foucault, M., 170
Freeman, Christopher, 122
Freund, J., 189
Friedman, M., 21, 39–41, 50–52, 123
Friedman–Savage theory, 231

Gadamer, 155
Galtung, J., 123
Garegnani, P., 60, 61, 64, 66, 72
Gerth, H.H., 212
Gesell, S., 30
Ghosh, P., 19
Giddens, A., 194
Giovanni, B., 208
glut controversy, 22; Malthus–Ricardo debate, 22
Goldmann, L., 163, 164, 168, 195
Goodwin, R., 88, 101, 115, 117–23
Gouldner, A.W., 206
Gustaffson, B., 209
Gramsci, A., 9–10, 15–16, 136, 147, 166, 186, 196, 200–10, 245

Hansen, A., 25, 115
Harrington, 170
Harrod, R., 23, 27–28, 88
Hayek, F.A., 94
Hegel, G.W.F., 21, 143, 145, 149–50, 153, 171, 176–77
Heidegger, 155, 164
Hempel, Carl, 214
hermeneutics, 135, 137–39, 149, 155, 167, 171, 174, 186–87
Hicks, J.R., 24–25, 28, 42, 45, 47, 68–69, 114
Hilferding, R., 59, 60, 110, 123, 125
Hindess, B., 152
Hirschman, A.O., 128
Hirst, P.Q., 152
historical science, method of, 186–87

Hobbes, T., 142, 170
Hobson, J.A., 125
Honaver, R.H., 114
Hung, Fan, 30
Husserl, E., 141

imperialism, an atavistic activity, 73
innovations, Marx on, 57–58, 79–81; Schumpeter on, 12, 74–78, 89–91, 94–95, 97–104, 106, 111, 116, 120–23
interest, Keynes' theory of, 25, 27–29, 42, 44, 70–71; orthodox theory of, 27, 70 (*see also* capital theory debate, neo-classical synthesis)
investment function, in Keynes, 28–29; Kalecki's treatment of, 29–30; role of inventory investment in Keynes, 46–47; in Hicks, 25, 46

Jevons, W.S., 59, 105, 115–16, 118
Johnson, E., 88
Joseph, F., 32
Joshi, P.C., 19

Kahn, R.F., 22, 88, 96, 114
Kaldor, N., 21, 34, 45, 103
Kalecki, M., 10, 20, 23, 28–30, 34, 55, 57–58, 60, 72, 97; dynamic theory of capital accumulation of, 58, 60, 72; influence of Rosa Luxemberg on, 20–21, 34
Kamien, M.I., 127
Kant, I., 186
Kantarovich, 114
Kantowsky, D., 16, 212, 221
Kapp, W., 227
Karve, D.G., 225
Kautilya, 228
Kautsky, K., 180
Kaviraj, S., 8–10, 14, 175
Kendrick, J.W., 95
Keynes, J.M., 7–13, 20–54, 57, 60, 64, 68–73, 86, 89–90, 92–95, 105–06, 112–14, 120–21; economic writings of, 11, 21–22, 50–53; founder of modern macro-economics, 21–22, 27, 60; internal logic of,

11, 30–33; philosophical tradition of, 11, 21–23, 26, 40–45 (see also neo-classical synthesis, capital theory debate)
Kitchins, 91
Knight, F.H., 23
Kondratief long-wave hypothesis, 12, 91, 96, 122
Korsch, 134
Krishnamurthi, B.V., 114
Krishnaswami, K.S., 114

labour, analytical importance of, 31, 65–68; essential to prove exploitation, 31, 66; metaphysical proposition (Robinson), 31; theory of value, 31, 61, 64–68, 75
Laclau, E., 153
Lafargue, L., 184
Lange, O., 24, 170
Learner, A.P., 28–29
Leinjonhufvud, A., 41, 69
Lenin, V.I., 55, 173, 201, 206–07, 209
Leontief, W., 88, 92, 115
Lewis, A., 96
Lewis, J., 187
Locke, J., 163, 170
Lucas, R.E., 40, 49, 95
Luckmann, T., 214
Lukacs, G., 134, 147, 164, 207
Luxemberg, Rosa, 20, 34, 55

Macpherson, C.B., 163, 164, 170
Maddison, A., 96
Mahalanobis, P.C., 105
Majumdar, T.K., 8, 19
Malinvaud, E., 41, 69
Malthus, T.R., 22, 114–15, 117
Mandel, E., 96, 122, 199
Mao Zedong, 208
Marshall, A., 7, 10–11, 20, 22–23, 27, 32, 41, 56, 59, 113–15, 117
Marx, K., 7–8, 20–21, 24, 30–33, 36, 54, 55–68, 71–75, 79, 81–88, 91, 100, 105–07, 110–11, 113–19, 121, 125–27, 129, 132–54, 156–73, 175–84, 189, 193, 197–98, 204, 206, 209, 214, 223, 233–34, 236, 239, 245, 257; conception of man in, 136–37, 175; economic basis, importance of, 176–77, 179, 182–83, 205–06; explanation of politics in, 15, 175–83, 197; method of, 176–79, 181–82; scientific project of, 82–85, 176–82, 197 (see also capitalism, innovation, profits, state, surplus based structure, technical change)
Marxian political analysis, 14, 132–40, 142–73
Marzani, C., 208
Meade, J.E., 24
Menger, C., 105, 114–15, 127
Mensch, G., 96
Metzler, L.A., 46, 115
Michels, R., 130
Miliband, R., 10, 17–18, 133, 257
Mill, J.S., 33, 114
Mills, C.W., 212
Minsky, H.P., 25
Modigliani, F., 35, 69
Mommsen, J.W., 193
monetarists, ascendancy of, 39–40; natural rate of unemployment, 35; policy prescriptions of, 39
money demand functions (Keynes and Friedman), 50–52
Morishima, M., 61, 66; fundamental theorem, 66
Mosca, Gaetano, 130
multiplier, theory of, 22, 26
Muth, J., 121
Myrdal, G., 227

Napolean, L., 257
Narain, I., 8
Narula, D.D., 8, 19
neo-classical synthesis, 11, 28, 57, 68–71; critiques of, 68, 70; Hicks as 'locus-classicus' of, 28, 68–70
neo-classical theory of value and distribution, critique of, 55–57, 60–61, 68; foundation of, 59; 'givens' of, 63; simultaneous determination of prices and quantities in, 63; weakness of, 56 (see also capital theory debate)

Ohlin, B., 23
Opie, R., 87
Orwell, G., 198

Parsons, T., 222, 223
Parthsarathy, G., 8, 19
Pascal, R., 163
Pasinetti, L.L., 58, 61, 64
Patinkin, D., 48
Petty, W., 59
philosophy of language, importance of, 136–38
Pigou, A.C., 22, 27, 107
positive time preference (Bohm-Bawerk), 107–08
Poulantzas, N., 153, 257
profits, Schumpeter on, 12, 74–81; theory of, surplus based (classical and Marxian), 65–66; zero rate of, 74–76, 107–09
Proudhon, P.J., 30

Quesnay, F., 89, 97, 105, 115–17

Racine, 163
Raj, K.N., 19
Rakshit, M., 10–12
Ramsay, G., 97, 105, 117
Ramsey, F., 25, 29, 114
Rao, V.K.R.V., 25
Raymond, A., 192
real and monetary economy, integration of, 42, 44
realisation crisis, 64, 82, 85
reserve army of labour, 64, 71, 82–88
Ricardo, D., 22, 31, 56, 58–59, 64–67, 86, 91, 93, 105, 113–17, 127, 130
Rickert, 186–87
Robbins, L., 23
Robertson, D., 8–9, 90, 95, 114
Robinson, A., 87–88
Robinson, J., 23, 28–31, 60, 68, 73, 88, 96
Robot, C., 198
Roth, G., 215–16
Ryle, G., 160, 162

Salvadori, M., 208
Samuelson, P., 88, 92–93, 114–15

Sartre, J.P., 147, 201
Say, J.B., 27, 30, 64, 92, 112
Say's law, 27, 30, 64
Schumpeter, J.A., 7–14, 20, 30, 32–33, 35–36, 57–58, 72–82, 85, 87–131; *Business Cycles*, 90–91, 95–97, 112–13, circular flow, notion of, 12–13, 73–80, 89–91, 94–97, 106, 119, 120; *Capitalism, Socialism, Democracy*, 91–92, 111, 120, 127–28; *History of Economic Analysis*, 92–93, 96; methodological individualism, proponent of, 13, 73–75, 77–81, 97, 110, 119–20, 123–24; philosophical trend of, 13, 32–33, 73, 92–93, 106, 119–20, 122; *Theory of Economic Development*, 88–89, 94–96, 101–03 (*see also* capitalism, profits, technical change, innovation)
scientific political economy, 59, 67
Sen, A., 10, 15–16, 203, 205
Sen, A.K., 114
Seton, F., 61
Shaw, B., 87
Shutz, A., 214
Sidgwick, H., 32
Singer, M., 225–28
Singh, Randhir, 10, 14–15, 19
Singh, Yogendra, 10, 16–17, 19, 227
Skinner, Q., 163
Smith, A., 58–59, 62, 67, 114–16, 127
Sobhan, R., 10, 17–18
Solow, R.M., 93, 95, 114
Spiethoff, A., 23
Sprondel, W.M., 215–17, 219, 229
Sraffa, P., 58, 60–61, 75, 97–98, 102, 105, 114, 117; prompting return to classical approach, 58
Srinivas, M.N., 225
Srivastava, S.C., 19
state, autonomy of, 17–19, 202–03, 233–38, 240–42, 256–58; conception of, 17, 35, 231–33; intervention of, 18, 237–46; partnership of and capitalist forces, 232–33, 236; relative autonomy of, 14–15, 178, 231–34
stationary state, 73, 103, 119

Steedman, I., 61
surplus based structure of classical political economy, resurgence of, 12, 55–61, 85–86; structural core of, 12, 55–59, 62–68, 82–86; value and distribution in, 55–59, 62–68, 82–86
Sweezy, P., 32, 61, 88, 91, 111, 115

Talwar, N.K., 19
Tarshis, 29
Taussig, F.W., 115
Taylor, C., 148
technical change, Marx and Schumpeter on, 12, 72–74; Marx on, 81–85; differences from Schumpeter, 81–82, 85
Therborn, G., 153
Tobin, J., 35, 50, 88, 115
Tolstoy, L., 213
transformation problem, 59, 61, 65–68
Tsuru, S., 199
Turgot, A.R.J., 116

uncertainty, in Keynes, 10, 24–25; and differences from Ramsey-de Finnetti approach, 25
unemployment, ascribable to imperfections and rigidities by neoclassicals, 71; transitory phenomenon (Schumpeter), 80 (*see also* capitalism)

Van Dujin, J.J., 96
Viner, J., 24, 92, 114
Von Bortiewicz, L., 61
Von Haberler, G., 92, 114
Von Newman, 98, 102
Von Thunen, J.H., 89, 106, 114–16

Walras, L., 13, 20, 56, 59, 69, 73–75, 89, 92–93, 105–06, 114–17, 119, 121, 125, 129
Weber, Marianne, 213
Weber, Max, 7–10, 15–17, 123, 134, 146, 185, 187–98, 201, 205, 209–30, 241; Indian experience in, 16, 17, 211–14, 218–30; methodology of, 146, 186–87, 189–96, 214–18, 220–23, 225–26, 228–30; on bureaucracy, 193–94, 197–98; on capitalism, 17, 187–97, 214; rationality in, 15–17; and typology of, 220
Weldon, T.D., 160
Wells, H.G., 123
Wicksell, K., 21–22, 56, 75–76, 114–15
Wieser, 114
Williamson, O.E., 126
Winckelmann, J., 212
Wittgenstein, W., 138
Worseley, P., 214